DYNASTIES

DYNASTIES

Irish Political Families

By Johnny Fallon

**NEW
ISLAND**

DYNASTIES – IRISH POLITICAL FAMILIES
First published 2011 by
New Island
2 Brookside
Dundrum Road
Dublin 14
www.newisland.ie

Copyright © Johnny Fallon, 2011
The author has asserted his moral rights.
ISBN 978-1-8484-0127-3

British Library Cataloguing Data. A CIP catalogue record for this book is available from the British Library

Typeset by Mariel Deegan.
Printed in th EU.

Cover Image Credits
Bertie Ahern: *Flickr user leppre*
John Bruton: *Flickr user FriendsofEurope*
Richard Bruton: *Flickr user infomatique*
Liam Cosgrave: *Corbis*
W.T. Cosgrave: *Bain News Service Collection*
Eamon De Valera: *National Photo Company Collection*
Enda Kenny: *Flickr user infomatique*

New Island received financial assistance from The Arts Council (An Comhairle Ealaíon), Dublin, Ireland

10 9 8 7 6 5 4 3 2 1

'Hence learn, whenever, in some unhappy day, you light upon the ruins of so great a mansion, of what worth he was who built it, and how frail all things are, when such memorials of such men cannot outlive misfortune.'

(Inscription on the foundation stone of
Leinster House)

To my Father, who made me what I am.

Contents

Acknowledgements

There are a number of people who assisted and supported in the writing of this book to whom I am eternally grateful. Eoin Purcell first approached me with the idea, and was willing to run the gauntlet of working with me again. I am indebted to Dr Justin Corfield for both his patience and insight. Everyone at New Island books gave me their help, support and co-operation. Peter Brennan, my colleague, was used both wittingly and unwittingly as a sounding-board for some of the theories in the book. All the academics and friends involved with the Political Studies Association of Ireland have always been helpful and supportive in my writings, and opened more than a few doors and challenged my thinking on numerous occasions. I thank the many political contacts and friends who gave their nuggets of wisdom on each respective dynasty. And finally I thank my wife, Annette, and my children, Maria and Michael, who were endlessly supportive and put up with many hours of my being locked away or talking about what my daughter refers to as 'the boring stuff'.

Follow Johnny Fallon on twitter:
www.twitter.com/@jonnyfallon

Foreword
David Davin-Power

One of the late Brian Lenihan's many endearing characteristics was his sensitivity to suggestions that he owed any element of his political career to the celebrated family dynasty. On one memorable occasion he reacted in spectacular fashion when my colleague Micheal Lehane asked him in an interview about the importance of dynasties in political life. This seemingly inoffensive question drew a volcanic response from the then Finance Minister.

'I'm where I am because of what I did, not who I am. I'm sick, sore and tired of this dynasty bullshit.' On he went for fully two minutes, railing in colourful terms about superficial commentators, shallow analysis, wrong-headed attitudes. Then he stopped.

'Okay, I've got that off my chest. The camera wasn't running, right?' It was. 'Okay, Okay, where were we? Just no more about this dynasty rubbish.'

To his credit the reporter persisted, lightly rephrasing the question. There was a momentary pause before the answer, a hint that a further eruption was on the way. But the politician kicked in and after a rueful shrug Lenihan took the question on the chin.

Brian Lenihan's unease with the dynasty issue was understandable on one level. Whatever he achieved was largely the fruit of his own energy, intellect, and occasionally his sheer bloody mindedness. But I have wondered since that exchange whether he detected a change in the political wind too. The last election swept away many political traditions and rubrics – did he foresee it spelling the end of so-called 'dynasties' as well?

True, some family names have clung on, but an increasingly urbanised and sceptical electorate has less time for the 'I knew your father/mother/uncle well' school of politics. Given the hostility towards politicians in general in the run up to the 2011 Election, bearing a well-known name proved a weighty millstone for some.

Within political parties, though, political lineage matters. The impact when a well-known name stands aside is considerable. Beverley Flynn was one of the first of the Fianna Fáil grandees to desert the battlefield ahead of this year's contest: her decision was met with incredulity by some of her colleagues and sent shock waves through the party. The news that 'a Flynn' had shirked the contest was a morale-sapping blow without a doubt, and of course many more were to follow as – in the eyes of many of their colleagues – household names lined up to show the white feather.

The shock engendered by the Mayo TD's decision highlights another aspect of the Irish dynasty: unlike celebrated political families elsewhere, the driving impulse here is to win elections, to pass on the torch of office rather than to perpetuate a particular political outlook.

Sometimes, the succession has more to do with resolving competing tensions within a constituency organisation. Opting for a relative of the incumbent can often seem the option least likely to prompt splits or defections. When an incumbent passes away suddenly, emotional factors are particularly likely to dominate.

As Johnny Fallon points out in this study of the issue, family traditions are if anything more pronounced in other walks of life. When a profession manifestly provides a comfortable living why would sons or daughters not opt for the familiar pathway? A study of the professional classes might well show that it represents the norm when careers are chosen.

On the other hand, given the opprobrium our politicians have had to endure in recent times, I'm sure many of them tried to inoculate their offspring against the political bug rather than encouraging them to follow suit. The wonder is that anyone would opt for the political life given the challenges we currently face.

In US parlance, 2011 saw a classic 'kick the bums out' election. There was no respect for the Haughey or the Andrews names but, less predictably, internal party vote management meant neither the Barrys nor the D'arcys made it back to the Dáil either. It remains to be seen whether the contest ushered in a new and more meritocratic politics, or whether fresh dynasties will emerge to replace those that have been swept away or been left tottering.

Either way, this is a timely look at some of the most celebrated Irish families, who have in the past done the State some service, and a reminder of a political system that was at the same time competitive and clannish.

Introduction

What's in a name? Quite a lot apparently, particularly if you are involved in Irish politics. Family dynasties have been a feature of Irish political life down through the years. In this book I take a cross-section of the more famous ones and analyse their impact. How did it start? Why are they so popular? Are there common beliefs or values that help family dynasties survive and thrive? The other purpose is to try to gauge whether they have been a positive or negative feature of the system.

It is important to recognise that family traditions are strong in most walks of life. There is nothing particularly unusual about children or relatives going into a family business or following in their parents' footsteps. Retailers, traders, lawyers, accountants, doctors, farmers, sports people – you name it and you can find a family that has generation after generation of people doing it. What makes politics unusual is that it is not necessarily a matter of just deciding to get a qualification or start in a business: it depends entirely on the moods of others. Establishing and maintaining a dynasty, in a highly competitive environment, where you can be unceremoniously booted out at any election, is no small feat.

Families with political traditions are not unique to Ireland, but the system of parliamentary democracy and

multi-seat constituencies does lend itself to quite a prolifer-
ation of them. Understanding this is often thought of as
difficult and much is made of efforts to break such cycles.
But the genesis of this template can be found throughout
the history of the western world. In ancient times the
Roman political system established itself above all others.
One of the reasons for this was that instead of having one
'monarch' or 'elite' concerned only with national issues, the
Romans had a system of 'senators' and 'clients'. Wealthy
Roman families produced generations of senators and 'con-
suls' (the highest office in the land). This was generally
achieved on the back of clients. Senators met with multi-
tudes of clients regularly, in scenes not unlike a modern day
Irish constituency office. They solved problems, met people,
and generally tried to assist those who came to them. You
could always go to another senator if one didn't perform to
your expectations. But the senator with the most clients was
usually the one with the most power, because that meant that
they had a host of people to call upon in an election, or
when needed, to exert their influence.

The crucial difference between the Irish and Roman systems is that in Rome there was a closed 'ruling class' or elite,
who inherited their political posts automatically. This makes
it unremarkable that a small number of families should
form long and powerful dynasties. In Ireland, though, the
proliferation of dynastic names does not appear to have
been unduly hampered by the inconvenience of getting
elected. This is all the more remarkable when you consider
that Irish politics is a career that, despite the perception of
some, remains very much open to anyone who chooses to
stand as a candidate. The varied nature and background of
many TDs is testament to this. It is also open to anyone to
try and establish a dynasty, whether they themselves had a
family background in politics or not. But so long as, unlike
in ancient Rome, your seat or your position is not something you can gift to a new generation, it is still the free

choice of the people to decide to follow you, and in particular your party organisation.

Irish politics at grassroots level, however, operates in a manner closely akin to the Romans' client-based system. Candidates are often selected by virtue of the fact that people feel they owe something to a particular individual – a situation perpetuated by the high levels of political access afforded to the Irish public by the current system of constituency based politics and multi-seat constituencies. A politician generally builds up a wealth of people who feel that they were served well by them. The politician will have a strong and influential inner circle who will be well versed in the art of winning elections in the constituency in question. These teams of volunteers are invaluable, but cannot be bought, and work instead entirely out of a dedicated belief in what they are doing. So when it comes to finding a replacement for a TD, the obvious place to start is with their family. The family member has a number of distinct advantages: they know the inner circle well, have gained their trust, and have usually soldiered with them in the past. Those around the former politician will move with much more ease to a family member bearing the name than one of their own number promoted above them. But perhaps most important of all is the 'favours' list, particularly when going before the general public. Good work done at constituency level rarely transfers along with the party badge, instead such loyalty in voting patterns is only afforded to the individual. So a son or daughter or relative can count on many of the people who voted for the name previously to continue to do so out of loyalty for work well done. A new candidate, without a recognised family name, will get little or no credit for any works done by their predecessor, and will have to establish a client list of their own from scratch.

But that's not where the advantages end. Those at the head of political organisations also know that the politician's life isn't for everyone. It is sometimes said that you either get into politics very young and know no different, or get into it much later in life having never been part of it before, in which case you don't know what you are getting into! There have been a number of celebrated cases where celebrity candidates have simply not worked out. Much of the reason for this lies with a lack of understanding of the processes and what the public really want. A family member will have grown up with the political system, they understand the importance of knocking on doors, they realise how humdrum and dull much of the experience can be. They know the hours are far in excess of those demanded in any other walk of life. They know that family life comes second to politics. They know it involves being out every night of every week and that you and your family are now public property. The family member can usually be relied on not to be shocked by the system or the demands, they understand about waiting your time for a promotion, they know how this game must be played. They are, in a word, dependable.

In a 2010 academic study '*keeping it in the family*', Doyle, McNulty and O'Malley argued that it was not culture that gave us political dynasties but instead personalised party organisations and a candidate-based electoral system that led to their growth. Observing the families contained in this book it is difficult to disagree with that conclusion, indeed everything would seem to support it. The focus of this book is an attempt to give a background and insight into the story of how some of these families attained power, and how it has been successfully passed along. Rather than trying to give an exhaustive survey of the subject, this book looks at the names that are instantly recognisable today, names that even a casual observer of the present Dáil will recognise. There are many other dynasties not covered here, especially from the past, whose stories are equally interesting and important.

What is not entirely clear is whether such families have brought anything distinctive to Irish politics that unconnected individuals have not. Perhaps there is a continuity in policy carried on from predecessors? Is there such a thing as raw talent in politics, and might it have a genetic element? Here we try to find out why some families become so obsessed with political power, and what the levels of political achievement associated with each one really are. Some have shown little continuity; some have manufactured an image; some have been proud servants; others have proved unwilling or unable to adapt or change with the times. Some have reached the highest levels of power and influence only for it all to crumble into dust. Nonetheless, such dynasties will remain a feature of Irish political life for the foreseeable future. As Michael Corleone might say, 'Don't ever take sides with anyone against the family'.

The Cosgraves:
Heirs to the Free State

The Irish State did not have an easy birth. Generations of rebellions finally culminated in the War of Independence and the new Irish Free State, minus six of the counties of Ulster. One of the hallmarks both of the Irish revolutionary movement, and indeed the Civil War that followed the establishment of the Free State, was the powerful personalities that led the respective groups. The Civil War sacrificed the lives of many talented people to the cause of Ireland, but probably the most notable casualty was Michael Collins. However, Collins was a military leader, and it is hard to say what kind of impact he would have had on the establishment of a civil state. One thing we do know is that in the absence of major figures and personalities the early Free State followed an unassuming man, a man of piety and conservatism, and in doing so established one of the first great political dynasties in Irish history.

W.T. Cosgrave was born in James's Street Dublin on 5 June 1880. He joined Sinn Féin as a youth, and made his first major break in politics by getting elected to Dublin Corporation in 1909. He was not just a politician, but a man of strong conviction, who during the 1916 rising had served under Éamonn Ceannt at the South Dublin Union. His part in this was rewarded with internment at Frongoch in Wales until early 1917. He was elected as an MP for Kilkenny North in a by-election later that year, but as an abstentionist he never took his seat. In 1919 he married his fiancée Louise and began the family that would be the basis of one of Ireland's first political dynasties.

Cosgrave supported the Anglo-Irish treaty, and sided with Collins and Griffith in this regard. He succeeded Michael Collins as the Chairman of the Provisional Government in 1922, and just a month later he took over from Arthur Griffith as president of the Dáil.

The Irish public was used to larger-than-life characters and personalities. Michael Collins had been a man of inspiration to many, and so had Éamon De Valera. The leaders of 1916 were equally flamboyant and decisive. Ireland faced an unenviable situation. The revolutionaries and dreamers had finally taken over, but with little experience of running a state or government. Most were men well used to war and insurrection and the disregard of established authority. But what happens when such men, and indeed women, win and in turn become the authority themselves? De Valera and Griffith were both recognised politicians, but with De Valera opposed to the Treaty and still part of an abstentionist Sinn Féin policy, and with the death of Griffith, the new Irish State needed someone who would be a reliable hand on the tiller.

Cumann na nGaedheal turned to W.T. Cosgrave, in no small part due to his experience of politics having served previously on Dublin Corporation. He may not have brought the same obvious passion or style to the role, but he brought something much more important at this time: an understanding of the dangers a new state faces, an awareness of *realpolitik* and knowledge of the limitations facing those who were now in control.

Ireland had suffered badly in the previous decades. It was, in the main, a poor society ravaged by major social issues and problems. Long-term poverty had left a scar on the society that seemed impossible to heal at the time. As well as the loss of lives, World War One had led to food shortages and dealt a blow to the economic stability of a country so dependent on Britain. The War of Independence did nothing to help economic matters once power changed hands: damage was still evident, lawlessness still gripped the State and many items of strategic governmental infrastructure were still damaged. The Civil War on top of all this had almost destroyed what hope there was of a bright future for Ireland. There was no doubt this was an extremely weak and fragile economy that seemed to have little chance of lasting for long.

Though Cosgrave had a very weak hand of cards to play, he got to work quickly, showing the kind of rigorous mind that he possessed for administrative thinking. He ended the dual executive system by merging the Provisional Government and the Dáil Government. While this was a natural step to take, it was also the foundation of the Oireachtas as we know it. This was quickly followed by the formulation of a new constitution and the purchase of Leinster House to become the seat of the Dáil and Seanad. Cosgrave was also adept at adopting British institutions and methods and putting them to work for Ireland. He possessed a keen understanding of government and the machinery necessary for a state to function. In these years, democracy itself was still something of an experiment. Ireland held close to the British system, but was well aware that the US, for instance, followed a very different one. Of course it should not be forgotten that the US and Britain were almost alone as examples, for much of the rest of the world was by now looking to Communism or Fascism as viable alternatives to democracy, which many thought to be a deeply flawed and unworkable system. Considering the political origins and beliefs of many members of Sinn Féin, the fact that Ireland did not fall into any of these traps is remarkable, and Cosgrave was central to this. In particular, Cosgrave was influenced by his experience of the parliamentary and democratic traditions, and this was a central reason he was chosen as leader. Brian Farrell

has pointed out that one of the reasons that Ireland managed to control its destiny and come through its traumatic birth was that the political movements benefited from their roots in the British parliamentary system. This tradition, strongly espoused by the likes of Parnell and the Irish Parliamentary Party, was at the fulcrum of the thinking that held the fledgling State together. Ireland was also fortunate in that politicians like Daniel O'Connell and Parnell had managed to settle major issues from Catholic emancipation to the Land Acts peaceably and through parliamentary procedure, giving the people a level of faith in the process that was absent in many other new democracies of the twentieth century.

Ireland faced major problems, and politics, at such a turbulent time, was no simple matter. Insurrection and rebellion still gripped a large portion of the population. The State faced ongoing threats and needed to bring lawlessness under control. Undoubtedly Ireland needed a strong hand to deal with such problems. However, Cosgrave was a man of very stern belief in this regard. Indeed some might contend that he was too stern. While many of his law and order measures might have been argued to be necessary, there is no doubt that few states today could get away with such proposals. In a time before Amnesty International or other such groups, Cosgrave showed a not so pleasant side to his character; a side that would stop at nothing to achieve what was essentially a military objective. In September 1922 he brought in the Special Powers Resolution Act, which was a truly draconian piece of legislation. It gave authority to the Army to hold Military Courts – often of questionable standing – and to impose the death penalty for certain offences. Such legislation may have been justifiable from a military point of view, but it raised serious humanitarian and civil rights questions.

Erskine Childers Snr was infamously one of its early victims after being found in possession of an illegal firearm. He was tried in secret, found guilty and sentenced to death.

By 1923, some 13,000 Republican prisoners were detained in camps around the country, and there is little doubt that such fearsome measures had a role in ending the Civil War. It could, however, be argued that the epublican cause was waning in any event, and less severe measures might have brought about the same objective. It is certainly difficult for a modern critic to approve of such legislation, and much higher demands would be placed on leaders today to find an alternative resolution. Cosgrave and his family were not immune to the ravages of the Civil War, however, as their own home in Templeogue was burned to the ground during this period.

Cosgrave managed to move on from this unpleasant business to focus on the establishment of the State, establishing Cumann na nGaedheal in order to fight the 1923 General Election as one united and identifiable party. Cosgrave certainly came into his own during the period from 1923 to 1927. He understood, even as a former revolutionary, that you do not throw out the baby with the bath water, and saved Ireland a great deal of stress and uncertainty by basing many institutions and in particular the legal system on that of Britain. Local government was put on a firm footing, a civil police force established, the civil service was made to fit the new State (which, as anyone looking at Ireland's current public sector reform difficulties knows, must have been no small task in itself), while currency and broad economic policies were also high on the agenda. The ESB was the first semi-state company to be established, and the construction of the power station at Ardnacrusha was a development that would terrify governments of far greater resources.

The Land Act of 1923 was a brave and necessary piece of legislation. In terms of statesmanship, Cosgrave led Ireland into its first international setting by joining the League of Nations. Governments must set priorities, and while housing was a major failure of his Government, as was any kind of coherent welfare policy, it is difficult to see how they could have addressed every issue that arose during that difficult time.

The assassination of Kevin O'Higgins marked a turning point for Irish politics. O'Higgins was seen as the tough guy in the Government, and his death brought into sharp relief just how questionable Ireland's credentials as a peaceful and democratic society truly were. Increasingly, Cosgrave faced questions about his policies, most notably regarding the extent to which he was willing to stay tied to Britain and dependent upon it. While this could be argued to be an economic reality that was largely impervious to political decisions, it also showed that Cosgrave, despite his revolutionary past, was still the product of the system and part of established political machinery. Cosgrave only managed to form a Government after the 1927 Election due to Fianna Fáil still refusing to take the oath of allegiance. However, the fortunes of Cumann na nGaedheal were on the wane, and Cosgrave must have seen the writing on the wall. When the world economic depression hit it was the last straw, and perhaps it was this more than anything else that highlighted a lack of charisma or ability to engender belief on Cosgrave's part. He was a safe pair of hands, but would never be an inspirational leader.

The Eucharistic Congress of 1932 was a very big event for Catholic Ireland; Cosgrave even held the General Election in February so as not to disturb the event in June. This proved to be an electoral disaster. One TD, Patrick Reynolds from the Leitrim-Sligo constituency, lost his life while canvassing, so the gun was still not entirely gone from politics even then. Fianna Fáil won the Election and came to power under Éamon De Valera, and yet again the revolutionaries had taken control. The changing economic wind had been harsh and Cosgrave helped form a new party: Fine Gael, but perhaps showed an error of judgment in allowing Eoin O'Duffy, of blueshirt fame, to assume the leadership. Two years later Cosgrave would have to take command yet again, and held the position until 1944.

Cosgrave was a pious and educated man, a Knight of the Grand order of Pius IX, and he received several honorary degrees. He was a conservative, and very strongly so, but that was not out of step with the times. A believer in the establishment of firm systems and law and order, even, it might be said, at any cost. He was not the type of man who was at ease mingling with the masses, but he certainly believed in service to his country. His Government was harsh in relation to liquor laws, and treated this as the great evil of the time. W.T. even considered a Senate entirely of theologians to provide moral advice to the Dáil, believing that this would be a Catholic and Church-run Senate to advise the politicians. It never came to pass. Many years later Éamon De Valera would describe Cosgrave and his Cabinet as 'magnificent', and in any kind of judgment of their administrative capabilities this is true. They may not have been a socially led Government, but then perhaps that was not the priority of a fledgling State still in its infancy. It is remarkable that although he continued to lead the opposition, Cosgrave almost fades from the pages of history once his term in government was up.

His son Liam took up the flag of the dynasty, and somewhat fittingly in 1965, the very year that W.T. Cosgrave died, his son Liam became the leader of Fine Gael. A family tradition was certainly in the making, and in 1973, with Fianna Fáil reeling from the arms trial, Fine Gael came to power and Liam Cosgrave became Taoiseach, thus giving Ireland its first, and so far only, father and son Taoiseach combination.

The story could not have been scripted any better in a Hollywood movie. W.T. had been instrumental in the founding of the State, but found himself unable to compete with the passion and political abilities of Fianna Fáil when they finally entered mainstream politics. He led the opposition to them, but in these years, apart from a short break, Fianna Fáil had a monopoly on power. Liam Cosgrave was to break this monopoly. He brought Labour and Fine Gael together in an unlikely partnership, and held them together as a cohesive Government, thus giving the Irish people an option other than single-party government, and an alternative to Fianna Fáil.

Liam Cosgrave's task in this matter should not be under-estimated. Fine Gael and Labour did not make easy bedfellows. Fine Gael was centre-right in policy, but Labour was very much left-wing. Fine Gael was highly conservative while Labour was far more liberal. Fine Gael, and in partic-ular the Cosgraves, had been particularly strong supporters of the Catholic Church and its position, while Labour included some of its fiercest critics. Fine Gael represented more of what might be described as the upper class of the time, while Labour naturally had its base among the working class. And keeping all these factions together had to be done against the backdrop of a Fianna Fáil party that was well-placed somewhere in the middle between Fine Gael and Labour on most of the issues, always threatening the support base of both should they be pulled too far in one direction.

Cosgrave had other problems to deal with too. Like any centrist party, Fine Gael was a broad church, and any coali-tion with Labour brought to the fore those who might be more disposed to that way of thinking within Fine Gael. There were many modernisers and reformers who found support for at least some of their ideas in the Labour party. Managing this was no small task. One thing we can certainly say is that the Cosgrave dynasty was ideologically consistent at this stage. There are many parallels that can be drawn between Liam and his father. Most noticeably, Liam showed a firm belief in law and order in the strictest sense, and while the troubles in the North escalated, he showed no willingness to allow any kind of overspill into the republic. And, like W.T., Liam was a conservative Catholic who placed great importance on the role of the church and in taking a cautious step-by-step approach to everything. For many he would be remembered for this. He once said that 'Jews and Muslims should settle their differences in a Christian manner'.

Liam was a man for whom religion, morals and faith had a deep effect, and he was unable to separate them from matters of State. In a scene that would be almost impossible to imagine in modern Ireland, Cosgrave actually voted against his own Government on a bill to make contraceptives more freely available. Such a move today would probably bring down any Government. Cosgrave was reflective of a debate and change already happening in Irish society that was eating away at both Fine Gael and Fianna Fáil. Cosgrave and his supporters felt a duty to their faith, to God and to a higher moral authority. Others saw the State as separate from the Church and considered that it should be run as such. For many in Ireland this debate presented a challenge. On one side there were those who felt that everything they believed was being stripped away, that morals were breaking down, that someone had to defend against an onslaught of change. These people were continually dismissed as unthinking, old-fashioned, and foolish. This stereotype only served to make their views more entrenched. Many of them, like Cosgrave himself, were sound thinkers, but there was a rush to dismiss many of their views.

Liam Cosgrave had much in common with his father. He strove to keep Fine Gael in line with the ideals his father had established, and with similar personality. However, Fine Gael was changing and he was almost powerless to stop it. The loss of the 1977 Election with a landslide in support of Fianna Fáil was the end for Cosgrave. He was succeeded as leader by Garrett Fitzgerald, who was a reformer, and his ascent marked the end of the reserved, conservative and understated Cosgrave approach within Fine Gael. As the era of personality was about to launch in Ireland, there was perhaps no other option for Fine Gael if they were to compete with Fianna Fáil. Ireland had changed and Fine Gael had to change too. But perhaps the most interesting fact was how the change would also affect the dynasty.

Liam Cosgrave has two daughters who still hold council seats, but neither ever succeeded in gaining election to the Dáil. His son, Liam T. Cosgrave, carried on the dynasty in the Oireachtas. He secured a seat in the Dún Laoghaire constituency in 1981, and managed to hold the seat through both General Elections in 1982. The power of the name was fading, though, and he did not mange to make a significant impact during the Fine Gael/Labour coalition from 1982 to 1987. The 1987 General Election saw him lose the seat. He made every effort to regain his position, but was defeated again in 1989. One final attempt was made in 1992, but this too met with failure, and it seemed the impact of the Cosgrave dynasty and its electoral appeal was to be consigned to history.

As is often the case, however, members of political dynasties who enjoy good recognition of their name can find refuge and rebirth in the Senate. Cosgrave secured a seat there in 1993, and also served as Cathaoirleach. This indicates that his stock still remained reasonably high among his peers, and also suggests that his career might yet have reignited. He did not contest the 1997 General Election, but was returned to the Senate, and this helped to nurture and strengthen his hand politically.

All things come to he who waits, and as the 2002 General Election beckoned, the window of opportunity opened for Cosgrave once again. Dún Laoghaire was always considered heartland territory for Fine Gael, but this had been cast into severe doubt in recent elections. In 1997, Monica Barnes and Sean Barrett both took seats for Fine Gael. Though this restored some pride, they did not intend to stand in 2002. Cosgrave, with his background and senate role, was the obvious choice to fill the vacancy. He was joined on the ticket by Helen Keogh who had defected from the Progressive Democrats having lost her seat in 1997.

Although Fine Gael was in no doubt that it faced a difficult election, Cosgrave had every reason to be confident. It could well be expected that even on a bad day this constituency would return one Fine Gael TD. There was also a feeling that the true Fine Gael vote would rally behind Cosgrave. However, John Bailey also contested the election for Fine Gael. Though he was well-known in GAA circles, Cosgrave had more heritage and experience. The three-candidate strategy was a surprise considering that polls indicated a tight election for Fine Gael, and that a two-candidate strategy had worked so well in 1997.

Of course, 2002 was an even worse disaster for Fine Gael than they had anticipated. Its bad strategy was found out in Dún Laoghaire, where its percentage share of the vote was just under half of what it received in 1997. Cosgrave received just over 3,000 votes, and Keogh was only marginally better, with Bailey bringing up the rear at 1,700. The candidates simply had far too much ground to make up, and bad strategy was exposed by the fact that although both the Progressive Democrats and the Green party received a smaller percentage share of the vote, they both took seats while Fine Gael was left with none.

It was a telling blow for the once mighty Cosgrave dynasty. Liam chose not to contest the Seanad elections, and even darker clouds were emerging on the horizon. His success was limited politically as he failed to make an impact on a party that seemed to have moved on so much from the Cosgrave era that it found it difficult to reach into its past and identify with the name any more. Cosgrave's own actions perhaps echoed this. In 2003, a Tribunal of Inquiry into payments to politicians uncovered a number of donations made to Liam T. Cosgrave. Such actions, while not uncommon to a core of politicians in his own era, were probably as far from the world of W.T. as one could get. Evidence perhaps that politics had moved on so completely. Fine Gael moved to expel Liam, and he suggested that it was an attempt to erase the Cosgrave name from Fine Gael history. His argument did not carry much weight, either within Fine Gael or among the wider public.

Liam T. Cosgrave pleaded guilty to a charge of failure to disclose a political donation from the lobbyist Frank Dunlop, and was sentenced to 75 hours community service. In 2010 he appeared again before a criminal court as part of the ongoing investigation. It will likely mark the end of any hope of a future political career. It was seen as a sad demise for the Cosgrave dynasty. But while this episode undoubtedly damaged the family name, it is unlikely that it will outweigh the significant achievements and reputation of previous generations when their history is written.

It was evidence that Ireland had become a very different country, and the Cosgrave family had been caught up in these changes and questionable practices. Toughest of all was the fact that it was perhaps an admission that those on the side of austerity and conservatism had lost the argument. Both Fine Gael and Fianna Fáil had sensed a changing mood among the public. The people wanted charisma and reform, even if it meant that other, less welcome, changes came too. Big personalities now controlled politics, and creating an impression was the secret of success. Politics was also becoming a costly business, out of all proportion to the pay in the '80s and early '90s, which was far from being lavish. The lifestyles that politicians now displayed, that went with their carefully crafted images to impress the public, were difficult to sustain. This led to a culture among a number who felt that supplementing their income with donations to defray election costs and indeed lifestyle costs was somehow acceptable. It became part of how things were done, and was a shameful period for politics. The fact that it was accepted by a few, or felt to be justified, did not make it right, and it constituted a serious abuse of position and privilege. This shameful behaviour in public office was encountered by all parties, but in particular by Fianna Fáil, who saw a litany of household names caught up in reprehensible financial practices.

As pay increased, such practices became more and more unacceptable, even among the politicians themselves. An increasing number of politicians who did not engage in such practices now had the resources to compete with the others who did. A lid had been lifted on Irish politics, and the public did not like what they saw. Clientelism was one thing, but corruption was another matter entirely. The Irish electorate could understand a favour, to say the least. They could understand the nature of political access and influence, but not when this was proven to be contrary to the public good and certainly not when money was involved. Some politicians might accuse the electorate of double standards, and there were many who argued that events were being viewed through more moralistic modern eyes than existed at the time. The reality is, however, that the electorate were pragmatic; they did not expect saints to represent them. They were willing to allow leeway to politicians to reach decisions and were generally accepting of *realpolitik*. However, open bribery, and politicians making money, not for the gain of even their party but for their own personal use, was just a step too far. Like a disapproving parent who finds a child has broken the fair and generous parameters they set out, the electorate felt betrayed and let down.

Well-paid positions were far removed from the origins of the Cosgrave dynasty. But in part it was the failure of politicians like the Cosgraves to modernise sufficiently that caused them to disappear in terms of influence, which handed the new culture its success. Many people would today hold much respect for both W.T. Cosgrave and his son Liam and their quiet and understated approach.

While W.T. and Liam Cosgrave showed that a family could have the same values passed father to son, some question mark might justifiably be raised over whether this was true of later generations. Such a question is difficult to appraise, in as much as the attitudes and principles of a politician must be judged in relation to the society in which they lived, and the rate of change of Irish society over the period in question meant that the various generations of the Cosgrave dynasty virtually lived in different worlds. What we do know is that this dynasty was remarkably influential, and lays claim to some of the most profound and long-lasting effects on Irish society. It is a name that will continue to hold a strong resonance in Fine Gael. But while the Cosgrave name was held in high esteem within Fine Gael, it never came to define the party or to be used as a benchmark for the future in the way that De Valera or Lemass would be referred to in Fianna Fáil.

The biggest problem for the Cosgraves as a dynasty was that they failed to move with the times and adapt to a new Ireland. The actions of Liam Cosgrave Jnr pointed to a willingness to adapt all too readily to other, less acceptable parts of the new political reality. But Liam Cosgrave Snr was unable to hold back the tide in Fine Gael. As reforming figures like Garret Fitzgerald emerged in Fine Gael, it became increasingly clear that Cosgrave was part of an old conservative Ireland that was beginning to pass. Honesty and integrity was still valued, but it had to be put in a new context. In time, the Cosgrave name became a symbol of austere, cold, conservative politics out of touch with Ireland. This clung to the family far more than its reputation for honesty, and it was in this regard the dynasty needed to move with the times. An inability to build upon the strength of the name, to incorporate new reforms into an older and more conservative agenda proved its undoing. That understated approach, with its attendant rejection of 'personality politics', was capable of being a great strength, but often proved a source of weakness, particularly as the political landscape changed around them. Despite generating two Taoisigh, the name will always be associated with decent and strong administration much more than with drive, passion, enthusiasm, charisma or personality. But each of these are qualities found in great leaders the world over; they are necessary ingredients to inspire a people and persuade them of the rightness of a cause. As Fine Gael searched for leaders it moved away from the Cosgrave approach, and indeed perhaps even the Cosgraves themselves were forced to leave the old ways behind.

While the name still boasts members at local government level, it is difficult to see it regaining its past glory in the near future. Of course, it could be argued that Enda Kenny's success in reforming Fine Gael, and in leading them to their greatest ever election result in 2011, is largely attributable to the Cosgravian approach of being understated, and if anything somewhat lacking in inspirational qualities. In recent years, a number of public appearances by Liam Cosgrave senior have lent some gravitas to the name. Notably, however, in the recent resurgence of Fine Gael there has been little reference to their past, or to the Cosgraves as representing any kind of ideological base for the future. Nonetheless, it remains a name that stood for something worthwhile and made a significant contribution to Irish society at the time when it needed it the most.

The De Valeras:
A Name that Says it All

If there is one name that dominates the history of the Irish State it is probably that of De Valera. It remains one of the most powerful names in politics, evoking images of high patriotism, idealism and honour for some, but of austerity, conservatism and outdated views for others.

The dynasty is still overshadowed by the image and strength of its founder, Éamon De Valera. As a dynasty that has produced two senior cabinet ministers in recent times, it is a perfect example of what having such a powerful founder can do. Carrying the De Valera name has proven to be a strong electoral asset, and all but guarantees a trouble-free journey straight to a senior and respected position, certainly within Fianna Fáil. However, it is equally a burden that is almost impossible to live up to. Love him or hate him, Éamon De Valera was one of the most dominant figures ever to grace the Irish political stage. When a politician can count among their achievements having fought in 1916, being imprisoned for their country, establishing a brand new political movement that becomes the most popular in the State, writing a new constitution that has stood the test of time for some decades, and leading their country through the Second World War, as well as being the only person to have held the posts of both Taoiseach and President, then it is always going to be a tough act to follow. Trying to establish your own place in political history with the De Valera name is thus an almost insurmountable task. It's a classic case of a dynasty carrying on with strength, yet still being completely overpowered by the views and personality of its founder. That these views cannot be shaken is the very thing that threatens the dynasty the most, and no successor to the mantle has ever been able to establish themselves sufficiently to modernise the name or what it represents in Ireland.

Many biographies have been written on Éamon De Valera, and an abundance of views exist, ranging from the patronising (that he was self-centered, limited and indecisive) to the outlandish (that he was an English spy). We will perhaps never know exactly what the true De Valera really encapsulated. We do know that his electoral record was impressive and, despite some high profile losses, he was a politician of the very highest standard by any form of measurement.

De Valera was a dreamer. He loved the Irish language and Irish heritage, like many of the 1916 revolutionaries; he thought a perfect world would be possible if Ireland was left to its own devices. This part of his personality would infect both his politics and those of every generation of De Valeras to follow. It was an ideal that, despite his general political pragmatism, held him fast to the dream of a very Irish Ireland – a dream from which he was never shaken. It hampered the view people had of him as time moved on. His radicalism also partially explained his stance on the Civil War. Michael Laffan described De Valera, as well as many others involved in 1916, as having made the move directly from cultural nationalism to military nationalism. Both in this respect, and as a latecomer to politics, De Valera could not be more different from W.T. Cosgrave. His military nationalist views and his comparatively late start in the political life of his country make his political brilliance all the more remarkable.

In time, De Valera showed a far better understanding of politics than most of his contemporaries. Perhaps his only equal in this sphere was Charles Stewart Parnell. De Valera also understood revolutionary politics very well. While Michael Collins possessed a brilliant military mind, De Valera was far more in tune with what needed to happen alongside those military maneuvers. Collins may have been the man who knew how to win, but De Valera knew what to do with a win to make it count. In this regard he sat neatly between the likes of Collins and Padraig Pearse. De Valera knew the importance of sacrifice, the importance of being seen as a nation, as a people. He knew how to win a propaganda war with Britain. Collins saw much of 1916 as a waste of life: they were battles he knew the Irish could not win, and that more covert methods were necessary. But these methods often allowed the British to portray the Irish as a brutal group of murderers. De Valera sought to change this. Padraig Pearse had known that Ireland had to face up to Britain as a country, and not just in small-scale activities. But Pearse was too embedded in the political dream. Pearse believed in patriotism even to the point of giving up his life. Admirable as that sentiment might have been, a dead leader was only a short-term help, and other, more pragmatic, methods had to be embraced to actually win against a superior enemy. Otherwise, you may simply run out of leaders.

De Valera ensured that while Collins caused havoc for Britain, the successes were seen in a positive light. He understood the fact even at this early stage that while guerrilla warfare could be a highly effective military strategy, it was also one that would not be accepted by the world at large. He knew therefore the importance of insisting that the IRA was a proper Army of the people, and of characterising its exploits as a fight with a foreign power.

It remains one of the great mysteries of Irish history that Éamon De Valera refused to attend peace treaty talks in Britain when the War of Independence, waged in 1920/21, had finally brought the British to the table. After many years of analysis and brilliant commentaries on De Valera we are really no nearer an answer that fits from all angles.

Diarmaid Ferriter's biography, *Judging Dev*, probably gives the most honest account of this period. While it is difficult to understand De Valera's true reasoning, it is likely that he believed he could send a team to negotiate and then wade in himself towards the end to drive for a better deal. De Valera seems to have genuinely believed that Collins and Griffith were wrong to sign a Treaty without ratification by the Dáil, and thought that they had kept him in the dark during negotiations. However, as Ferriter points out, if either of these were the case then it was De Valera who had failed to make the position clear and who had caused the ambiguity.

Of course De Valera chose to oppose the Treaty, and opposed the Free State during the Irish Civil War. It was a bloody and pointless waste of life. Both sides engaged in horrific and unforgivable acts of brutality. De Valera was a talented politician, but the Civil War was not his finest hour. In the decades that followed he would regain his ability to think and act in line with that talent. During the Civil War, however, De Valera found himself at the head of a group of rebels with no funds, poor weapons and no real idea of what they were going to do if they won. De Valera dithered, second guessed himself and seems to have been racked by doubts. On the other side, Collins was decisive, single-minded and perfectly suited to this kind of pseudo-military state. In almost every aspect of the Civil War, Collins came out on top. He did not wait or procrastinate, and he did not fear the situation. In modern terms, one could say that Collins cared little for, and did not feel, 'the hand of history', but took his decisions and dealt with the consequences leaving no room for debate or doubt.

Some of those who supported De Valera most vociferously were women. In fact all six female TDs voted against the Treaty, and Dr Tom Garvin has argued that incidental evidence would suggest that in the wider population women were more likely to oppose the Treaty than men. This is perhaps explained by the fact that there was still a view that women should not be involved in politics, and this meant that those who were, or had opinions on such matters, tended to be more radical in their views, this being a precondition of stating an opinion in the first place.

The Treaty split proved a factor that is intrinsic to dynasties: the personal nature of Irish politics. Evidence suggests that people picked a side based on their love of, or loyalty to, others, in particular to De Valera or Collins. Harry Boland said himself that he 'could not let Dev down'. On the other side, it was famously opined that 'If it's good enough for Mick Collins, it's good enough for me'. The way these views were stated points away from principled political ideology, and towards the power of name and personality; factors that still dominate allegiance to political parties in Ireland to this day.

As the Civil War ended, it appeared that the pro-Treaty side had well and truly won. The nation at large had tired of fighting and had no stomach for any more division and warfare when a peaceful future was being offered. De Valera and the anti-Treaty side were a defeated bunch. They had lost their ideal of a free, united Ireland, and had lost any argument to keep a fight going when they had been soundly beaten militarily, particularly with the aid of British equipment and arms. The Free State was established and very much in control, and it was clear that that was not going to change. The future must have looked rather bleak to De Valera at that point. The new Ireland was moving on, and he was not at the helm.

That was not helped by a political movement in Sinn Féin that seemed unable to grasp the new realities. De Valera led a push to change its abstentionist policy, quickly coming to appreciate that being on the outside shouting might be a principled stand, but it also meant you could never effect any serious change or have any impact on the lives of the people. Any man of action as opposed to just words knows that it is in implementation rather than policy discussion that the real reward lies.

The majority of the Sinn Féin party, however, still held fast to the abstentionist policy, being more concerned with the old traditional values and visions than any pragmatic advancement. This caused a major problem for De Valera and his followers. The political wilderness beckoned, and the only option was to get out.

This decision was a fateful one. It consigned Sinn Féin to being little more than a political fringe group for the rest of its days. De Valera was supported by the leading lights in the party, and some of its most noteworthy figures. His right-hand man, Seán Lemass, was a key figure as regards organisation. Frank Aiken was a former IRA Chief of Staff. Sean MacEntee, Gerry Boland, James Ryan, Sean T. O'Kelly and Margaret Pearse were all individuals with impeccable republican credentials, and leading political thinkers of their time. It was an illustrious set of names, and these charismatic men and women were not equalled on the opposite side of the division. The challenge was to harness these talents into a functioning, coherent and purely peaceful political movement.

This led to the formation of a new party, Fianna Fáil, for that very purpose. It encompassed everything that Ireland was so desperately hungry for at the time, and De Valera had assembled a political outfit to give the people exactly what they wanted. It was a party committed to constitutional pol-itics, which was welcomed by a war-weary public. Yet it still contained that whiff of sulphur that the Irish still admired so much: it was as anti-establishment as establishment poli-tics can legitimately be, peopled by men and women who came across as fearless reformers and the true heirs to the spirit of 1916. While the party made strong noises about a united Ireland, the truth was this was a new movement that acted out what might or perhaps should have happened for Sinn Féin if they had taken over the full country. It was a party designed for the 26 counties that could represent the ideals of those who had fought for a free Ireland.

One of the key factors in trying to understand De Valera and perhaps the De Valera dynasty, along with many of the other dynasties that were founded under the Fianna Fáil banner, is to understand the thinking that informed what those inside this new organisation believed it to be. The party was highly pragmatic. Despite De Valera's belief in self-sufficiency, it was clear that men like Lemass knew how to promote business, and quickly those with wealth and property began to feel that they could identify with this new party and had nothing to fear from it. It was not a communist party that might seize land or profits. The roots of the party were with small farm holdings across the country, its leaders always most at ease with the smaller-scale farmers, who where many times more populous than their larger counterparts who favoured Cumann na nGaedheal. Its republican traditions lent it a left-wing idealism, in the sense that it was a party that still favoured public enterprise and was concerned with the plight of workers and individuals who were struggling. This gave it a reforming nature, and meant that no matter what your background, no matter what your outlook, Fianna Fáil was a compromise that could bring everyone together in one great family of Irishness. At least that was how it was sold and perceived by its members.

De Valera was instrumental in that. He managed to blend being a political visionary with being a man who could accept harsh practical realities. This was exemplified by the agreement of De Valera and Fianna Fáil to take the oath of allegiance in order to take their seats in the Dáil. This had supposedly been a reason for the Civil War, but with a law now passed effectively banning abstention as a policy in the wake of the murder of Kevin O'Higgins, De Valera and his supporters, no matter how principled, had run out of options. They could either put up with that new reality, or could effectively give up politics. In a style that would become typical of Fianna Fáil throughout its existence, they swallowed their pride and suffered the ignominy of taking the oath. For some it was the ultimate humiliation of the republicans. Indeed, De Valera himself described it as 'contrary to all our former actions and... painful and humiliating'. But in truth their ability to take the blow and keep going allowed them to grow and to assume control in the new State, effectively pushing the victors of the Civil War into the role of onlookers for the following 80 years of its history. The ability to espouse political principles was important when it came to being an inspiring and magnetic personality who could gather popular support, but it was the ability to quietly jettison those principles when it became politically expedient to do so that mattered when it came to taking power and maintaining that position.

The Church did not support the early incarnation of Fianna Fáil. Indeed, they had excommunicated De Valera and his followers during the Civil War. The Church was not sure what to expect from this organisation. But, being a political organisation not unlike Fianna Fáil itself, it quickly began to mend bridges with the party once it saw that it was becoming an unstoppable machine in the towns and villages across the country. In typical fashion, religious opinion was divided, with many Bishops and key church figures still favouring Cumann na nGaedheal. But the ordinary priests on the ground, often deeply embedded in the daily lives of the people in their parishes, were becoming more and more convinced of the merits of Fianna Fáil, or at least its prospects for significant political power.

Fianna Fáil began to realise those prospects, coming to power for the first time in 1932. Perhaps not surprisingly given its republican leanings, it did so with the support of the Labour party. This arrangement only lasted for a year, however, as De Valera showed the true nature of the Fianna Fáil beast by quickly going to the country in 1933 when the times were better, thus allowing it to dispense with another party having to be appeased, and leaving it free to implement its own policies at will.

De Valera has come in for much criticism as a politician. He waged a financial war with Britain that did great damage to Ireland economically, although it also created a national sense of spirit that was perhaps De Valera's aim all along. He knew then just as he did in 1916 that a policy does not have to be successful to still achieve a desired result. The protectionist policies were part of something De Valera believed in deeply. That kind of thinking was something that would mark his views and his dynasty. The De Valera name would always be associated with a proud, if insular, view of Ireland. That view was reoinforced when heirs to the name, Síle De Valera and Eamon O'Cuív, both expressed serious doubts about the EU during the Nice Treaty Referendum. In fact, you could say that by doing so they reinforced the brand.

Protectionism did create some jobs, however, in the protected industries, and these were sold well by a propaganda machine. It is often forgotten that during World War Two, when the world markets effectively closed, Ireland also benefited somewhat from its protectionist past when people had learned to work within the economic confines of the island. Self-sufficiency helped the people survive. It was, however, a small victory. Protectionism and self-sufficiency were always nice ideas and visions but completely unpractical. De Valera unfortunately found this hard to accept, and it was left to Lemass in later years to save the country from being a backward and ostracised island.

It is beyond any reasonable argument that protectionism was a failure, and Ireland would have benefited from Lemass coming to power a lot earlier. De Valera's personality must be understood in relation to how he viewed the world. Across Europe countries had ravaged themselves and each other with political ideologies, as communism, fascism, socialism, capitalism and a host of other ideals caused strife for millions. The leaders ranged from the plain mad to the idealistic dreamers, but the results were often the same: pain and suffering for ordinary people. This would have given De Valera an extreme scepticism about mixing with other countries and importing their ideals. He understood probably better than anyone how dangerous an ideal can be. It could seduce an entire people into believing its worth, but such experiments were usually costly, and De Valera himself had been responsible for such flirtations in his more radical past. De Valera had become a firm proponent of the status quo. It is perhaps something he learned the hard way from the Civil War, which must seen as the one time when pragmatism deserted him and he let idealism take full control.

This reflects another important aspect of the dynasty's position in Irish society. It had somehow completed a journey from being excommunicated and revolutionary to becoming an important part of the establishment, to the extent of being almost synonymous with it. There the name would firmly remain, becoming the focus of all future 'revolutionaries' ironically raging against the image it portrayed.

In 1937 De Valera gave the State another gift in the form of a new constitution. While the document has undergone enormous change since it was first ratified, along with numerous amendments, it was a significant achievement on De Valera's part. It contained much of De Valera's vision and, strangely enough, it is these national visions that most citizens are inclined to accept and agree with. It is other more personal, technical and belief-based areas, from abortion and divorce to political establishment, that have caused more widespread dissent, much of which has more to do with a changing society and politics than any personal fault of De Valera's. There is a strong case that the 1937 constitution, which still stands as an extremely intricate document that imparts political principles and confers basic rights, was the greatest achievement of De Valera, and the one for which he deserves the most credit. It is fitting for a man who spent most of his life endeavouring to fight for the freedom or in the service of the Irish people that he had the opportunity to frame the political principles of the emerging State.

De Valera did fail his party and people in other ways, however. In the aftermath of World War Two he could lay claim to most of his great success and finest moments. It was an opportune moment to call time on an illustrious political career. Up to that point much could be said that was positive about his policies, even to some extent to support the ill-fated protectionism of the time. However after the War the world changed, and an economic boom was experienced during the '50s by all but Ireland. De Valera stayed at the helm of Fianna Fáil until 1959, which was at least ten years too long. There is little during this period to commend either De Valera or his policies. The once-great man seemed past his best, and his refusal to change protectionist policies in the face of overwhelming evidence now began to hurt as never before. Had Lemass led during this period Ireland might have become a much stronger country.

In politics, recognising when it is the right time to go is a vital and rare talent that is imperative in the creation of legacy. De Valera undoubtedly hung on too long. The country had changed and new generations no longer saw De Valera as the revolutionary, instead he was just an old politician who had been around forever. This created a tendency towards unfair sneering at his approach and vision. While some criticism was undoubtedly merited, so much of the good he did was brushed aside by generations tired of his presence and dominance.

Leaving his role as Taoiseach was not easy for De Valera, but he found solace in Áras an Uachtaráin, becoming President in the same year, 1959. He was re-elected in 1966 at the age of eighty-four. This election was a narrow victory, and signalled that the nation was growing weary of De Valera and was moving on from his vision of society. On the other hand, it is still remarkable that De Valera was one of the oldest Heads of State ever to be elected, and continued to serve until he was ninety years of age, by which time he was almost blind and had little to offer the country in terms of policy. Nothing could signal the power of a name or the stature of the man more clearly than the fact that he could still win this election at that point in his career. Much is made of how close he came to losing the election, as if this portrays some kind of weakness. On the contrary, the truth is that in the Ireland of the 1960s it is astounding that such a figure could even begin to hope to get elected in the first place. It was an election he had little right to contest, no right to win, and any other eighty-four-year-old in the world would have been lucky to get a handful of votes. But it wasn't somebody else, it was 'Dev'.

De Valera came from an era when politics was not scrutinised under the media microscope in the way it is today, but it had more than enough other stresses that could quite literally be a matter of life and death. Family life certainly suffered. Síle De Valera admitted that it was not until much later in life that De Valera himself got to partake in family life. He, however, was probably always aware of such sacrifice and felt it justified. It is reported that when De Valera offered Jack Lynch his first cabinet post, Lynch replied that he wasn't so sure as his 'wife wouldn't like it,' to which the experienced De Valera replied: 'We all have trouble with our wives'.

He died aged ninety-two, and was undoubetedly a man of significant achievement. He will remain a focus point for polarised views for generations to come, and that in itself is testament to his influence. Éamon De Valera will always remain a colossus in Irish political history. Ferriter described him as a 'unique and noble politician'. That is perhaps a succinct and fair epitaph that De Valera himself would have appreciated.

Éamon De Valera's son, Vivion, was similar to Eamon himself in that he was a thinker and took great interest in the scientific world. He was privately educated at Blackrock, before going on to study science at UCD and then becoming a barrister. He was also a Major in the Irish Army during the Second World War. He followed his father into politics, serving as a TD until 1981. He died in 1982. His career in politics, however, was comparatively undistinguished. The weight of the name was crippling, and he also had the difficulty that Eamon himself was still an active force in politics for much of his son's early career. Vivion was far more recognisable in his role as MD of the *Irish Press*. That was a role he took very seriously and the paper was one of the most important newspapers in Ireland for many decades. It ran into a series of problems after De Valera moved on, and finally collapsed in the early '90s. Vivion did keep the De Valera name and tradition alive, but from the perspective of the ordinary public he had done little to either enhance or change the image of the dynasty. It was perhaps a lot to ask, particularly in an era that seemed so intent on moving on from De Valera policies and when Eamon's image still hung large over the nation.

Síle De Valera was probably one of the most recognisable faces in Irish politics for many years. She has in the past recounted family get-togethers at Áras an Uacharáin when De Valera became president. One of the things that she recounts as standing out in her memories of growing up was an insistence on fairness and a lack of bitterness towards opponents. The family was always taught not to personalise arguments, and De Valera had little time for such personal attacks as they became increasingly the stock and trade of modern politics. Logical debating and argument was always promoted in the De Valera household. It must certainly have been a major influence on the family to have grown up in the surroundings of the Áras and with the knowledge and weight of history that their name possessed. There is little doubt but that within Fianna Fáil carrying this weight could be an awesome burden, but also a major advantage.

Síle De Valera was first elected to the Dáil at twenty-three years of age, continuing a pattern that is common to many dynasties in that it seems far more likely that you can get elected as a very young TD if you have a dynastic connection. This endorses the theory that dynasties build their vote on predecessors' achievements in the first instance. It also underlines the idea of the electorate seeking a 'comfort blanket' in that they expect to get a certain set of values and policies from a particular name. Continuity is important. If the electorate liked your predecessor, then they are likely to want 'more of the same please'. Equally, political parties know that a family member is already well attuned to political life, they know the realities and strategies involved and have a much shorter learning curve than someone arriving on the political scene for the first time.

Síle was quick to establish herself on the scene, carrying all the confidence of someone who appreciated their role in history and felt a duty to act. She was ambitious and well-liked in Fianna Fáil. She was duly elected in the Mid Dublin constituency and was the youngest candidate to take a seat in the 1977 Fianna Fáil victory. She followed this by securing election to the European Parliament in 1979. This was an interesting move as it was the first batch of elected representatives in the Parliament, and showed a willingness and desire to interact with Europe and to welcome the outward-looking Irish State. This in itself could be seen as an attempt to modernise the dynastic name, whether or not it was intentional.

On the other hand, Síle held fast to the old revolutionary and rebellious spirit that went with the younger days of the great name. She was highly critical of Jack Lynch, and this was a serious departure in party political terms. Sensing a mood and the desire for change, she also became a strong supporter of Charles Haughey, like many of the brightest and best in Fianna Fáil at the time. She certainly proved that she was not going to be a respecter of authority just for the sake of it.

Never far from controversy, she spoke in favour of the hunger strikers in Northern Ireland, and even went so far as to ask Fianna Fáil voters to continue their preference and vote for hunger strike candidates after Fianna Fáil. Given that Fianna Fáil traditions had always been to vote exclusively for Fianna Fáil candidates and not to continue a preference after that, this represented a significant departure, and ruffled a few feathers. This was a serious statement, for the times were heated and controversial. The hunger strike candidates also stopped Fianna Fáil getting an overall majority, and this in party terms was not good business. But, like her grandfather in his youth, Síle carried a certain firebrand approach that was not willing to be silenced in order to make life easy for someone else. Nationalism and patriotism were an important part of both her political armoury and inheritance.

A redrawing of constituency boundaries forced her to move constituencies to Dublin South, where she was on the same ticket as Seamus Brennan. He was one of the most formidable operators in Fianna Fáil. He had opposed Haughey, and this was seen as a serious division in the constituency. Brennan knew the Fianna Fáil organisation better than anyone, and it is no small achievement that although Brennan did not side with Haughey, who was considered ruthless, he still held his respect and was appointed to the Cabinet. Brennan did not back Reynolds in his November 1991 bid, but yet was one of the few Reynolds continued to appoint. Brennan would go on to serve under Bertie Ahern.

The new constituency was tight, and although De Valera ran it close she lost out to Brennan and Niall Andrews, who took the seats. She ran again in February 1982, but her vote diminished and it was obvious that she was never going to take a seat in Dublin South. If dynastic names do carry electoral weight, it was likely that the Andrews name would hold more sway in Dublin in any event. However, her difficulties during these elections also showed that carrying a dynastic name does not grant anyone an automatic right to be elected. Seats are not hereditary and cannot be taken for granted.

In the Election the following November she decided to move to Clare. This was a clear attempt to build on the dynastic connection. Clare had been Éamon De Valera's old constituency and she was moving to an area where the name would still hold a powerful meaning. Unfortunately, she had no time to build any kind of base, and the name alone was not enough, especially considering that her grandfather's departure from constituency politics had occurred some twenty-three years earlier. Even so, the period in opposition allowed her to start building on that base, and she met with a very receptive public.

In 1987 she returned to the Dáil in a moment that was not short on history or mention in the media. It was not to be a dramatic return to the top. Her career effectively stalled on her return and she was consigned to the back benches to learn her trade. Haughey did not promote the young supporter, and it is likely that her stormy and somewhat controversial approach in her earlier time as a TD contributed to this. She took quite a while to find her feet again in the Dáil, perhaps realising that whenever she spoke she carried the weight of a name that meant her comments were assessed more closely than most. This could be a help or a hindrance, and meant that she had to be far more considered in her approach.

Unlike many ambitious back-benchers, Reynolds's revolt seemed to just pass her by. Indeed, she only really came to national prominence in 1993 when she resigned from Fianna Fáil over the decision to end the enforced Shannon stopover for transatlantic flights. It is perhaps characteristic of Síle De Valera during this period that it would be a constituency matter rather than anything of national importance that would cause her to come to public attention. But for a De Valera to have resigned from the party was in itself no small matter, and she knew that.

Of course by the end of 1994 Reynolds was gone. The Shannon stopover was also gone, and gone forever. Even her constituents had now accepted this fact. So when Bertie Ahern took over there was a chance for a new beginning. Ahern was determined to mend all bridges and create a united platform, and he went about this with great efficiency. It was perhaps a mark of Ahern's political ability. He kept many of the Reynolds faithful; he appeased all his friends in the Haughey camp by bringing back Ray Burke and promoting others like John O'Donoghue and Dermot Ahern. Bringing Síle De Valera back and promising her a front bench position gave Ahern a final piece that linked his team to the past.

She served as Minister for Arts, Culture and the Gaeltacht until 2002. During this time she was seen as a relatively safe pair of hands. She remained a strong figure, although for many she lacked the charisma and energy that they were looking for in this new era. It was certainly apparent that the old firebrand was gone. Her career was perhaps similar to her grandfather in this regard. She and her cousin Éamon Ó Cuív did cause controversy over the Nice Treaty however, with De Valera voicing concerns on the influence of Europe saying that EU regulations 'can often seriously impinge on our identity, culture and traditions.' She also said that she was 'seriously concerned' about the future direction of Europe.

Thus she became as something of a eurosceptic within the party. This was a shock for Fianna Fáil, as it was now suffering from a pronounced fissure of doubt on the matter of Europe generally. However, if her early days had done something to bring the De Valera name into the new age, this time of her career did little to help that. She was often seen as a parody of the De Valera name – safe, conservative, and now on top of all that inward-looking and distrustful of anything outside of Ireland. While she argued many valid points on Europe, it was the last thing the dynasty needed, harking back as it did to the De Valera's disastrous protectionism.

She was not reappointed to the Cabinet in 2002, and instead served as a junior minister in the Department of Education. She showed no ill will and served her role well and with some credit. She did, however, announce in 2005 that she would not seek re-election. This suggested to many that her continuance as a junior minister should be questioned. Such posts carry great electoral weight and, when in the hands of someone who is not going to seek re-election, a very definite opportunity is lost to another politician.

This reached a mini-crisis in 2006. Bertie Ahern had effectively snubbed another member of a dynasty, Sean Haughey, in his promotions to junior ministerial ranks. The controversy reflected badly on the Taoiseach and backfired in spectacular fashion. In the effort to diffuse the situation, Ahern needed to find another post to which he could promote Haughey, and the obvious choice was that Síle De Valera would resign, thus allowing him to do so. However, she appeared for some time to be unwilling to do so. Perhaps she resented being used to help Ahern out of a crisis he created himself. Perhaps even though she was not standing she just did not want to lose her office. Eventually she did concede her position and the crisis was averted. If not a service to Ahern, she did perhaps give one last service to her party by agreeing.

Síle possessed great ability, and by attaining a cabinet position had certainly played her part in the De Valera dynasty. She could retire proud of her career. Yet that strong, modernising influence seemed to have been choked somewhere along the way. Perhaps the level of expectation was simply too great. She offered the best chance to paint the name in a different shade, to bring it into a new era, but ultimately this amounted to a missed dynastic opportunity.

Síle De Valera was not the only hope for this particular dynasty, of course. Éamon Ó Cuív, grandson of Éamon De Valera and nephew to Vivion De Valera would also throw his hat into the political ring. Ó Cuív suggests that, while he knew

Éamon De Valera, and was very much aware of his achievements as a statesman growing up, it was only when he himself moved to Connemara that he began to understand Fianna Fáil. Ó Cuív quickly began to understand that the secret of Fianna Fáil was not the actions of those at the top, or some of the great people that had shaped the party, but instead the unwavering, loyal, committed and insightful supporters that it had amassed on the ground. Ó Cuív was very close to De Valera in his understanding of what makes a party strong: ideological aims, practical policies and good organisation.

In terms of politicians from dynasties, Ó Cuív came to the game relatively late in life. He was thirty-seven when he first stood for election in Galway West in 1987. His first outing was, however, to be a disappointment. Ó Cuív was a co-operative manager in the Gaeltacht, a career of which his grandfather would surely have approved, and many had already noticed a similarity in his approach and ideals, although this did not translate into votes immediately. From this we can see that just having a dynastic connection does not mean that elections are necessarily plain sailing. It might also be suggested that not holding the De Valera name directly was also an impediment. Certainly, Ó Cuív made a poor enough showing in 1987, family connection or not.

Tenacity is a key ingredient that seems to be passed among all dynasties, and Ó Cuív was back for another shot in 1989. While he still failed to take a seat, his vote had improved significantly, and this at least was encouraging.

Ó Cuív then took the Seanad route beloved of many dynasties, and secured a position on the Cultural and Educational Panel, which afforded him a platform in politics in the years that followed. This was to prove invaluable in building his base. Ó Cuív recounts that the election he remembers most fondly was 1992 – unusually for a Fianna Fáiler as it was a tough election. It was, however, the one that saw Ó Cuív elected for the first time, and on the first count at that, heralding a dramatic change in his electoral fortunes. This was to remain the case in elections to follow, where he was comfortably returned at each time of asking.

Yet again, Ó Cuív displayed something of a revolutionary spirit in his early days. He was a confident speaker and sought out opportunities to speak, especially on national issues. In particular, in 1994 he suggested Ireland could consider rejoining the British Commonwealth as a gesture to Unionists. This was incendiary and dramatic stuff, particularly coming from the source it did. During this period many suggestions were made, even Albert Reynolds indicated a willingness to consider a set number of Unionist seats in a future Irish parliament if Ireland were ever reunited. So perhaps such suggestions were just mere discussion. Nonetheless, due to the statement coming from a grandson of De Valera it was particularly powerful, and showed a desire on Ó Cuív's part to contribute to this debate and perhaps try to modernise the name and show a different face to the one that had been commonly assumed.

However, on closer examination it was perhaps not as shocking a move as might be imagined. While Éamon De Valera had been a major opponent of British rule, and had shown little desire to co-operate with Britain, he had stopped short of taking Ireland out of the Commonwealth or indeed of declaring it a republic. This honour actually went to Fine Gael and the inter-party Government of 1949. It is surprising that De Valera as the great leader of the Republican Party had allowed his opponents this opportunity, and speaks perhaps to a deeper policy belief on his part that it was not a wise decision. Ó Cuív, rather than recasting the name that seemed so anti-British, was perhaps simply restating a family belief that was long held.

Having spent his time on the back benches, Ó Cuív was seen as a strong character, and the type of politician Fianna Fáil needed if it was to bring in new faces. While Fianna Fáil was in opposition he served as the party spokesperson for rural development and the islands. So, when Bertie Ahern became Taoiseach in 1997, he appointed Ó Cuív as a junior minister. Interestingly, Ahern chose to have Ó Cuív serve in the Department of Arts, Heritage, Gaeltacht and the Islands. The senior Minister in the Department was of course his cousin Síle De Valera…

It was particularly interesting to see a senior and junior minister from the same dynasty in the same Department. However, it may also point to a difficulty that the dynasty was experiencing, which was to shift the focus and perception away from being just Gaelgoirs and lovers of all things Irish into a more meaningful economic profile. It would seem that Ahern had decided that the members of this particular dynasty had talents best suited to more rural, artistic and cultural ends: areas he was not all that fond of dealing with himself.

Ó Cuív performed well and became a well-liked figure among the Fianna Fáil grassroots, particularly due to his connection to Éamon De Valera and a strong physical resemblance to the party's founder. He was also seen as a strong voice for rural communities and a man who understood the party faithful. This may, though, have contributed to the perception of his general abilities as only lying in such spheres. When a reshuffle occurred in 2001 he was moved to the Department of Agriculture, Food and Rural Development as a junior minister. This appointment was welcomed, yet it served to pigeon-hole the view of Ó Cuív further. Ideally, the De Valera name would have needed a voice on real economic issues and tangible figures if it was to change its image.

For Ó Cuív, such an assumption may not have sat well, but he was undoubtedly used to it at this stage of his life. It was particularly ironic that he was seen as someone who only understood rural affairs and was obsessed with the Irish language, especially considering the fact that he was born and raised in Dublin. In fact, as a child he shared his schooling with Michael McDowell.

As we have seen, Síle De Valera voiced particular concerns about the EU in the wake of the Nice Referendum in 2001. That defeat seemed to allow a particular strain of euroscepticism to arise in Fianna Fáil. Síle De Valera was not alone in her doubts; indeed Charlie McCreevy suggested the result was a 'healthy development'. This built upon widespread doubts among the Fianna Fáil grassroots about the European project. Later studies clearly showed that while Fianna Fáil members broadly supported Europe, they had misgivings, feeling that its influence had to be kept in check by national government, and that the benefits it brought were in fact hard won by successive negotiating teams. Ó Cuív went slightly further than any of his colleagues. Indeed, he went further than many of the grassroots supporters who had stayed away from the polls out of apathy. Ó Cuív, having campaigned for a 'Yes' vote, later announced that he had actually voted 'No'.

This episode was particularly defining, making Ó Cuív a hero for a small number, but casting a significant doubt over him for many more. While Fianna Fáil has always been a party that has had vociferous debate and division, it is also a party that has little time for anyone going against it outright. As the pain of losing the Nice Referendum began to hurt the party's pride, it brought significant weight to bear on Ó Cuív for actually being part of that defeat.

Outside of Fianna Fáil, Ó Cuív's view was not appreciated at all, and his political maneuvering was seen as duplicitous, particularly considering that he had not voiced his concerns before the Referendum was held. In terms of the dynasty, the fact that Síle De Valera and Ó Cuív had both found reason to doubt Europe seemed to suggest that they still felt a hankering for a more insular or isolated Ireland, and despite being part of many positive decisions on Europe since, they were reaching a breaking point where they felt that things had gone too far. The fact that both had voiced these fears cleared the way for the argument that Éamon De

Valera would not have liked the new Europe, and that Ireland was moving further away from its conservative past. Brian Cowen was of course Minister for Foreign Affairs at this juncture, and the loss of the Nice Referendum was a particular blow to his reputation. Many suggested that he was very annoyed with Ó Cuív as a result of this, and indeed in the Dáil debates, when the opposition attacked Michael McDowell for also expressing fears about Europe post the Referendum, Cowen quipped: 'At least he voted for it.'

Bertie Ahern was a very different type of leader, and saw no reason for causing major upset as a result of this defeat. As was his style, he allowed voices to rage until they finally wore themselves out, then spoke with the individuals quietly, causing little fuss. He had an election to fight in 2002 and needed a united team.

Ahern also had a reputation for promoting those who caused problems, not being a man to insist on discipline. This has often been cited as a failure of Fianna Fáil in the last decade, and one that has caused particular concern in recent times. However, after the 2002 Election, Ahern responded to Ó Cuív's varying achievements and opinions by promoting him to a full cabinet position. Ó Cuív found that he then had little difficulty telling people that he voted 'yes' in the subsequent Nice II Referendum. This he ascribed to the guarantees received by the Irish Government in the meantime.

Ó Cuív was now Minister for Community, Rural and Gaeltacht Affairs. Yet again it was a pigeon-holing of both himself, and indeed his dynasty, but it was a welcome promotion all the same as Ó Cuív was now fifty-three and any further delay could seriously jeopardise his future career. Like many dynasties, there was mixed news accompanying his promotion, for it coincided with the demotion of his cousin Síle. Thus Ó Cuív now became the main standard-bearer of the De Valera dynasty.

Although his new Ministry was not an easy one with which to make a mark, Ó Cuív did perform well. While not a media favourite or a particularly strong communicator, Ó Cuív was seen as straight and objective. The people affected most by his Ministry liked him, and this was what mattered most to Ó Cuív. He continued to be a strong and resolute voice for rural Ireland and a strong defender of its traditions. Some fears were expressed for his future when Brian Cowen became Taoiseach. Ó Cuív was now approaching sixty, and many felt that Cowen was about to overhaul a Cabinet that had spent a long time in the public eye. Some felt that he may decide to follow the road of his mentor Albert Reynolds and introduce many younger faces to change the perception of his Government. Cowen, however, showed far more likeness to Ahern and preferred a much more cautious approach. He was loathe to remove anyone from their positions, and made very few changes. When he did, he tended to promote older figures rather than younger or more energetic voices. Cowen placed a high value on experience and caution. The only exceptions to this were the rapid promotions of Brian Lenihan and Mary Coughlan within the Cabinet, to varying degrees of success.

If Cowen held any animosity to Ó Cuív for his stance on Nice, it was now long forgotten, as Ó Cuív continued to serve, and when a further reshuffle occurred in 2009, speculation was rife that Ó Cuív may face the chop. However, Cowen gave him a huge vote of confidence in effectively promoting him to be Minister for Social Protection, at the expense of one of the top performers in Cabinet, Mary Hanafin.

This move was a significant step for Ó Cuív. While not an economic ministry *per se*, it was one of the biggest spending departments and, in the midst of a recession, one of the most important in social terms. While the Ministry may have afforded a chance to make a more significant mark, timing and circumstance were against Ó Cuív and there was little from this period that would make a mark for the De Valera dynasty.

Perhaps the most significant thing that was to happen was that the great movement that was Fianna Fáil, once the all-powerful and all-conquering machine, was now on its knees. The party convulsed as poll ratings plummeted to as low as eight percent. Brian Cowen was challenged as leader by Micheál Martin. Cowen showed strength and acumen in defeating Martin in the initial vote, but Martin knew that he possessed the support of the grassroots due to promises of radical internal reforms and changes. Cowen attempted to reshuffle his Cabinet, but completely misread the public mood and was forced to resign. It was interesting that during the initial tussle for leadership, Ó Cuív chose to back Cowen. While there was no doubt a favour owed personally, it could not have been easy for Ó Cuív to watch the party so synonymous with his family falling apart around him. Ó Cuív's backing of Cowen was a boost for the leader, as was that of the Minister for Finance, Brian Lenihan. However, all failed to read the obvious signs, and by backing Cowen and failing to take a stand as Martin had done, they all seemed too afraid and lacking nerve.

After Cowen's resignation, Ó Cuív stood for the leadership and put in a respectable showing, though he was a long way behind Micheál Martin. Ó Cuív was seen as simply too old at this stage to take on the job. Few believed his ideas were radical enough, or that the public would relate to him. There was little doubt, however, about his love of the Fianna Fáil organisation and his understanding of it. Internally, the party was very angry at how it had been treated – they wanted heads, and Martin seemed to be the man willing to swing the axe.

The 2011 Election was a disaster for the Fianna Fáil party. To say Éamon De Valera would be turning in his grave would be an understatement. The party had forgotten the highly involved characteristics on which its organisation had thrived, and now seemed to have moved a long distance from the 'fearless guardian of Ireland' that the party fondly imagined itself to embody.

Éamon Ó Cuív was one of only twenty Fianna Fáil TDs to survive the electoral massacre. As the public mood became more eurosceptic after the EU aid package imposed strict terms, and not insignificant interest charges, on Ireland, Ó Cuív may yet find that the De Valera voice of euroscepticism becomes more widespread within Fianna Fáil. For many years this euroscepticism was not seen as a positive for the dynasty. This was mainly due to the fact that it was clear from any fair analysis that Ireland had benefited hugely from its membership of the EU. Doubts about the ultimate aims of the EU were therefore put on hold, even though many in Fianna Fáil harboured serious reservations. Fianna Fáil wanted to support Europe, but it never believed in a federal state – for them it was a club of nations where power resided at the table where the Heads of State or Council of Ministers sat. More recently, efforts have been made to shift ever increasing amounts of power to the European Commission. This marks a more federal approach, where the power of national governments is reduced. Fianna Fáil is not at ease with this. Ó Cuív and the De Valera dynasty have now come full circle, and their argument is now very well received within Fianna Fáil. It may indeed mark a central plank of Fianna Fáil policy going forward.

While Ó Cuív was appointed to the Fianna Fáil front bench, it is clear that there is little he can now do to change radically the view of the De Valera dynasty. An opportunity does, though, exist for him to assist in the reformation of Fianna Fáil and in its restructuring. Ó Cuív may yet become a champion of the grassroots supporters, particularly if the new leader, Micháel Martin, fails to deliver on his promises of 'major surgery' for the party, and if he proves too forgiving to deliver the heads of those that many blame for the organisational demise of the party. This allows a particular opportunity to leave a mark within the party, and should it ever return to its former glories it may perhaps be fitting that someone from this dynasty played a role. If there is to be a platform for future generations to build upon, then it will require a vision and toughness of character that has not been seen since De Valera and Lemass first took to the road to spread their message. At the time of writing Fianna Fáil is still in a perilous state. Interestingly, Ó Cuív's name came to the fore as a potential Fianna Fáil presidential candidate, and while he disagreed with the policy of abstaining from the 2011 Presidential Election, he was overruled. It would have marked a very interesting journey for the dynasty were he to have attempted to follow in his grandfather's footsteps to become President. Whatever happens, there is little doubt that Ó Cuív still has a role to play in the fortunes of Fianna Fáil, whenever he is called upon and in whatever capacity.

The name De Valera will always be synonymous with Irish history. Anyone who carries a link to that name will always be a force to be reckoned with. However, the modern age has focused almost obsessively on the failings of Éamon De Valera and the dynasty he founded. Diarmaid Ferriter's recent biography presented the most balanced picture seen for some time. There is little doubt, however, that if the perception is to be changed then it will require a future inheritor of the dynastic tradition to become a key government figure, particularly in an economic role, and one who can successfully modernise the name in order to restore it in the hearts of Irish people, where it has long lost its appeal outside of the Fianna Fáil family. The fate of the De Valera name is inextricably interlinked with the fate of the Fianna Fáil party, and, as I write, the political future looks bleak for both.

Family Business: The Lenihan Legacy

The Lenihan family has been influential in Fianna Fáil and Irish politics since the 1960s. The Lenihan legacy is also fascinating because it is probably the only dynasty where a successor to the throne had the opportunity to completely redefine such a famous name and to surpass the achievements of such well-known figures from the past. That is something that does not happen often in politics, but it is likely that when the Lenihan name is mentioned in future it will be associated with Brian Jnr, and that is no small achievement considering the power and strength of his father, and indeed his aunt Mary O'Rourke.

The Lenihan dynasty has always been something of a mould-breaker. In fact, it is difficult to say where one should start in assessing it. Brian Lenihan Snr was the first of his family elected to Dáil Eireann in 1961. In an improbable dynastic reversal, and for the only time in Irish politics, his father Patrick Lenihan followed him into the Dáil in 1965.

As the most senior member of the family, it is perhaps best to consider Patrick Lenihan first if one is to understand the dynasty. Born in County Clare in 1902, Patrick started out in life with the revenue commissioners before turning to business, principally with Gentex textiles in Athlone.

He had fought in the War of Independence, but as a strong admirer of Michael Collins he had taken the pro-treaty side in the Civil War. When he encountered Lemass, Lenihan became a convert to Fianna Fáil. He was a strong and affable character, and during the period when he owned the Hodson Bay Hotel in Athlone his hospitality and stories of all night sessions and good times became the stuff of legend.

Patrick Lenihan always had a strong interest in politics, and was close to Seán Lemass, the Taoiseach. He instilled this belief and vision into his family, culminating in the election of his son Brian in 1961. Four years later he was elected himself, but whereas Brian sat for Roscommon, Patrick represented Longford/Westmeath. Athlone straddled both constituencies and this helped the dynasty to get off to a strong start. Patrick had been heavily involved in Brian's election, and he faced no small task in getting elected himself as he faced General Sean McEoin of Fine Gael, a man with legendary standing in the Longford/Westmeath constituency. McEoin had been a formidable IRA leader during the struggle for independence, and led one of the most famous and successful flying columns of the period. Patrick Lenihan used every ounce of his enviable campaign nous to secure the seat for Fianna Fáil. He successfully defended the seat in the 1969 General Election, but died suddenly in 1970. So far he remains the only TD from the family who has not been appointed a senior or junior minister.

Patrick Lenihan passed on considerable knowledge and political ability to his children. The children were encouraged to read as widely as possible, and had access to a large library in the family home. Brian Lenihan and his sister, Mary O'Rourke, would both serve at the Cabinet table. His third son, Paddy, served as a councillor, but defected to support another powerful dynasty: that of Neil Blaney and his Independent Fianna Fáil movement.

It was Brian Lenihan Snr who would etch the Lenihan name in the annals of political history for the first time. He would become one of Ireland's best-loved politicians, and a man who would remain dear to the heart of a huge number of Irish people for as long as they would live. He was an avid reader, and was known for his insatiable appetite for more books, often reading in the car while going from one function to another.

Brian was a barrister by profession, but he didn't practise for very long. He was determined to enter politics, and having stood unsuccessfully in the General Election in 1954 aged just twenty-three, he secured a seat in the Senate in 1957. This gave him the opportunity to build a base and make a name for himself, and in the following Election of 1961 he made the breakthrough.

Seán Lemass was determined that Fianna Fáil and the country needed to modernise. Part of this involved bringing a host of new faces to the Cabinet table. Lenihan was one of those who were tipped for greatness, and he was appointed parliamentary secretary and then Minister for Justice in 1964. Lenihan was charismatic and a powerful speaker. He had the ability to bring people with him on issues, and was seen as a strong and steady figure at this time. In Justice he tackled many difficult issues including censorship and succession rights. Lenihan proved early on that he was typically pragmatic, a value that is highly esteemed in Fianna Fáil, and he had no fear of reform or of change. He was no stranger to personal tragedy either. While his career may have been on the up he lost his second-eldest son, Mark, to leukemia in 1965 aged just five years old.

Such figures can rarely expect to avoid controversy. When in 1968 he became Minister for Education, Lenihan again began to make waves. This time, however, not all of his policies were received well. His predecessor, Donogh O'Malley, had proposed the merger of UCD and Trinity College, believing that through shared resources much more could be achieved, and that their continued separation was just another part of Protestant/Catholic segregation. Lenihan tried to follow through on this proposal. However, he underestimated the antipathy towards this in academic circles, and also underestimated the rivalry among the student bodies that were fervently opposed to the idea and forced its abandonment. Lenihan did successfully secure a rationalisation of services at both universities, and also will be remembered for increasing significantly the number of college places available. It was Lenihan who also proposed a new university in Limerick, as well as what is now known as DCU, then called NIHEs. This move served as one of the enduring benefits to Limerick city and to the mid-west region.

Following Fianna Fáil's success at the 1969 Election, he moved on to the more sedate role of Minister for Transport and Power, and after Patrick Hillery became an EU Commissioner he was appointed Minister for Foreign Affairs. By achieving probably the most senior ministry after Finance, Brian Lenihan had illustrated the high regard in which his abilities were held, and the high esteem with which he was viewed by his peers. However, things were not quite so rosy on the ground. When Jack Lynch became leader it appeased many by stopping Fianna Fáil falling into the hands of a particular faction. But Lynch was a frustrating leader in the wake of Lemass, and the party edged back from radical reforms to conservatism and caution. Fianna Fáil suffered electoral defeat in 1973. It was an Election the party had expected to win, however, rocked by the Arms crisis and facing a strongly unified opposition with a pre-arranged voting pact in place, Fianna Fáil lost out. Lenihan had been attempting to win a second seat for Fianna Fáil in Roscommon, and his high-wire vote strategy encouraging voters to vote for his running mate cost him dearly. Lenihan's home turf in Roscommon has a slight reputation for being fickle and perhaps a bit impetuous, and this was a famous occasion when Lenihan lost his seat to the shock of many people nationally. Lenihan was forced to fight for his survival through the Senate, and once he was elected it was easy to see that his peers' impression of him was far from dented as he was elected Fianna Fáil leader in the Seanad.

During this time, Lenihan decided that it was best to change constituency, and he moved his base to Dublin West. Lenihan was never a fan of the constituency system, or of the clinic as a place for the public to make demands on politicians. As a man who was highly protective of his family its intrusion into the family home in the early days was not welcomed. Lenihan had supported attempts to reform the electoral system to introduce single-seat constituencies and a straight vote with this very much in his mind.

As Lenihan searched to make his mark in Dublin West, he was helped by another Dublin family: that of P.J. Burke, and in particular his son, Ray, who had recently been elected a TD. The two struck up a friendship that lasted through the years.

During this time Ireland was in the unusual position where the first MEPs were not elected but appointed. Lenihan was part of the Fianna Fáil team. He encountered an early difficulty in Europe for Fianna Fáil. The party was in a quandary as to where it stood politically within the Parliament. Fianna Fáil as a party sat neither to the left nor the right. Lenihan was always to the left of the Fianna Fáil spectrum, and he would have happily joined the Socialist grouping, but others wanted the Liberals, some the Social Democrats and Haughey himself had no idea. It resulted in the ridiculous situation where Fianna Fáil ended up seated to the right of the fascists. In reality, Labour and Fine Gael had already aligned themselves with the Socialists and Social Democrats respectively, and there was no room for Fianna Fáil to place itself in a distinctive political position. They ended up forming a new grouping with the French Gaullists, but this indecision and inability to define the kind of Europe the party wanted lasted right up until 2009.

Lenihan was regarded as very successful within the European circuit, where his unrivalled powers of retention and ability to appreciate arguments served him well. He continued to work assiduously to build a base in Dublin, and this work paid off with his re-entry to the Dáil in the Fianna Fáil landslide of 1977. He was immediately re-appointed to the Cabinet as Minister for Forestry and Fisheries. Lenihan was never at ease with 'auction politics', and had been a critic of those who pushed such agendas in 1973 and 1977. During that period, political parties vied to outbid each other in an effort to win the electorate over. If one party promised a tax cut, the other had to offer an even bigger one. Interestingly, Charles Haughey was Lenihan's ally in opposition to all of this. The Election of 1977 had brought a lot of new talent into Fianna Fáil, largely from a background in business: the likes of Ray McSharry, Albert Reynolds and Charlie McCreevy, all of whom were open to a more realistic style of politics. But Fianna Fáil was about to enter a period of extreme turbulence as Jack Lynch resigned and the battle for leadership became a race between Haughey and Colley. Neither side particularly saw Lenihan as a friend. Colley viewed him suspiciously as one of many new charismatic figures, and knew that Lenihan had famously been friends with Haughey and Donogh O'Malley, and these young reformers' escapades and late-night drinking sessions were well known. Lenihan admired Colley's integrity, but felt that otherwise he was limited as a politician. Haughey did not feel he could count on Lenihan at this point as Lenihan had a tendency to respect tradition within Fianna Fáil. Haughey also knew that Lenihan certainly had leadership potential, and could easily have been a compromise candidate. Many years later he said that he had supported Haughey in the end, but many at the time believed he had voted for Colley. In fact, Lenihan was one of those jostled and intimidated by Haughey supporters after his victory. Lenihan has been quoted as saying the choice was between 'a fool and a knave,' but he opted for Haughey in the end. Meanwhile, his friend Ray Burke sided with Colley.

Charles Haughey was eventually successful. He was no respecter of names or reputations, but knew Lenihan had become one of the most powerful and formidable figures within the party. To find yourself on the wrong side of Lenihan could quickly spell immense trouble as his reputation among grassroots supporters was second to none. Whether or not Haughey believed Lenihan supported him, he made sure to quickly befriend him by giving him the coveted post of Minister for Foreign Affairs. Lenihan spoke his mind, and was often accused of thinking aloud too often. Many also suspected that Lenihan was an incredibly loyal figure, and therefore he was used by successive Taoisigh as a stalking-horse for ideas. He was willing to say things others were not. One such instance occurred after an Anglo-Irish summit where Lenihan suggested Irish unity could be brought about within ten years. This angered the British and of course the Unionists. Some felt it was typical of Lenihan, thinking aloud and not putting a whole lot of thought into it at that. Others felt that it was fair comment – he was believed to have a strong republican streak and such an outcome was one he would desire. But it could also be argued that Charles Haughey showed little regard for the Anglo-Irish process, or for Margaret Thatcher. Haughey did not seem to feel there was any progress to be made, and was aware that republican sentiment was running high in Ireland at the time. Fianna Fáil is particularly prone to strong nationalist feelings, and Haughey was always quick to portray himself in this light. It is equally plausible that Haughey used Lenihan to shore up nationalistic and patriotic Fianna Fáil support at a time when the party remained divided. It was perhaps a case of putting his leadership and party ahead of what was good for the country.

Lenihan showed considerable ability and intelligence when dealing with other crises of the time, which included the murders of two Irish soldiers in the Middle East and the Russian invasion of Afghanistan.

But for all the hope that many had expressed, and Haughey had courted, of stable government based on sound finances, he did not deliver during this term of government to the disappointment of many in his own party and even more among the electorate.

Fianna Fáil lost power again in 1981. The Fine Gael/Labour coalition that followed was shaky, and dependent on independents for support. When Finance Minister John Bruton failed to get a budget through the Dáil, Fitzgerald advised that he would seek its dissolution. While Fianna Fáil could expect to benefit, for some unexplained reason Haughey decided that he would attempt to form a government without an election, and tried to communicate this to President Hillery in order for him to refuse dissolution of the Dáil. There was nothing wrong with this action, however surprising it might have appeared. However, President Hillery was uneasy with it and saw the situation as placing undue pressure upon him. It remains open for debate as to whether this was the case. Ultimately, this issue comes down to the question of to what extent the President of Ireland should be involved in matters political; a question which is yet to be adequately resolved.

When Fianna Fáil regained office in 1982, Lenihan found himself in the somewhat less influential Agriculture post. Lenihan showed no evidence of disappointment, though, and worked through the setback. He opposed Haughey's anti-British position on the Falklands war and suggested privately that if he had been Minister for Foreign Affairs he would have had to resign. In any event the Government only lasted ten months before losing power once again. This time, Fianna Fáil was set for a long period in opposition.

Lenihan was immensely loyal to the idea of the party and to party unity. He supported Haughey through numerous heaves because he believed no one else could reasonably take over. This often cost him friends, for Lenihan was a man who would defend the indefensible and was always happy to carry the fight when others shied away. Due to this, Lenihan became seen as someone very close to Haughey, but in truth it was a friendship that owed at least as much to Lenihan's desire for a successful unified party as it did to any personal belief in Haughey. If Haughey had been defeated, Lenihan intended to contest the leadership, but ironically it was his work more than any other and his understanding of the grassroots and organisation that kept Haughey in place. Lenihan had little time for Des O'Malley judging by his public utterances with regard to O'Malley's actions and his eventual expulsion from Fianna Fáil. This must be understood not in terms of the personal relationship, but instead through Lenihan's overriding loyalty to party. Lenihan saw little to admire in any man who was not loyal, or who would desert their party and those who were in it.

That relationship was not helped by O'Malley's formation of the Progressive Democrats. Lenihan remained to the left of the Fianna Fáil spectrum, and he had little truck with most right-wing politics. He simply did not believe in a right-wing approach, and any animosity with O'Malley, who was most definitely to the right of the political spectrum, was only further heightened by this ideological divide.

Haughey and Lenihan both led opposition to the Anglo-Irish agreement that was signed by Garret Fitzgerald. This surprised many people but was typical of Fianna Fáil intransigence on the issue during this period. Haughey was playing a very strong nationalist card, and it seems Lenihan was following suit. While Lenihan was undoubtedly nationalistic he was also very loyal to a party leader. This loyalty was one of the qualities for which he was most admired by people on the ground. Fianna Fáil as a unit opposed the Anglo-Irish agreement at Haughey's insistence. Albert Reynolds, who rarely spoke on Northern Ireland, was the only one to offer it any degree of support, which, although it raised some eyebrows at the time, was quickly forgotten.

Lenihan's loyalty paid off, and on Fianna Fáil's return to Government in 1987 he secured the post of Minister for

Foreign Affairs and Tánaiste. This was the pinnacle of Brian Lenihan's career. The party grassroots loved him. He thrilled Ard Fheisseanna with his speeches, and was viewed by many as the true heart of Fianna Fáil. The stories of excessive drinking often only served to improve his reputation with a nation that loves some humanity in their politicians. Lenihan was renowned for being a good sport and good company. Haughey seemed to have finally learned some political lessons, and took serious and correct measures to save the country. He allowed Ray McSharry to introduce necessary but unpalatable finance measures, he allowed Albert Reynolds to handle Industry and Commerce with a free rein and, importantly, he recognised that Lenihan was vastly superior to himself on European issues and infinitely more capable at understanding inter-governmental relations, and was content to let him control the arena of Foreign Affairs.

Shortly after his appointment, Lenihan began to have serious health problems and needed a liver transplant. It is important to point out that while Lenihan may have been famous for his hospitality and his drinking sessions with many self-confessed alcoholics, he was never an alcoholic himself. His liver illness was not due to alcohol but to the fact that in the early 1960s he suffered a liver infection and heart problems, but these remained concealed from the wider world for most of his life. In 1989 he travelled to the Mayo Clinic for the life-saving operation. In many ways the prognosis was not good: the operation itself was still relatively new, and Lenihan was the oldest person to have ever undergone the treatment. Rarely in Irish politics was such an outpouring of goodwill seen from all sides of the house and among so many people on the ground of various political views. Lenihan was always a unifying force for those involved in politics – even when they did not agree with him, most of his peers found him an eminently likeable person. His bravado was there at all times, always putting on a fearless face, but, as he recounted in his own book *For the Record*: 'I was dying and I knew it'.

He was re-elected by the people of Dublin West in his absence as he underwent surgery. After this election he was appointed Minister for Defence as he returned to the hectic schedule of politics. He was greeted with open arms and good wishes by all in Dáil Eireann. Even though Lenihan embraced his second chance with gusto, his doctors were under no illusions, and he continued to undergo strict monitoring and needed to take heavy doses of steroids and other medications. Lenihan was instrumental in helping Fianna Fáil adjust to sharing power with the Progressive Democrats. Again, his ideals of doing what was good for the party caused him to put any personal distaste aside. But he was well aware that other influential figures such as Albert Reynolds were opposed to the idea, and now began to entertain serious doubts as to Haughey's judgment and reasons for clinging to power.

Lenihan had one more ambition, however, and his efforts in this regard would open one of the most painful chapters in Irish politics for his many supporters. In 1990 he declared his intention to seek the Fianna Fáil nomination for the presidency. Neither Lenihan nor his family entirely trusted Haughey to support his candidacy. John Wilson was an influential member of the Country and Western set and was probably the favoured choice of that group. Lenihan was a man of strong character, and all who knew him could attest to his immense intellect. He had been the one there for Haughey's crisis of indecision, and knew more than most he was not the confident man in control that he portrayed. He also knew Haughey, who once had been a great reformer, had been happy to embrace baser instincts when it suited him. As a man from a background thought to respect hard work and earning your way to the top, there can be little doubt but that Lenihan had suspicions of Haughey's financial dealings.

Lenihan did manage to secure the presidential nomination, and was seen by most as a shoo-in. Earlier that year in May 1990 a Fine Gael activist and UCD research student Jim Duffy asked Lenihan if he would assist him by giving an interview. Lenihan agreed as he was always wont to do. The interview took place just after Lenihan had undergone crisis rejection treatment for his liver and was on a serious dosage of medication. He was not fit on the day to be answering any questions, nor recalling any situations with a reliable degree of clarity. But letting someone down was not in his nature and he honoured the request. During the interview Lenihan said that back in 1982, when calls were made to president Hillery to refuse dissolution of the Dáil, he had in fact made one of them, and actually got through to Hillery, who was quite annoyed. The transcript of the interview was never sent to Lenihan for correction as would normally be the case in such interviews.

Duffy wrote a series of articles referencing this in *The Irish Times* and it was seized upon by Fine Gael. When Lenihan was later confronted on *Questions and Answers* he denied he ever made a call. Jim Duffy then made a series of calls to *The Irish Times* and played the tape. Most academics advised him that the tape should not be published given the circumstances. But a storm was gathering, and he became a hunted man who eventually found refuge in an *Irish Times* car that took him to their lawyers' offices. The tape was duly made public. Lenihan appeared on the six o'clock news to protest his innocence, stating that on 'mature recollection' he had not made any such call and the assertion on the tape was incorrect.

The tragedy for Lenihan was that if he had said he did make the call then it would probably not have been as big a deal. Most commentators looking at the evidence and the testimony of other ministers such as Sylvester Barrett would accept that, given the sequence of events, Lenihan knew of the calls and was well-briefed on everything that was said, but never lifted the receiver himself.

The treatment of Lenihan within the Government was equally abysmal. The Progressive Democrats were playing both sides of the moral coin and demanded Lenihan's resignation in order to keep Haughey (the man who had instigated the phone calls) in power. Unlike Albert Reynolds, Lenihan had supported the Progressive Democrats' entry into the Government and had worked hard to ease tensions, putting personal feelings on the back burner. There was little thanks for it: O'Malley and others still disliked Lenihan personally and were happy to see him go. On the other hand, Lenihan was a loyal friend to Haughey, although that relationship also cost him personally. Haughey, clinging to power, agreed to sack Lenihan. In *For the Record* Lenihan recounts amazing scenes in Athlone, his heartland, where on one hand Padraig Flynn and Bertie Ahern, working on Haughey's orders, sought to convince him to resign at a meeting in a hotel room, while outside a crowd of thousands, stoked up by fiery speeches from his sister Mary O'Rourke and Albert Reynolds, shouted 'No resignation!' for all to hear.

Lenihan was a loyal man who always put himself second, and he paid a price for that. Those he helped on so many levels were those who let him down. But he bore no animosity. Many years later shocking revelations would show that Haughey, in financial peril, diverted a surplus of funds collected for Lenihan's treatment for his own personal use.

Lenihan received by far the most first preference votes in the Presidential Election, but a voting pact between Fine Gael and Labour ensured that Mary Robinson won the Election on transfers. The story goes that in typical fashion one of Lenihan's last actions of his campaign was to instruct the driver of his campaign bus to drop Gene Kerrigan of the *Sunday Independent* to his local polling booth before the bus was decommissioned. He did so, where Kerrigan duly voted for Mary Robinson.

Lenihan and Fianna Fáil took a battering. After this, Lenihan, although much loved by the party still, was to be sidelined to a watcher of the unfolding game. He had supported Bertie Ahern as the man to lead Fianna Fáil after Haughey, showing no animosity towards Ahern for his closeness to Haughey. Lenihan knew it was all a game, and everyone was just trying to play the cards they had. He was dismayed by the Country and Western set's activities in trying to bring down Haughey. Lenihan never liked cabals or coups of any sort. He supported his sister Mary O'Rourke for the leadership when Ahern said he would not stand, but even so he is said to have had grave doubts about this as now Reynolds was clearly going to be leader and he believed in a united front. But that was Brian: the party, above all, to the very last.

Lenihan did have one more important role to play. All his life he had supported the closeness of the Labour party and Fianna Fáil in terms of roots and vision. After a disastrous General Election in 1992, Lenihan was one of those pushing hard for a coalition with Labour. Others like Padraig Flynn were strongly opposed, but Reynolds, who was far removed from ideology and driven purely by results and pragmatism, was siding with Lenihan's argument. It was nothing short of a dream come true for Lenihan to see Fianna Fáil and Labour enter Government together. He supported Reynolds as passionately and loyally as he had every leader of his party. And although the relationships were torrid and often difficult, and the Government collapsed after two years, it did not detract from the fact that it was in terms of policy and achievement arguably one of the finest governments in Irish history.

While holidaying in his native Roscommon in 1995 Brian Lenihan was rushed to hospital in severe pain. He was suffering from a blood clot and, although rushed to the Mater hospital in Dublin, there was nothing that could be done, and an immense legend of Irish public life passed on. The outpouring of grief from all shades of political opinion was genuine and heartfelt.

Brian Lenihan certainly had established the name of a formidable and much-loved dynasty. His loyalty was admirable, but perhaps he was the definition of being admirable to a fault. Lenihan never forgot his friends or evaded doing a good turn for someone where he could. He was perhaps a poorer judge of character, and his unfailing loyalty caused him to overlook some fatal flaws in some of his friends. However, while some may have let him down, the affection he was held in by so many of the Irish public and among the grassroots of his own party showed that he had many friends who would honour him long after he was gone.

Lenihan's political abilities were shared by his sister, Mary. While she shared many similar features, she also possessed a very different streak that made her quite a different politician. A teacher by profession, Mary served her apprenticeship in Irish politics at local level in Athlone UDC and Westmeath CC in the 1970s, and was unsuccessful in her first attempt to win a Dáil seat in February 1982, having been elected a Senator just a year before.

Another opportunity came in November of that year, and this time she succeeded in taking the seat. She was already well known in the constituency of Longford/Westmeath. Her elections were hard-fought and territorial. It may have been because she had learned a hard lesson from her brother about the dangers of vote management, but one thing was clear: Mary O'Rourke did not concede territory easily. Her constituency colleague, Albert Reynolds, was from a similar mould, and the two enjoyed a difficult relationship; at times very much united and in agreement but at times diametrically opposed. Within the constituency they stayed and guarded their own borders jealously. Unlike her brother, Mary O'Rourke was a solid vote-getter but never in the kind of numbers that allowed for large transfers or enough to guarantee a running mate's entry. Like Brian, though, she was held in high esteem by those close to her and by all who had any depth of interaction with her.

When Fianna Fáil returned to power, O'Rourke was appointed Minister for Education by Haughey and, along with her brother Brian, became the first brother and sister to serve in the same Cabinet. O'Rourke has often said that this Cabinet was perhaps the finest that she served in. Many would agree it was a Government and Cabinet that marked a turning point in Ireland's economic story, with a little help from a Dáil of similar mind, particularly with Alan Dukes as the leader of Fine Gael with the Tallaght Strategy. O'Rourke did not have an easy time: education faced harsh cuts in order to bring public finances under control, and she handled the portfolio with abilities far greater than one might expect from a new appointee. She oversaw course revisions and the planning of the introduction of the new Junior Certificate curriculum to replace the old Inter Cert.

Following Albert Reynolds's sacking in November 1991, O'Rourke was given the Health portfolio in the subsequent reshuffle. O'Rourke obviously had not backed Reynolds. Similar to her brother, she had little time for what she saw as an attempt to push Haughey before he was ready. While she had grave reservations about Haughey in the wake of the Presidential Election of 1990, it is clear that she saw Ahern as the man to lead Fianna Fáil forward as opposed to Reynolds.

Of course, her stay in Health was short lived. Only three months later Haughey was gone, and O'Rourke contested the leadership of the party against Reynolds. Reynolds was always confident of victory, even from the day he was sacked. Albert Reynolds was a gambler it's true, but his secret was that he was very good at gambling. His timing was perfect and, once Haughey was gone, there was always going to be a rush to the Reynolds flag. No other politician aside from Ray MacSharry engendered as much confidence or exuded such strength of character as Reynolds at the time. Bertie Ahern was an equally smart politician and, while he had very strong support, he was still even at an optimistic appraisal several votes short of being able to defeat

Reynolds. Such a split would be divisive, and Ahern knew and read correctly that if Reynolds won then you really wanted to be on his good side. He duly withdrew from the race and backed Reynolds.

O'Rourke did not. She and Michael Woods challenged Reynolds, but with Ahern gone nothing could stop Reynolds and he cruised to a crushing victory over both. While Woods survived the subsequent cull, many did not. Mary O'Rourke was demoted to a junior ministry, but showing similar traits to the family name she did not complain publicly but took the post and continued to work away believing she would have another day. She could draw strength from the fact that Reynolds had decided to completely modernise the face of Fianna Fáil and had savaged the Cabinet ranks and now had a cabinet-in-exile on his back benches. The most illustrious of these was Ray Burke, a man with whom no one in the party, apart from Reynolds, would have trifled. Burke did not take his punishment lying down and worked assiduously to bring about Reynolds's downfall. While his good friend Brian Lenihan listened, he had little time for disloyalty to any leader. O'Rourke may have been slightly more receptive, but she did not like any public showing of disunity either, preferring to bide her time. Burke rested all his hopes on Bertie Ahern. While Brian was to the left of the Fianna Fáil spectrum, Mary O'Rourke was slightly more to the centre and felt that Bertie Ahern occupied a similar space.

The turnaround was not long in coming. When Albert Reynolds resigned in 1994 the stage was clear for Bertie Ahern to assume the leadership of the party. O'Rourke was duly rewarded by being appointed Deputy Leader of Fianna Fáil. This reflected several strategic considerations that were in play. Firstly, and most importantly, Ahern recognised the asset that O'Rourke was. While she and Reynolds might have been caught up in constituency politics, she was now the leading figure in the midlands and someone liked by the grassroots. Her easygoing approach and unvarnished style appealed to many. In his early days, Ahern was not all that sure who he could count on, being particularly aware that he needed to bring the Country and Western set onside. Brian Cowen and Marie Geoghegan Quinn were the leaders of this section, and Ahern wasn't sure if they would always support him. O'Rourke on the other hand was loyal and believed in him and he knew it. She was also in a key constituency heartland where many of those in the Country and Western side of the party still admired and respected her.

When Fianna Fáil came back to power in 1997, Ahern gave her the key portfolio of Public Enterprise. This was no easy task with such a wide-ranging Department. She took to the job with gusto. She was instrumental in taking a long-term view of Dublin's traffic problems and, rather than trying for a quick fix, was one of the first to see the need for a real solution that could last in the form of the Luas, and eventually an underground. At the time, many decried the proposals as crazy. But, unlike many ministers before her, O'Rourke knew that a tin of paint on a few bus lanes and the widening of a few streets or closing of a few others would not solve the issue. It would take resources and commitment, and she showed incredible courage in getting the proposal through. O'Rourke would not be there to see the Luas unveiled some years later in 2004, and it also suffered many setbacks along the way. Probably the greatest of these was the opposition from traders which saw plans for a connecting line dropped, and instead when the Luas came on stream it had two lines that were totally separate. The senselessness of this is now apparent, and plans are being made to go back to the original idea for a fully connected service. Further extensions to lines are also planned in the future. It is important to note, however, that the Luas currently carries some 90,000 passengers a day, and operates without a state subvention, unlike other forms of transport. It has therefore proven itself sustainable and highly popular with commuters.

She also found herself embroiled in controversy with regards to the privatisation of Telecom Éireann. Here, O'Rourke was caught between the proverbial rock and hard place. On one hand she represented the taxpayer, and in doing so it was her duty to get the highest price possible for eircom shares. In order to do this it had to be marketed, pushed and essentially talked up. In this regard the flotation of eircom was a good piece of business with the taxpayer getting a good price for the shares. Unfortunately, politics is seldom black and white. Many of those who bought shares were private citizens who purchased shares because they believed the marketing line and believed the company was much stronger than it was. Some even took out loans to buy shares. However, within a few months the shares had fallen in value, and many felt that they had been duped into buying the shares and were now at a loss. On one side the majority of taxpayers, most of whom did not buy any shares, had received a boon in terms of the State coffers. On the other, a large number of private investors felt the Government had a responsibility to them. It would colour all flotations in the future for Irish governments where it was seen from then on as a general principle not to make good political sense to offer shares to the man in the street who perhaps is not prepared for the harsh realities of the stock market.

Mary O'Rourke was one of the highest profile members of the Fianna Fáil parliamentary party. Yet it remained that her personal vote, while solid, was never exorbitant. In 2002 this created a serious problem. Fianna Fáil was incredibly popular. Taxes were reduced, money was being spent on improving services like health and education at rates never seen before and the country was at near full employment. The party was on course for a resounding electoral victory. The opportunity existed for a third seat in Longford/Westmeath. Donie Cassidy secured the nomination as a high-profile candidate in his own right. After much heated debate a carve up of the constituency was agreed which saw

O'Rourke give up some key areas. This forced her to try and eke out a higher than ever vote from her Athlone base. In the end, this proved a bridge too far, and in an election where Fianna Fáil was victorious the woman who had become affectionately known as 'Mammy' lost her seat. Yet again, the similarities to her brother Brian were quite evident.

Such similarities did not end there, as she was nominated to the Seanad by Bertie Ahern. Just like her brother before her, she immediately assumed the position as Leader of the House, showing that she was still considered by her peers in Fianna Fáil to be a force to be reckoned with and a politician of considerable standing and talent.

Yet again, O'Rourke kept plugging away and loyally working, and this period saw her becoming increasingly outspoken about a variety of issues. She was less inclined to just toe the line, and quickly became a media favourite as someone willing to shoot from the hip and tell it like it was. Her turn of phrase was often archaic and even old-fashioned for some, but it only endeared her to many more. She was astute and played the role of school marm to perfection, often scolding opposition figures, and being both a master of the backhanded compliment and dry wit she seemed impossible to antagonise or defeat in an argument.

Mary O'Rourke has never slowed down in politics; it is a game she readily admits to loving. But she does not take it to heart or see it as the be-all and end-all of everything. She cites her grandchildren as the most amazing thing in her life and the reason she keeps going every day. She is an almost unique figure in Irish politics. Some already want to see her run for the presidency, but she says that it has far too many rules and constraints for her. It's hard to doubt her on that score. She has never been a politician who took well to being told what to do, or that there were limitations on what could be done or achieved. In that she was very much a visionary like her brother, although she did not share some of the misty-eyed ideology or the willingness to always step back for the sake of someone else and the party. O'Rourke was very much a real world politician, a pragmatist, and was a lot more direct and unequivocal than the men she supported in Fianna Fáil such as Haughey and Ahern. Perhaps she was more like Reynolds in personality than she cared to admit, and perhaps that is why they didn't always see eye to eye. In the massacre that was the 2011 Election, Mary O'Rourke lost her seat. It was perhaps one battle too far and, despite her national profile and the long connection and service to the town of Athlone, it was not enough to save her from the fury that the public was directing at Fianna Fáil. Although her vote collapsed she took the blow with grace and bowed out, bringing the curtain down on a truly epic journey in politics.

While not similar to him in all respects, O'Rourke shared many attributes with her brother and carried the family name, even if she never used it directly, with distinction.

In many cases this would be enough to constitute a dynasty in itself. There is enough in the preceding paragraphs of this chapter to mark the Lenihan name indelibly on Irish history. Yet, that would not be the style of this family. Ever the mould-breakers, there was more to come with Brian's two sons Conor and Brian Jnr serving as Minister of State and Minister for Finance respectively.

Conor Lenihan inherited many of his family's famous traits. He was outspoken and generally seen as honest. He is, like his father, always considered good company and outgoing. His manner and approach to interviews has followed with striking similarity that of his aunt, Mary O'Rourke. But Conor Lenihan is experienced in his own right, having worked as a journalist in Ireland and the UK, covering the House of Commons and also European matters.

His entry into politics was no surprise to many. In 1997 he stood for the first time in the Dublin South West constituency. In what was considered a very tough battle, Lenihan edged in to take the last seat. It was a considerable achievement in that it was a gain of a seat for Fianna Fáil at the expense of the Labour party, and the margin was narrow at just over one thousand votes.

Conor quickly established himself as an outspoken voice on many issues. He continued his journalistic exploits by writing for the *Evening Herald* and also by helping establish an internal Fianna Fáil paper called *The Nation*. However, Lenihan was often critical of policy decisions and indeed of Bertie Ahern himself. In 2004 Ahern responded to this in typical fashion by promoting him to the role of Junior Minister with responsibility for overseas aid. This certainly ensured that Conor was now less vocal in any criticism. Lenihan took on the role with enthusiasm and the establishment of the 'Irish Aid' programme to assist developing countries was a primary achievement.

Being outspoken to the point of flippancy, Lenihan continued to court controversy. In 2005 he told Joe Higgins to 'Stick to the kebabs' in response to an angry speech by Higgins attacking the Government. Lenihan was referring to an earlier incident where Higgins had been defending Turkish workers. This did not help his image, and indeed the remark was at odds with everything the dynasty he represented had stood for. Lenihan apologised and has always made the case that it was purely a throwaway comment that he regretted, meant only to respond to what he saw as taunts from Higgins and not to be directed at the workers. Yet it showed Conor Lenihan's tendency to speak sometimes without due consideration, another trait he may share with his august father.

After the 2007 General Election there was some support for his promotion to a full Cabinet position, however this did not materialise, and with the simultaneous advancement of his brother Brian in the Cabinet, it seemed unlikely that the Taoiseach could afford two such positions for the family. Instead he was reappointed as a junior minister, but this time with responsibility for integration policy. Under Brian Cowen in the 2009 reshuffle, Lenihan was moved again, this time given responsibility for Science, Technology and Innovation.

Like many politicians, Lenihan has often faced criticism for a lack of experience in certain roles. This argument is without merit in a true democracy, where the very idea is that a Government of the people is established, most often without particular expertise, but rather to act as representatives of the public and to question, challenge and encourage expert thought that would exist in an area in any event. Lenihan has never appeared particularly ruffled by such criticisms. His style is what attracts critical comment, and is seen to be a drawback in his efforts to be taken seriously from an intellectual point of view. In many cases he has found himself to be an easy target.

A typical example occurred when he agreed to launch a book written by a constituent of his. The book put forward an argument against the theory of evolution. Many felt that it was not appropriate for a junior minister with responsibility for science to launch a book that flew in the face of accepted theory. The writer asked Lenihan not to launch it as a result of the embarrassment that would be caused, but ever since Lenihan has faced comment and remarks suggesting he does not accept evolution as a theory. The whole episode was typical of Lenihan's ability to end up in a controversy where none exists, however it was also highly ironic that it was felt that the Minister for Science could not launch such a book, for that in itself was an approach to debate that mirrored the inability of those in the Church and other such institutions to accept questioning when Darwin first put his theory to the public. It is likely, however, that the controversy had less to do with the role of science and debate and a lot more do to with the fact that it was Lenihan in the role.

In early 2011, as Fianna Fáil lurched and heaved its way to collapse, Conor Lenihan was one of the few who spoke out publicly. He challenged the way Fianna Fáil had been run and those who had allowed its organisation to rot away.

While many accused him of having a personal aim, there is no doubt whatsoever that he was at least voicing the concerns that were being expressed by ordinary Fianna Fáil members and voters across the country. Had they been listened to earlier Fianna Fáil might have avoided at least some of the trauma.

Throughout a tense couple of months, Lenihan faced considerable attacks for his stance. He faced it in typical fashion, only becoming agitated when his personal integrity was impugned in any way. Conor had one problem, however, in that while his criticism was valid there did not seem to be a real plan or suggestion as to what should happen to resolve the situation. It is highly likely that this was affected by the resistance of his brother Brian to declare his position. Conor found himself therefore caught between a brother he would eagerly support, but who wasn't making the right noises, and someone like Micheál Martin, who was probably the only person who could defeat Brian Lenihan for the leadership, and was making all the right noises.

His utterances fell on deaf ears when the electorate went to the polls. Fianna Fáil was completely obliterated in Dublin, and Conor Lenihan was among those who got swept away in the wave of anti-Fianna Fáil sentiment. It was clearly a day that even the strongest of dynasties could not withstand.

At forty-seven, Conor Lenihan still has the potential for a career in politics. As one of the main critics of how the organisation was run, his words will carry some weight in this new Fianna Fáil reality. His voice will be seen as a barometer of feeling on the progress of the party under Micheál Martin. Conor Lenihan demanded swift action and change, and while many criticised him for not delivering it himself, there is no doubt that his view is still widely shared. He has served the dynasty well in terms of actual political progress, and has also continued the idea of it being a friendly, open and gregarious dynasty that is made up of straight talkers. However, unfortunately for Conor Lenihan, he also became representative of some of the criticisms of it, exemplified by his inability to hold his tongue, a tendency to create controversy and act or speak without due caution. These are serious impediments in government. Yet it is clear that they can be overcome. Certainly the input, impact and influence of Conor Lenihan are not yet at a conclusion.

Brian Lenihan Jnr may yet do what few have ever done in political dynasties. He may yet surpass his illustrious predecessors in terms of historical notoriety. Indeed, some might argue he already has, although that might be with the insular self-importance of the present day clouding the judgment.

Brian Jnr found himself in the most important ministry in the country in one of the most perilous times in the history of the State. Make no mistake, democracy and independence are fragile things. Talk of plans and economics is cheap. Real action is far more risky, and beyond the realms of theory lies a land where repercussions can be serious and permanent. It is still too early to judge Brian Jnr's achievement, but if Ireland does survive this crisis, if the country does keep afloat, if NAMA proves as some observers expect to be a major but not unbearable burden, if Ireland recovers and can tackle its unemployment again with the next five or six years, if public spending is controlled, then perhaps Brian Lenihan will take his place in the pantheon of Irish political greats. He showed no shortage of courage in his task. He became respected worldwide for his efforts, even if many of the measures were not popular at home. One day someone will either berate Lenihan's decisions as flawed and disastrous or they will be seen as the bedrock that saved a country.

As the eldest son of Brian Lenihan Snr, it was no surprise when Brian decided to stand for election. He was largely hidden from the public eye for many years as it was his father's protective wish for his family. When the death of his father in 1995 caused a by-election in Dublin West, though, at thirty-seven Brian Jnr was the ideal candidate. However, Fianna Fáil had not won a by-election since 1985. Being in opposition in 1995 presented them with a better opportunity, though they would still face an uphill struggle even if a strong sympathy vote turned out for Lenihan. This was due to the presence of a charismatic speaker and Socialist by the name of Joe Higgins. Higgins presented a difficulty for all of the established parties. This was because while they all felt they had the potential to be in government and therefore tempered their comments and expectations to reflect this, Higgins had no such ambition and could oppose and propose with impunity and without fear of repercussion.

The by-election was hard-fought, and Lenihan did secure the vote. Despite Higgins's ability to attract transfers from other candidates, Brian Lenihan took his father's seat and was returned to the Dáil.

Having qualified and practised as a barrister, Brian Lenihan Jnr was already a formidable figure. His private school education was something that did not sit well with a Fianna Fáil party that was notorious among its membership for being opposed to such institutions, but none the less he carried a respected name, and had inherited his father's ability as an orator. In the 1997 General Election he was returned at the top of the poll, and many felt he was the brightest prospect in Fianna Fáil. Indeed, many were surprised when Ahern chose not to make him a junior minister and instead Lenihan was given the role of chairman of the all party review of the constitution; a role to which he was well suited in a technical sense, but one that was seen as a particular under-utilisation of his talents up the 2002 Election.

He remained, for many, Fianna Fáil's best-kept secret. Despite impressing time and time again in debates, and among those he met and interacted with, he did not secure a promotion.

It soon became apparent that the reason for this rested with the Taoiseach Bertie Ahern. The simple answer was that he did not like Brian Lenihan. It has been suggested that Lenihan came across as far too smart for his own good. Unlike his father he was not shy of his intelligence and did not try to hide it. Perhaps Ahern felt Lenihan would be a threat in the longer term. Perhaps there was also a slight throwback to times and divisions gone by. However, no matter what the reason, there is little doubt that Bertie Ahern's dislike of Brian Lenihan stunted his political career.

As Ahern sealed his grip on power and became more confident in his position, he had less reason to doubt Brian Lenihan. The swell of support for his promotion was growing all the time within Fianna Fáil. There was a definite mood among commentators that if Fianna Fáil was going to introduce some new faces to the Cabinet after the 2002 Election, then Lenihan would certainly be one of them. But while Ahern did finally bow to the pressure, it was not to make Brian Lenihan a full Cabinet Minister but instead to appoint him a Junior Minister at the Department of Health with responsibility for children.

If Brian Lenihan was disappointed he certainly did not show it and, like his father, he showed considerable loyalty to the party and its leader. The promotion was of course a welcome step in the right direction. Lenihan was immediately at the heart of a strong policy agenda improving resources for the vetting of childcare workers, and changing rules on adoption and internet protection of children. He was quickly established as an authoritative figure not afraid of reform or action.

The Cabinet reshuffle in 2004 had been seen as an opportunity for Fianna Fáil to recast its image. The timing was perfect for the promotion of Brian Lenihan. However, to the surprise of many, the expected promotion still did not come. It was at this point that people began to seek an explanation for what had happened and stories of a rift between Ahern and Lenihan came to the fore. Lenihan was no timid creature and was, in the same vein as his father, a man of considerable political ability and muscle. He worked through a serious programme of reform on children's affairs, and eventually both the internal calls within Fianna Fáil for his promotion and the policy platform he had put in place coincided. In effect, Lenihan had pushed for a much higher profile for children. It must be stressed that this was a definite policy belief on his part. However, the establishment of the Office for Children and its role across several departments would require a minister of some standing. So, in 2005, something of a compromise was reached politically. Lenihan as Minister for Children would in effect be a 'Super' Junior Minister. In other words he could sit at the Cabinet table but would not have a vote. This meant that matters relating to children's rights had greatly increased importance and visibility at governmental level, which represented a significant policy shift.

For Lenihan, it at least meant some further progress, but undoubtedly he had to do it the hard way, fighting for promotion every inch of the way despite an impressive record. In 2006 he described Bertie Ahern's acceptance of money at an event in Manchester in the mid-nineties as 'unthinkable'. Lenihan was certainly of the view that such actions were wrong. This would appear in keeping with the attitudes of his dynasty: his father, for all his links to Haughey, was not embroiled in tribunals, and such actions would always seem out of character. Indeed, Brian Lenihan Jnr would have been painfully aware of the fact that Haughey had used some of the surplus money raised for his father's medical treatment for his own personal use. This must surely have left a mark as regards the ethics of any man engaged in such activities.

The 2007 Election was tough for Fianna Fáil, but they had managed to come through it in impressive style and return to Government. There was little doubt in anyone's mind that the Election had been won by Brian Cowen and many of the Cabinet members, for it was their performance that allowed Bertie Ahern's more personal attributes to shine. It signalled, though, a weakening in Ahern's position. He finally relented after the Election and made just one new promotion to the Cabinet. Brian Lenihan would become Minister for Justice at the age of forty-eight. For one so highly regarded it had been a long time coming. There was another dynastic connection in that it was of course a portfolio that his father had also once held.

Most commentators felt that it was as far as Ahern would be willing to let Lenihan go for now. But politics is all about patronage. Bertie Ahern's resignation marked the coming to power of Brian Cowen. This was a man with a very different approach, and someone who respected Lenihan highly. Cowen understood two things clearly from the Taoisigh he had served. Reynolds taught him that a Taoiseach must have a new team, and people he can trust in the Cabinet. Ahern had taught him the art of compromise and how to avoid making enemies. Cowen attempted a half way house. On becoming Taoiseach he did not sack any of the old Ahern Cabinet or show a radically new team to the country. Within the Cabinet, though, he elevated the people he trusted most to the key positions, so that his 'kitchen Cabinet' would be loyal and dependent on him. In doing so, Mary Coughlan was elevated to Tánaiste and Minister for Enterprise, Trade and Employment. This move was a huge surprise, and many considered that in hindsight it did not work out. Micheál Martin was a future threat but was kept close in Foreign Affairs. But perhaps the biggest surprise of all was Cowen's elevation of Lenihan to a position above all other ministers by awarding him the finance portfolio.

Few doubted Lenihan's ability or talent. But many felt he was not experienced enough as a minister, and that such a promotion had risks. However, Cowen undoubtedly felt Lenihan's ability justified the move. It also meant that this key Ministry and the usual springboard of Fianna Fáil leadership would be occupied by a man who owed Cowen for the elevation and who in the normal course of events could not expect the party to grant another step up to leadership for some time.

The obvious key phrase is 'the normal course of events'. From the time when Lenihan first took the Finance job, nothing was normal for Ireland as a country. A worldwide banking crash heralded disaster. With banking in turmoil, the Irish debate on stamp duty had already stalled the housing market for months, leading to a rapid decline in confidence. What faced the country by 2008 was nothing short of fiscal armageddon.

It is easy to assume that life will always continue as before, that economics and politics can only make so much of a difference. The ancient Greeks once thought so, as did the Romans, and many more after them. Democracy and our current systems are still in their infancy by comparison with other systems in history. The threats posed by the world crisis shook every element of western civilisation to its core.

Lenihan was faced with an unenviable task. Fianna Fáil and Brian Cowen and Bertie Ahern took an early hit, being blamed as Ireland went from extreme wealth to bankruptcy overnight. In those early days many doubted Lenihan's ability to handle the crisis.

Banks were the problem. In layman's terms, banks had seen an opportunity to make a lot of money during Ireland's property bubble. They gambled with developers and mortgage products to win a greater market share. The risks were high and the figures staggering. However, the banks were not worried. Like the Department of Finance, they made two catastrophic assumptions. Firstly, if the property market underwent a crash, then, even though it accounted for over fourteen percent of GNP, the rest of the economy would still be going strong, exports, I.T. etc. So there were other markets from which they could still make money, and no reason to assume that any Irish property collapse would affect them to the point of breaking them. Secondly, they assumed that if they were hit for heavy losses in Ireland they could cover this by borrowing internationally and spreading the risk. What they did not allow for was a worldwide crisis that would engulf all sectors of the world economy, so that every company in every sector in Ireland found its market shrinking. Ireland's output dropped, and banks couldn't make as much money from other areas to compensate for the loss in construction. This was combined with the fact that the international financial system had undergone a similar collapse, and so there was little prospect of raising money internationally to cover domestic losses. Loans simply were not there. Irish banks now had a liquidity problem and could not cover their exposure.

It is also clear from the reports into the banking crisis that the relationship between the Government and top level banking and business had become far too close and trusting. No evidence has yet been produced to say that corruption existed at a political level that led to the banking crisis, but there is much evidence to suggest that far too much trust was extended. The banks were at best frugal with the information given to the Government. At worst they hid and sidestepped the attentions of their political masters and sought to mislead them. In short, the banks told the regulator a story, the regulator saw no reason to doubt them or their auditors, the regulator confirmed the story with the central bank, and the central bank told the various ministers. There was a pervasive element of groupthink, and the politicians all too readily accepted what they were told which was, after all, exactly what they wanted to hear.

Brian Lenihan found himself in a very awkward position. He had never been a fan of Bertie Ahern, and his promotion to the Cabinet had come very late. The weakness in the Irish cabinet system was plainly evident: while collective responsibility exists in theory, there is little or no room for a minister to challenge either a Taoiseach or a Minister for

Finance on their approach unless they intend to challenge them outright and cause an election. We don't know if Lenihan had doubts, but he certainly hinted that some existed. The reality was, however, that with an opposition that was equally committed to high spending up to the 2007 Election, and with few voices calling for less spending, there would seem little point in any minister causing a general election by challenging the theory. As soon as Lenihan became Finance Minister, his first act only a month in was to introduce over €300 million in cuts. His predecessor had gambled on the property market and the gamble had gone wrong. That predecessor was now his boss as Taoiseach. Lenihan was left in an invidious position having to deal with the fallout as best he could.

Irish banks were close to collapse. One fateful night in September their representatives arrived at Brian Lenihan's door needing to make a decision before markets opened and they collapsed. Lenihan was in a situation that no minister has ever been asked to handle before. The entire future of the country was now at risk, and something had to be done that night. As private entities, Lenihan or the Department of Finance had limited access to bank files in those hours. Equally, any advice they would have sought would be based purely on guesswork. In the aftermath, while AIB and BOI had problems, it was Anglo Irish Bank that proved the poison in the system.

Irish banks were small fry on world markets. All over the international stock exchanges and among agencies major banks were taking hits. Panic had engulfed the entire system. Lenihan could have decided to let Anglo fail, while saving the likes of BOI and AIB. Perhaps he would have if he had access to the true depth of Anglo's problems, which would not become apparent for another full twelve months. On the other hand he faced international markets opening to yet another day of panic within hours. If he let

Anglo fail, the international markets were unlikely to take the view that the problem was limited to Anglo Irish Bank, but would more readily assume that Ireland's entire banking system was tainted.

He had a decision to make. He could guarantee the lot, in which case the problems of the banks would became liabilities of Ireland and its taxpayers for potentially a very long time to come, but at least Ireland could decide in time what it needed to do from there itself. On the other hand, he could let Anglo fail, give a partial guarantee, and gamble the entire country on a panicked market hoping it would see sense and take note of what Ireland was doing. Some still feel the market might have grasped this and Ireland could have saved a lot of money. Others believe that given the circumstances the risk would have been too great and the markets would have devoured all the banks. With other bondholders and major investors now terrified, and with no banking system, Ireland as we know it may have ceased to exist. Lenihan chose to guarantee them all and face the consequences of his decision in his own time and in a manner the country could decide. Serious questions must be asked about how the banks got to this point, and about the fundamental failings of the system, both financial and political, to prevent it. The new Governor of the Central Bank, Patrick Honohan, pointed out repeatedly that certain actions could and should have been taken earlier. In assessing Lenihan, who only came to the role in mid-2008, Honohan made clear that none of the options facing the Minister on that night in September were good, and that all options suggested carried huge risks and potentially enormous cost no matter what was done. He suggested that Lenihan took the best option given the conditions and fear that existed on the night in question.

Hindsight is a wonderful thing, and much comment has been made about slight changes in the decision that could have been implemented. It has also been suggested that as the Department of Finance lacked the particular intricate expertise in house it should have sought assistance that night. However, it clearly remains the fact that such experts, academic or otherwise, would not have been in a position to make any better or more informed choice at that point, even if now with hindsight and more information they can make an alternate case. Some commentators have suggested that the Government could have asked the EU to assist and use some of its financial expertise on that difficult night, but this was clearly not an option. Despite having a wealth of resources it has taken the EU considerable time to vet the decisions on Anglo Irish Bank and, despite the urgency of the markets, the EU seemed unable to assist Ireland in coming to a conclusion on its costs, acting instead as a watchdog rather than a partner. The slow decision making process of the EU and its careful weighting of the impact on all members meant that a phone call to them in such extreme circumstances would be a waste of time for they would not have been able to assess the situation or make such a decision. The banks were also less than honest: loans were covered and hidden, and meanwhile they failed to inform the Government that the problems they faced were not just of liquidity, but of insolvency.

The bank guarantee was a fateful choice, and one that will forever be attached to Lenihan. For some it placed a noose around the taxpayers' necks and saved the banks at huge cost to the public. For others it was a seminal decision that had to be taken, and rather than abdicating his duty and letting the markets decide, Lenihan chose to step in and bear the consequences. It was for some a moment when the country was saved, even with huge cost, from absolute ruin, and a decisive action that put the Government in control of the country's fate, even if this meant that from there on it would take all the flak. There is little doubt, however, that if all the information had been put before the Minister, if the Department of Finance and the Government had all the facts and could have forseen the sheer depth of the problems, particularly in Anglo, they would most likely have taken some form of different decision. No doubt that would also have had negative implications that we would be discussing today, but it is highly likely that if the Irish Government had had a crystal ball at least some elements would be radically different.

The bank guarantee was no more than a first step. Lenihan had hoped that it would prove a 'cheap' solution. He was wrong in this, and it showed just how little information the Government was actually in possession of, particularly in relation to Anglo. The markets remained in turmoil and the Irish economy was in a deep crisis, now hemorrhaging money at an alarming rate. It was clear that Ireland as a nation was living like a company executive despite having the income of someone on the dole. Something had to give.

In order to calm nerves, Lenihan moved forward his first budget to 14 October 2008. Although it was billed as a hair shirt budget, and had the nation trembling in fear in the lead up to it, it did little to inspire confidence. It did not go anywhere near far enough and most people knew it, although it was likely to be as much as Lenihan could convince backbenchers and coalition partners to bear. A decision to end universal benefits such as the medical card scheme for the over 70s drew enormous criticism. However, Lenihan argued that those who were wealthy enough to afford treatment should be willing to pay, as by doing so it ensured even better treatment for those who could not afford it. Otherwise everyone lost, and this affected the poor disproportionately. Brian Cowen when he was Minister for Health had echoed this viewpoint. For some it is a right-wing approach to end any form of universal benefit. For others it is the heart of a left-wing ideal that those with means should be willing to pay to help and support those with none. It was a debate that would not be resolved and is unlikely to ever be resolved either in Ireland or the world at large.

The Government did increase the limits at which the medical card cut off applied, however they did not back down and rescind the decision. It was apparent after only two months into the new year that the problem was growing larger and the figures were way off target. At a political level it began to dawn that tougher measures were necessary, and that while it would cause pain and upset many people, action had to be taken. Lenihan acted with courage, introducing another budget in May, this time tougher and harder hitting. The party and the public, while not happy, began to accept the reasoning as the fear spread throughout the country. And rightly so. At this point Ireland faced an abyss where its very sovereignty and existence was threatened. Lenihan quickly established the primary objective of his tenure: to stabilise public finances and get the country back on budget.

The budget also saw the proposal of another major institution arising from the banking crisis: the National Asset Management Agency. It was a decisive and bold move, but highly controversial, and carried with it considerable risk. The nature and viability of NAMA is a subject of far more in-depth assessment than would be appropriate here, however some simple facts can be extrapolated as they apply to Lenihan's views.

Firstly, it remains a matter of debate among many commentators as to what the final outcome of NAMA will be, and there is undoubtedly potential for it either to turn a reasonable profit or to end in significant loss. The truth is that no one can predict the outcome either way with any degree of certainty, and it will only be possible to assess Lenihan's decision to establish NAMA at least a decade hence. It is clear that Lenihan believed in NAMA and its potential to solve the problem and, while many disagreed with him, it is likely the decision was taken in good faith and for good or ill was made in the belief that it was the right thing to do. It has presented the Irish people with an enormous risk and burden, and the country can only hope that it will be successful, for if it fails it carries a terrible price. Lenihan was less than impressed by the behaviour of the banks during this saga, stating that at every juncture his worst fears were realised. As the Government tried to solve the crisis the figures from banks kept changing and getting worse, and rather than facing the issue they seemed obsessed with trying to portray a best case scenario. He also described the figures involved for Anglo Irish Bank as 'horrendous'.

Lenihan went on from this to introduce one of the toughest budgets ever to face the Irish people. It was well received under all the circumstances, and even gave a slight bounce to a Fianna Fáil party that had collapsed, indeed if the party had been better organised or served at this point it may even have been a springboard for recovery. Again Lenihan showed that he would make no attempt to curry the favour of the electorate or particular interests that might make his life easier. The cuts to public sector pay and pensions were harsh, but showed a man who believed in what he was doing and was prepared to face the consequences, whatever they may be, in order to do what he believed was necessary. This again was in line with his father, who opposed auction politics and the refusal of Fianna Fáil and indeed Fine Gael in the early eighties to accept reality and admit that one could not keep people happy and at the same time do right by the country in such circumstances.

Lenihan remained popular even though his party and many of his decisions caused people to turn from him electorally. Internationally, Lenihan was seen as a guiding light; someone who cast aside electoral politics and popularity and took the necessary decisions to save the economy that employed him. In this respect he was very close to the self-sacrificing nature of his father, but taking it even beyond his party and beliefs to a national level.

During 2010, international markets began to lose faith in Ireland once again. In many respects, this was understandable. While Ireland had impressed them with the decisions that were being made and the willingness of the people to work through the crisis and accept the measures in December 2009, the markets had seen the Greek economy collapsing, with larger and larger countries threatening to need bailing out following close behind. The feeling on the markets as Ireland approached yet another tough budget was that the people would not be willing to take it again, and that the Government would welch on its commitment to reduce spending, particularly in light of the high cost to the taxpayer of Anglo Irish Bank. Some within Fianna Fáil have suggested that Lenihan actually went to Brian Cowen and suggested that they call a general election as there was a danger the country was going to be bounced into a deal with the IMF. Cowen, it is said, rejected this idea.

Ireland was now in a very difficult position. Rates of interest on borrowing were reaching exorbitant levels. Lenihan tried to calm the markets by promising that Ireland would stay the course and the budget would deliver. However, problems were mounting on a number of fronts. Ireland was part of the Euro, and this made it a player in a bigger global game in which its actions could have serious worldwide repurcussions far beyond what its size merited. The Euro was going to come under pressure as indeed was the entire European project. Ireland itself had a vested interest in this project with a significant agriculture sector almost completely reliant on the survival of the EU. So, on this front the EU began to pressure Ireland towards resolving the situation to end the pervasive uncertainty which had characterised the State's finances for long enough. The EU solution was for Ireland to accept an aid package, the interest charged would still be punitive but at least it would be several points less than what the market would charge and it would give stability.

In order to try and strengthen his negotiating hand, Lenihan needed the markets to ease up on Ireland in order to lessen the rates of interest with which Ireland would be saddled, but the markets would not give up until they saw a budget. Lenihan could not present a coherent budget until he had finalised a plan for the next four years to give it much-needed credibility, but that plan could not be finalised until the EU was happy with it and was willing to sign off on the figures for Anglo Irish Bank. The EU was finding it difficult to come up with figures and seemed to take an eternity to put a number on Anglo and to assist with the four-year plan despite all the resources available to the Commission. In essence, the European Commission played a significant part in the delay that was causing problems while the European community at large was eager to press on and make decisions.

Eventually, Ireland succumbed to the pressure and the EU/IMF rolled into town. This must be the lowest point for the Lenihan dynasty, to have had a man on point duty when such a catastrophe occurs. Brian Lenihan himself became somewhat cocooned, and was poorly advised during this period. He issued denials about the existence of talks with the IMF and even allowed ministerial colleagues to go on television to deny reports that talks were underway. This may have been a technical ploy or civil service attempt to keep the talks under wraps to avoid public pressure and remain in control of what the IMF would do, but it was particularly disastrous PR at the very least to be caught feeding a litany of lies to the general public in this way. How much of this was Lenihan's personal plan and how much was a Department approach only time will tell, but it is clear from interviews since that Lenihan certainly felt bounced into the deal and had little control over events during those weeks. Central Bank governor Patrick Honohan has since stated that he, Lenihan and many others had initially thought that the negotiations would carry on for some time, which may go some way towards explaining Lenihan's actions. It is possible that he did not see the escalation in contact as part of the negotiations proper, and probably believed that it would involve some level of political negotiation at some point, which would be what he considered formal negotiation. As it was, what occurred in the week the IMF and EU came to Ireland was very little negotiation. The interest rate was set by a formula used everywhere else and the question of bondholders and burden-sharing was outside the scope of the discussion. While the Irish Government probably thought they would be sitting down at some point to hammer these out at a more senior level, the EU were aware that Ireland had no choice but to accept whatever terms it chose to provide. They knew that Ireland needed some sort of assurance before the budget, and by talking up the negotiations they ensured that the markets would force Ireland into an acceptance of a deal because in the absence of such acceptance the Irish budget a fortnight later would be a farce given the interest rates.

Ireland thought the EU and IMF were coming as partners, that the discussions would be quiet, and final agreement would be reached over a couple of months. Instead, they found a group that ensured the negotiations were leaked, and when Patrick Honohan effectively confirmed the negotiations were ongoing it did two things: Ireland now had to get a deal before the budget and the politicians were pretty much sidelined. The deal would be one done by officials based on set formulae with little discussion, and it was clear for all to see that the elected Irish Government was no longer running Ireland.

The economist Morgan Kelly suggested that a Finance Minister had never been so deftly cut off at the knee as Honohan had done, possibly unintentionally, to Lenihan. It is also true, however, that it was easy for the EU to do this because the Government themselves were so unpopular. Had Ireland had an election and had a new government taken over, then things might have been different, and it might not have proven so easy to completely sideline political negotiation. It is quite shocking that at a time when such a massive decision was about to be taken on sovereign finances, there was so little going on at a political level. One would naturally expect the Taoiseach and Minister for Finance to be seen marching in to such negotiations along with the leaders of the ECB and perhaps other Eurozone countries. Instead, Patrick Honohan has given an account where he suggests that there was no discussion on rates of interest as it was based on set formulae and generally viewed as being academic. Brian Cowen and indeed Brian Lenihan must take some responsibility for allowing the elected Government to become so unpopular that their view hardly seemed to matter. This was not good politics.

There can be no avoiding the fact that history will show that Brian Lenihan was Minister for Finance when the IMF came. This is something no minister would be proud of, and it took a serious toll on Lenihan personally. The poor handling of the news and what many saw as a craven acceptance of a punitive interest rate left many doubting Lenihan's ability and motives.

He did, however, come back to launch his four-year plan, which today still forms the bedrock of the plans for the recovery of the Irish economy. It has been attacked, and is considered to be far too optimistic by many, but thus far it remains the only plan in town. Lenihan proceeded to introduce another tough budget, and again showed no desire to break from his plans in order to fit a more populist approach. There is no doubt that Lenihan could have made himself far more popular by telling the EU where to go and by introducing big stimulus plans in his budget. He did not, and therefore some regard must be given to the fact that he was not willing to play politics with the future, even though had he done so he would have been hailed by many serious economic commentators.

It is difficult to judge whether Brian Lenihan Jnr retained the left of centre beliefs of his father, because thecircumstances that he found himself in presented little scope for change or ideology if the country's finances were to be rectified. It would be easy to suggest that due to the cuts imposed and the measures affecting medical cards and social welfare that Lenihan had moved significantly from the beliefs of his father and was more right-wing in approach. In truth, though, ideology is a child of resources. To make that assumption at this point in time is like suggesting that Charlie McCreevy was more left-wing than Proinsias De Rossa for he oversaw much greater increases in social welfare and pensions. Judging it primarily on the figures can taint the picture.

The new Fine Gael/Labour Government finds itself upon election faced with unpalatable choices on social welfare and issues affecting those on lower and middle incomes, irrespective of how much it may wish to avoid this. Of course, the argument can be made that it is not the implementation in itself but how fair it is seen to be. For many, the cuts took little note of the people they impacted upon. While there was an understanding that everyone had to bear some pain, many felt that the overriding aim was how much money would be raised. This meant that excessive focus was on cuts to the majority of people at the lower end rather than some of the more 'symbolic' cuts that would hit wealthy individuals. Such measures might not raise much revenue, but they are important when people are being asked to bear pain themselves. A prime example was how lower civil servant grades were hit but higher level civil servants managed to find a loophole and avoid the punishment. It should be noted that politicians, to be fair to their much maligned image, did take pay cuts and pension levies, and the Taoiseach and ministers also took hefty cuts to their income. This was only as it should be, it is only right that they would be the first to accept the hit, the only problem is that they should have gone even further. However, it is interesting that others in organisations from the HSE to the civil service steadfastly refused to accept similar level cuts. The politicians were not particularly heroic, but at least they took some level of cuts in their salaries. While this act of leadership was plainly much too little and too late, it still proved to be more than could be expected of many of those well paid people around them, who saw no compelling reason to do the same.

In December 2009, Brian Lenihan was diagnosed with cancer. The prognosis was not good. A television station receiving a leak of the news over Christmas decided to contact him and tell him they were going public with the story in the national interest. Lenihan was faced with the awkward task of ringing family and friends over this period to inform them of the news before the story broke publicly. The TV station was justified in that: the story was certainly of national interest. Indeed, the story would undoubtedly have been broken by someone, and if they didn't do it they would be usurped. However, a question mark still hangs over the desire of the public for news and over the fact that the need to be first with a story can sometimes overrule the right to privacy.

Lenihan faced his illness in stoical fashion, much like his father. It is still too early to fully assess his impact on the political scene. However, if Ireland does recover from the economic collapse, and all indicators are that it will, then Brian Lenihan may yet be accredited in history with playing a part in this survival. There is little doubt that in years to come many of his decisions will be proven incorrect or poorly based. Nonetheless, his first priority as a public servant must be the survival of the country and its economy, and while in time some may say things could have been done differently, if history shows that Lenihan took the measures that broadly stabilised the problem in Ireland and laid even a scant foundation for a recovery, then it will no doubt be one of the most immense feats in Irish political history. Many agree that Lenihan was not at fault for this crisis, and there is an acceptance that he deserves some credit for trying to rectify it. Lenihan, it is true, did not seek to bring down the Government when it engaged in excessive and obviously unwise spending. He did support general Government policy as a TD. This must be remembered, but it should be in the context of a wider sense of responsibility from which the country must learn. Politics let us down. All parties supported high spending, not one sought to rein in spending in their promises of 2007. In truth, there was also no appetite among the public for it either. From hospitals to roads to schools, all services needed more funding. The political system must admit a core failure to identify problems and predict events. Sadly, the fact is that the politicians were not in control as they should have been, and this is an indictment of all. But Lenihan must take specific responsibility for the bank guarantee however, and only when the full impact of that can be assessed with regard to the information available will the public be able to judge this action. He was also the Minister for Finance when the IMF started funding Ireland, and this is a tag any minister would rather not have. However, such is the enormity of the decisions that Brian Lenihan took in this regard that it is impossible to judge any of them fairly so soon after they occurred. Indeed, it may take a full fifty years before a thoroughly honest assessment of Brian Lenihan and his decisions can be made. Right now it would be easy to dismiss everything he did as disastrous, but that is in light of the conditions Ireland now faces. At a future time, and in less heated circumstances, some of the positives may be able to be assessed in a way that is impossible now. He is in the unique position whereby in many decades to come, when people mention the name Lenihan, they will think of him before any of his illustrious predecessors. That is rare in any dynasty.

When Micheál Martin moved against Brian Cowen there was a widespread belief that if Brian Lenihan joined him then Cowen would resign. Lenihan prevaricated and then said he had other things on his mind besides leadership challenges. This was contested by many within the parliamentary party who claimed to have discussed the matter with him. Lenihan's support for Cowen was seen as an attempt to secure the Fianna Fáil leadership for himself following the election with a defeated Micheál Martin out of the way. In this regard he greatly underestimated both Martin and the depth of feeling among the Fianna Fáil membership. Coming on the back of the PR disaster surrounding the communication of the IMF negotiations it did not help Lenihan's cause.

The circumstances in the lead up to Cowen's resignation again underlined the trust that had existed between the Government and the banks. It was revealed that Cowen had spent a day golfing with senior figures of Anglo Irish Bank in July 2008. While there was nothing wrong with this in itself, it shocked many Fianna Fáil back-benchers and members that such bankers could get an entire day's access to the Taoiseach when they would struggle to obtain 15 minutes on a policy issue or to get the Taoiseach to attend an event. It is still unclear if Brian Lenihan as Minister for Finance was even informed by Cowen that he was meeting with representatives from Anglo Irish Bank or if the Taoiseach sought the opinions of the new minister on an approach to what was happening in banking. Considering that the bank guarantee occurred only a couple of months later, it again indicated that Cowen trusted the information he was receiving from the banks to a detrimental level, and perhaps to the exclusion of others.

After Cowen resigned, Lenihan again went one step further than his father by contesting the leadership, and there is little doubt that his father would have taken huge pride in this. He was, however, unsuccessful. But the ensuing General Election proved what a political collossus Lenihan was. He was the sole Fianna Fáil survivor in Dublin. The city was a nuclear wasteland for the party in political terms, and that puts Lenihan's achievement in being elected into some perspective. His ability to argue his case and his courage on a personal level are testament to such strength. There were, however, even bigger battles facing Lenihan. After the Election he was re-appointed Fianna Fáil spokesperson on Finance. Shortly after, his absence was noted by many. Lenihan's battle with pancreatic cancer was coming to an end, and it was one he simply could not win. On 10 June 2011, Brian Lenihan Jnr passed away at home surrounded by members of the family that had held him in such high esteem. He was aged just fifty-two, and there is no doubt that but for his illness he would still have had a lot more to offer to the political life of the country. It was an enormous blow to the Lenihan family and to the Fianna Fáil party at large. The general outpouring of grief from all sides of the political divide was hearfelt. No matter what people said about Brian Lenihan or what arguments they engaged him in, all remarked that he never allowed it to sour a personal relationship and he never held a grudge against others.

He was a remarkable politician and, like his father, had won enormous respect and admiration even from those who did not agree with him. This was perhaps underlined when he was the only Fianna Fáil politician to be asked to address the Michael Collins commemoration at Béal na mBláth. He faced adversity with courage, and never uttered a word to seek sympathy. He served his country selflessly. Had Lenihan resigned as finance minister it would have caused serious problems for how Ireland would have been perceived internationally as he seemed to be the one ray of light that the markets appreciated. Without doubt he is a loss to politics, but he did his name proud considering the impossible hand he had to play, and the short time in which he had to play it.

The Lenihans are a dynasty of genuine power and influence in Irish politics. While not always on the same hymn sheet they also share many similar qualities. Thus far three generations faced with political adversity and personal difficulty have all faced their problems in similar fashion. Talking to politicians around Leinster house from any political background you choose, it is difficult to find anyone who does not respect the Lenihan name. Recent events and decisions taken by Brian Lenihan Jnr hold perhaps the key to how that name will be viewed by history. However, most would agree that even if they disliked his policies Brian Lenihan was at least more decisive than many of his colleagues. Talking to people involved in politics about the Lenihans one finds one particular trait being quoted time and again in one form or another: that they acted out of genuine belief and conviction. Perhaps no greater compliment can be given.

Building the Haughey Name

For many people, the Haughey name defines an entire era of Irish politics. Charles Haughey was one of the most charismatic and divisive figures ever to grace the Irish political stage. He was followed by his son Sean, who not only maintained the Haughey presence but also maintained through his mother the Lemass presence in the Dáil right up to the 2011 General Election.

Charles Haughey was not exactly what one might expect from an Irish politician when he entered politics. He was very different to the generation of austere War of Independence heroes who had gone before him. But, as the Cosgrave story shows, Ireland was changing by the time he entered the Dáil. Most of that change started with Seán Lemass.

Those who had fought for Irish freedom in the early twentieth century had unifying goals despite some different underlying political approaches. They wanted a free Ireland that was ruled by its own people and master of its own destiny. They wanted an Ireland of social justice. To a large degree they wanted to be left alone to get on with things. The world, however, was changing fast, and isolation – social, cultural or economic – was no longer an option. Leaders like De Valera and Cosgrave quickly found that the dream they once had was largely unsustainable, and indeed became practically impossible in the wake of World War Two. Ireland had become master of its own destiny in name and democratic terms, but remained economically dependent on the UK and others. The simple reality was that it could not even support its own population, many of whom were emigrating to the US, Europe and Britain. The 1950s and early 1960s were bleak days for Ireland. Charting a more prosperous course in the future would mean a move away from sentimental idealism and ideology towards an acceptance of realities.

Cometh the hour, cometh the man. Seán Lemass rose to the position of Taoiseach from streetwise veteran of the War of Independence. Lemass was known as 'the Boss': a name that Charlie Haughey would later try to emulate. He was the ultimate pragmatist. He was probably the only politician who had the vision and ability to see through the plans that civil servant and visionary of an economically vibrant and free-trading Ireland T.K. Whitaker had created. Lemass embarked on major reform, a significant industrialisation of Ireland and, perhaps most importantly of all, he gave up on the well-meaning and attractive mantra of self-sufficiency and indigenous employment in preference for engaging in global trade. He knew that for Ireland to be successful it was always going to rely on foreign direct investment, and the sooner it upped its game in that regard the sooner it would start to make progress. Lemass seized upon the new, outward-looking spirit in Ireland. It sprang from a generation that that had not known the struggle for independence, and by the 1950s had very little regard for it except in patriotic terms. Business development became the key to the economy.

The electorate never honoured Lemass with an overall majority, perhaps illustrating that he was ahead of his time. Although it would be unfair to the electorate to suggest that under Lemass there was nothing but good news. The growth in figures and economic indicators seemed to have few practical benefits to the man on the street, and it was not until much later that the true worth of Lemass's policies could be appreciated, when jobs and investment began to flow. Lemass, being a practical man, was the first to understand the importance of institutional fund-raising and corporate support, which introduced a vein in Fianna Fáil that would cause them serious problems, and perhaps, at the time of writing, some of its opponents might suggest was the root cause of its imminent collapse. Economic success was a necessity, but Lemass gave no real sign of an interest in culture or the arts. Everything made way for progress. This may have represented necessary policy during a time when Ireland was playing catch-up with the rest of the world, but for some it was at best a soulless type of growth.

De Valera had given the party idealism and loyalty tempered with a large dose of pragmatism. Lemass made pragmatism the overarching *modus operandi*, allowing idealism to fall far down the list. So, while it was a major positive that things like protectionism were abandoned, and real economic growth began, while it was a massive boost that Ireland now began to truly address the needs of its people, this came at some cost, particularly for Fianna Fáil. With the reform came new breeds of politicians: businessmen as opposed to idealists, who were more apt to have financial backers than any harsh political principles.

Another significant move that showed Lemass's strength and pragmatism was opening the door to the North in discussions with Unionist leaders. This was yet another positive policy. But again, it came at a cost to the party. It had to abandon yet another old ideal of being freedom-fighters and totally opposed to the six-county State. Loyalty to Lemass was immense, perhaps even greater than that given to De Valera. The party was incredibly well run. However, Lemass was a man whose head could not be turned by those with money. He was not afraid to go back on a political ideal or principle if the good of the people required it for progress, however he was a man of personally high ideals and principles. Therefore such an approach caused no difficulty. To understand this it is necessary to distinguish the public figure from the personal man. As a politician, Lemass was not closely wedded to any particular ideology or principle other than an idea of serving the greater good. On the other hand, on a personal level Lemass held principles of honesty, integrity and fairness very close to his heart. As a result he took decisions based on what he personally believed was right and proper – if this meant the reversal of an older public position taken by him or his party he saw no difficulty with that. He was simply being honest with himself and the people as he saw it. It was not yet apparent that in another man's hands such an approach could easily be twisted, and there were those who would follow into Fianna Fáil who did not share the same level of devotion or belief, or perhaps standards, as 'the Boss'.

Lemass was a man who certainly did not seek personal enrichment, and seemed unable to understand those who did, or appreciate why they would do it. Maureen Haughey recalled that when her father found himself out of the Cabinet, after Fianna Fáil lost an election, he was dropped home by his driver and had to borrow his son's car to go to town the following day, later purchasing a modest Ford for his transport. He also told his daughters that he was unlikely ever to be able to leave them any wealth, so to make up he would ensure that they would get a good education. Lemass was a man of vision, perhaps one tempered by the loss of his brother Noel, who was arrested and then executed during the Civil War in a suspected reprisal for the killing of Michael Collins. This affected Lemass deeply, but it is a mark of the man's character that he was convinced that the desire for violence and revenge were useless emotions that would accomplish nothing. He buried the pain and put his country first. However it is likely that it also influenced his view of material things. It caused him to realise at a very deep level that there are things in life much more important than acquiring wealth, and he seems to have resolved to pursue those things in his political career. Lemass never seemed impressed by possessions or wealth and was known among friends for being somewhat frugal.

There is a celebrated incident that is often quoted to illustrate Lemass's lack of materialism. During a time when tea was rationed, a wealthy diplomat sent Lemass a large chest of tea for his family. Lemass returned it, saying that if the Irish people have to do without tea so too would the Lemass family.

Seán Lemass named his only son after his brother. Noel Jnr was to follow his father's footsteps into the political arena. He was twenty-seven when he stood in a by-election in Dublin South-West in 1957, and took the seat. Even if his family name was an advantage in getting elected, it proved to be of little help in forging his subsequent political career. Seán Lemass was a man who did not like the idea of nepotism. He was also a man who was wary of the effect politics could have on life. He famously offered Charles Haughey a junior ministerial position saying, 'It's my duty as Taoiseach to offer you a position, and my duty as your father-in-law to tell you not to accept it'. The pragmatist in Seán Lemass would have had no difficulty with his son seeking election and winning it. No doubt his name helped, but it was still up to the people to decide. Promotion by his father's hand once elected was a different matter, and one that would have left Seán Lemass uneasy.

When Seán Lemass retired, Noel found better opportunities, and Jack Lynch quickly promoted him to Parliamentary Secretary (or junior minister) in the Department of Finance. He served in that role until 1973, and did so at a difficult time politically as he first served under Haughey and then under Haughey's great rival George Colley. Fianna Fáil entered opposition in '73, and Noel's career was cut short by his sudden death in 1976 at the age of forty-seven. It was unexpected and tragic as he had lived his political life in the shadow of his father and, despite his nineteen year career, his family link could be said to have stunted his emergence as a politician in his own right, only finding political office at the end of this tenure.

The resulting by-election was contested by Noel's wife, Eileen Lemass, a lover of the arts and long-standing Fianna Fáil councillor. However, despite her record and name, she was unable to hold the seat. The difficulty for Fianna Fáil at this point in its history was well illustrated in this by-election. Eileen Lemass secured almost thirty-nine percent of the vote, and almost three thousand more votes than the eventual winner, Brendan Halligan of Labour. Despite the impressive numbers, with only one seat on offer she did not make it on the first count, and the transfers from eliminated Fine Gael and other candidates formed a solid anti-Fianna Fáil bloc that ensured Halligan would overtake her and gain the seat.

She did not have to wait long for another opportunity, and in the 1977 General Election she regained the seat for Fianna Fáil. However, it was only the start of a difficult career from an electoral point of view. Despite carrying the Lemass name, she was unable to build a consistent and solid base. She was re-elected in 1981, but lost the seat again in February 1982, only to regain it again in November of that year.

Other opportunities presented themselves, and she decided to run for the European Parliament in 1984. Considering the emphasis that Seán Lemass had put on the European project and Ireland's participation in it, there is little doubt but that this was a move of which he would have approved, and also found interesting. Eileen Lemass was successful in her bid, and as a result retired from national politics at the 1987 General Election. Her career would face another challenge when she sought re-election to her European seat in 1989. This time she was again defeated. Now aged sixty-six, it was one defeat too many, and she decided to call time on politics.

The true inheritor of the Lemass tradition as a result was Charles Haughey, through his marriage to Maureen, the daughter of Seán Lemass. It was during the time of great social upheaval and change that was brought about by Seán Lemass that Charles Haughey began to make a name for himself. Fianna Fáil and Fine Gael were both undergoing huge change that was reflective of Irish society in general. Austere politicians were gradually being replaced by fire-brands, men of large personality and sweeping vision. Despite the dynamism and strength of this new generation of Irish politicians, they also brought with them many short-comings, as history would testify.

Whereas Cosgrave found himself the defender of the old ways in Fine Gael, and fighting a losing battle, Haughey proved himself a much different animal in Fianna Fáil. He did not lead a charge against the old guard, although many of them disliked him. Haughey infiltrated them instead. He built a reputation for being a charismatic man, a man who could get things done, someone who was typical of the new Ireland, not hung up on words but a politician of bold action. He could, however, use words to great effect when he wanted to, and frequently painted himself as the defender of the old rebellious spirit of Fianna Fáil and linked to the fight for independence.

Haughey was described by the Lemass family as always being reserved in the presence of Seán Lemass. They were very different men, but both shared an appreciation of for-ward thinking and reform. Doubtless Lemass had little knowledge of Haughey's true approach to money, and would have disapproved severely. In Michael O'Sullivan's biography of Lemass, the following paragraph probably best depicts the differences between the two men:

After a party that Charles and Maureen Haughey gave in their former home, Grangemore, to mark the Lemasses 40th wedding anniversary... Lemass casually asked his host how much the event had cost him. "Knowing Lemass's form on money matters," recalls John O'Connor [Lemass's son-in-law],"Charlie said it had cost £200." Utter incredulity was written all over Lemass's face as he hastily wrote a cheque and disappeared into the distance frantically puffing his pipe. When he was out of earshot Charles Haughey said, "Well, it's just as well I didn't tell him it cost me nearly £2,000."

Lemass certainly did not share Haughey's ostentatious approach to life. It is odd to the point of being notable both that Charlie took the cheque in any event, and that Lemass obviously felt obliged to pay for a party thrown in his honour.

Haughey married Maureen Lemass in 1951. This was a major piece in the jigsaw of building a political name. Haughey now had one of the most glorious political names attached to his own; his dynasty would forever be linked to that of Lemass. It was a complete infiltration of the old guard that brought many people to his standard and allowed him claim a lineage of which others could only dream. It did not assist him immediately, as he failed to take a seat in the 1951 General Election. Indeed, he had to wait until 1957 to take a seat in the Dáil.

Haughey was an extremely charismatic individual, whose very presence could change the attitude of an entire room. Haughey worked hard to mould this image and portray it at every opportunity. Behind it all was a very human man, racked by self-doubt and often in need of others like Brian Lenihan to reassure him and guide him.

In his early days, Haughey was busy building and creating his name, and as a minister he was forward thinking and reforming, always seeing the bigger picture in the policies he implemented. It was this vision that caused so many to follow him and believe in him so passionately. Haughey had a view of the world that could be quite seductive.

His rise to the top was meteoric, and has been well documented in various tomes. But apart from his visionary and reforming nature, the principal characteristic that would define his contribution to the dynasty was his nationalism. Haughey was no doubt a believer in Irish nationalism on a personal level. It is almost strange nowadays to note that Haughey, out of a loyal and nationalistic pride in the GAA, refused to attend international rugby matches. He also refused to holiday in Greece while the Army remained in control there. However, he also recognised the uses of such sentiments as a tool, particularly within Fianna Fáil; a party that has never given up the ghost on a united Ireland . Haughey was at the top of the political food-chain in 1969 when the arms crisis erupted.

His career prior to this is noteworthy in its own right. He pioneered new ways of thinking, and led some highly reforming policies across a number of departments. In Justice he opened the new Garda Training College in Templemore, and was involved in the abolition of the death penalty. In Agriculture he was successful in improving prices and markets for produce, and played a pivotal role in the introduction of farmers dole in 1965, although problems with falling milk prices were a substantial blot on his copybook during this period. He also introduced four budgets, and most notably he ran a surplus on the current budget and succeeded in cutting taxes. This would not happen again for twenty-five years.

While he would never describe himself as a 'socialist' in the manner of Bertie Ahern, Haughey certainly appreciated the power of left-wing politics and knew how to use this when implementing policies that he believed could improve social conditions. He oversaw the implementation of more socialist policies than many socialists could hope to achieve, from the introduction of free travel for pensioners to free TV licences and fuel allowances.

This was perhaps Haughey, the young politician, at his best.

At the end of the 1960s, problems were starting within Northern Ireland, and by 1969 they had reached crisis point. This created a deep and difficult dilemma for Fianna Fáil. This was the party that had opposed partition: it was founded on a belief that the abandonment of those in the North was fundamentally wrong. However, as we have seen it was also a party designed to operate within the twenty-six county State making only gestures of opposition towards the North. For many in the organisation this was still a core reason for following the party. The stories of ill treatment and discrimination against Catholics in the North sat uneasily for decades and seriously damaged the party's image. The crisis in 1969 seemed to open up the wound and Fianna Fáil could no longer ride both horses. On the one hand this was for some the very opportunity that the party had been waiting for; this was the reason the 'revolutionaries' had taken power and suffered: to be in control at this moment. For this group, the situation was clear: idealism, nationalism and ideology all dictated that the honourable course was for the Republic to defend its brothers; to show them they were not left alone. The consequences and chances of failure might be apparent, but honourable action demanded no less. The consequences could not dictate the stance any more than they could in 1916.

Fianna Fáil contained many, indeed a majority, who felt that reality should come first. They believed that the party had committed itself to constitutional politics and must accept the limits that imposed. Any moves to help Northern Catholics could only be diplomatic. They believed that Fianna Fáil and the Republic had made enormous strides on behalf of its citizens and it could not and should not put this at risk. It was in the twenty-six county State and it had a primary duty to protect the safety and security of the people within its borders. Crucially, this group recognised that any military action in the North was futile and would damage Ireland as a whole, perhaps irreparably. International eyes were watching the Irish Government at this time. It must be remembered that it was only during the 1960s that Ireland had begun to recover its shattered reputation following its neutral stance in World War Two. The idea that Ireland, at this point, could find international friends to back it against Britain was simply fantasy. That group, led by Taoiseach Jack Lynch, won out. The period is important, however, as it marked a type of civil war within Fianna Fáil: it forced it to face a demon within and confront an awkward question on the North. It split the party, and many families, right down the centre in terms of how it was viewed.

The decision was to finally set up field hospitals near the border, and there was a small fund established to help Northern communities. As Minister for Finance, Haughey had control over this. The story of what happened next is covered in much more detail elsewhere. However, for the purpose of this book it is important to note that it caused Haughey to be faced with the same dilemma as the party because nationalists inevitably came looking for arms to join the struggle. The plans to import arms were made and were found out. Haughey and Neil Blaney were dismissed for their part, despite protesting their innocence. The Government persisted with an unsuccessful prosecution, which only served to make Haughey a republican hero.

For most politicians, this episode would have ended a career, but in the case of Haughey it only added to his name. The minority who had wanted to make a move on the North now had a hero within Fianna Fáil, while he still had time to bring the others around to his way of thinking.

He did this by proving that he understood the core of Fianna Fáil. Yet again it was not of great importance what those at the top did if you cultivated and promoted what those on the bottom were doing. Fianna Fáil's strength was in its grassroots. Haughey had learned this at Lemass's side when he undertook a major and brilliant reform of Fianna Fáil that lasted up to current days. Aided by P.J. Mara, a man who was unrivalled in his understanding of ground level politics, he hit the country, visiting local units everywhere and anywhere, small crowds or big crowds, and in a very short period of time his accessibility and promotion of the views of those on the ground made him a hero, and the demand for his reinstatement grew. This culminated in Haughey's return to the Cabinet in 1975 as Minister for Health.

Jack Lynch was a highly popular man among the public. He was for many people the epitome of what they expected from an Irish politician. He was understated and quiet, but this hid a very strong character, as the events of the previous decade had shown. Lynch was helped greatly by his background as a GAA player. It is no accident that '69 and '77 were two elections that seemed to go the opposite way to what many expected. Fianna Fáil was attracting a lot of young voters, and for these a spirit of revolution and change was strong. Fine Gael under Cosgrave was as far from reforming or revolutionary in their minds as it was possible to get. Fianna Fáil on the other hand had the personalities and characters that captivated many who thought real and lasting change was possible. Lynch himself had one major weakness: despite being a very well-liked politician, he did not have the personality that could lead this emerging generation, even though his party certainly had. Lynch also failed to appreciate the hunger or need for change. He, like Colley, his chosen successor, did not sense the party changing from the bottom up. He didn't seem to grasp the fact that it was the party rather than himself that was delivering the large vote. This was as much to do with the reformers as it was the party grandees. Lynch was an admirable man and was a politician of the highest calibre, but he was no match for Haughey when it came to understanding the grassroots or playing the political game. As regards the general public, Lynch lost out in that he failed to appreciate the new economic circumstances. Similar to Fine Gael, what is most surprising is that the old conservative wings of the parties were the ones that understood the economic crisis the least.

Lynch and Colley were very much fans of 'auction politics', and for the pushing of policies that took little account of what was necessary. In a strange twist, it was Haughey, Lenihan, McCreevy and other politicians in Fianna Fáil along with the likes of Fitzgerald in Fine Gael who were supporting more austere measures. The new generation just seemed to understand.

Haughey came to the leadership with a huge reputation. He also had enormous popularity within the party and seemed destined for great things in the Fianna Fáil leadership. However, he still faced ongoing battles for control within the party. This was a cloud over Haughey. Similar to every leader who takes over mid term there is always an unfair and damaging criticism that they have no mandate or were not elected. In Irish politics this is nonsense as the people do not elect a Taoiseach but rather the TDs, and those TDs then select the Taoiseach – a very different basis to a presidential election. However, such a criticism was levelled at Haughey, to his annoyance. The implication was that it was Lynch's majority. If Haughey was ever to take full control of the party, or establish the Haughey name above all others, then he had to prove that he was no fluke. Polls suggested that the party could still achieve a majority, and Haughey, brim full of confidence, chose this moment to call an election. It was a gamble, but Haughey calculated that if he won he would silence all critics and have absolute control.

Some very basic maths was forgotten in this calculation. The number of seats in the Dáil had been increased from one hundred and forty-four to one hundred and sixty-six, creating twenty-two new seats that were very much 'up for grabs'. Fianna Fáil was on the back of maximising its vote in '77, leaving little room for growth after such a surge. The party had also to face the fact that, like all governments, there was a disappointment that after coming to power the world didn't change dramatically for most voters. This is an inevitable fact of life, and one that costs almost every government votes when seeking re-election. On the other hand, Fine Gael and Labour had lost many seats at the last election that they expected to win. They had ready-made candidates who had strong electoral records ready to stand for the new seats.

It is perhaps too easy, and indeed lazy, to characterise everything that happened during this period as political intrigue and turmoil. In understanding the dynasty and what it was expected to stand for, we need to note that Haughey continued to endeavour to portray a strong image that people could support. He had several successful and laudable policy initiatives that showed the kind of beliefs that came with the name. He continued with his prioritising of the aged, over-seeing the introduction of successive pension increases. He was a strong patron of the arts, more so than perhaps any Taoiseach since. This included the Aosdána scheme to sup-port artists and the establishment of the Irish Museum of Modern Art in Kilmainham. He also removed VAT from books, which was a major and progressive step, perhaps underappreciated in terms of the statement it sent out.

Adjusting to opposition was not easy for Haughey, and he seems to have launched into a period of opposition for the sake of opposition. The Fine Gael/Labour coalition strug-gled to deal with the many problems they faced, and there was more than enough ammunition for Fianna Fáil on the economy alone. Not content with that, Haughey also chose to go against all attempts made in Northern Ireland such as the Anglo-Irish Agreement and New Ireland form, to the surprise of many. He was particularly argumentative on social issues too, and seemed to take the view that constructive opposition simply would not pay. Indeed, if the period of 1982 to 1986 could be characterised then it should probably be one of bad government and equally bad opposition.

But a long period in opposition had done much to quell Haughey's adventurous spirit. He had learned many lessons the hard way, and had begun to return to some of his early ideals. Essentially, he understood that the country needed drastic action, and that this was what the people wanted and would respect. The view was that they might not repay you with electoral dividends, but it was better to be judged by history to have had one term and done the right thing than to have had several and be remembered as ineffectual or having made things worse. By 1986, Haughey had effectively defeated any rebels and was in control of the party. He could select his own team, and Haughey was highly capable of spotting talent. Two men were also coming to the fore who would dominate economic policy: Ray McSharry and Albert Reynolds. Both swung Fianna Fáil very much away from being a party of auction politics and electoral populism towards being a party determined to implement policies that might actually work.

Irish politicians faced a very stark choice at the time. They could either get their act together and do what was necessary for the country, thus risking increasing unpopularity with the electorate, or face the risk of national bankruptcy. Aided by Alan Dukes, who in trying to plot a longer term course for Fine Gael came up with the Tallaght Strategy, Fianna Fáil began to put the finances on a proper footing and to take tough but necessary decisions.

During this period, Haughey was a changed man from the one who had been Taoiseach initially. He returned more to the roots that had brought him initial popularity, and showed a tremendous talent for managing his Cabinet and keeping things under a tight rein, while also leaving ministers just enough room to plot their own course within their departments.

The tough course of action that Ray McSharry took between 1987 and 1989 was instrumental in laying the foundations for Ireland's future economic success. But cuts imposed in Health and Education were met with strong resistance. Haughey showed the strength of his resolve by holding fast to the policy and backing his Minister. He began to show the style that had led to his reputation as a statesman.

Despite the harshness of the measures imposed, the public seemed grateful to the Government for its course. Opinion polls showed astonishingly high ratings for Fianna Fáil given the austerity package proposed, and the general mood was that the Government was performing well. As a result of this, an old trait returned to Charlie Haughey. In this sense he did not learn from his father-in-law Seán Lemass, for despite doing the right thing, and having a minority Government performing well, Haughey was still tempted again in 1989 to risk it all and gamble with an election in the hope of securing the elusive majority.

The move was an error, with Fianna Fáil losing vital seats and making the continuation of the minority Government impossible. It would prove to be Haughey's last election. He returned from this escapade facing a loss of power just when he had finally gained the respect of most commentators on the economy. He had little room to maneuver. Haughey decided that he would swallow a bitter pill and seek to enter government with the Progressive Democrats and Des O'Malley. This hurt, and there is little doubt about that. Probably the only thing that made it possible was that by 1989 both men had been chastised by the electorate for their behaviour, and O'Malley had gone from being a powerful new force in Irish politics to being just another small fringe party.

The move annoyed many in Fianna Fáil. Haughey also began to illustrate that he was again changing his *modus operandi*. Reynolds and Ahern were tasked with sealing a deal with the Progressive Democrats, yet it was Haughey who agreed the terms separately with O'Malley personally. It was a move behind Reynolds's back that was not appreciated, but clearly Haughey felt that his future would be decided by him, and him alone.

Haughey showed that he had an amazing ability to work with people, even those whom he didn't like, when it suited him. The Government with the Progressive Democrats was a success in policy terms, although many in Fianna Fáil remained ill at ease with the party being pulled to the right. Brian Lenihan was foremost among these. Albert Reynolds, meanwhile, was now Minister for Finance and, following on from McSharry, he kept a tight rein on public spending, yet began to stimulate the economy through a series of tax cuts that would be the first of a major three part package that would later, in conjunction with enormous injections of funds from the EU, and to some extent a dividend accrued through the peace process, lead to the Irish boom.

Haughey gave much more attention to Northern Ireland at this point. Secret talks were held with Sinn Féin with regard to what could be achievable, but Haughey was very much afraid that any open association with them could end his career. He was correct in that. At the time, any government figure talking with terrorists would be completely unacceptable to the vast majority of the Irish public. For Haughey, of course, the issue was particularly incendiary, given his alleged involvement in illegal arms smuggling. He knew that he would not be forgiven if he started to suggest that talks could be held, and this made any progress on the issue particularly difficult.

The 1990 Presidential Election saw Haughey at perhaps his lowest point in terms of stature. For a man who had frivolously entered elections in the past, he seemed nothing short of broken when the Progressive Democrats demanded the head of Brian Lenihan. Haughey clearly sent a signal that there would be no more elections for anyone or for any reason, his remaining Taoiseach was now the priority. It was not what Fianna Fáil party members expected or wanted and they felt let down.

Seán Lemass had shown two admirable traits that were sadly absent in Haughey. First, he just got on with the job, electoral success and popularity came a distant second to this and therefore he did not rush to face the electorate. Secondly, Lemass knew how to set an agenda, how to work it to its completion, and when to recognise that time is up.

Haughey couldn't see this end coming. In the wake of the 1990 Presidential Election, Haughey was on the way out. Few in Fianna Fáil may have seen it so early, but there is little doubt that his career was facing its immediate end. Questions began to gather pace as to when he would resign and who would take over, to the extent that it began to irritate Haughey. While he had always maintained that he had a timetable in mind, there is little evidence to suggest that this timetable was ever agreed or discussed at length with his colleagues, and even less to suggest that even if the timetable were in place Haughey would stick to it.

He found a formidable opponent in Albert Reynolds. While he easily won the vote of confidence within the party, and subsequently sacked Reynolds, the bravado shown in its wake was merely a thin veil. Haughey was finished as a leader, and his opponents gathered pace behind Reynolds. When Sean Doherty announced that Haughey had known about phone tapping in the early 1980s the game was up, and the most charismatic, sometimes inspiring and yet divisive and corroding influence on Irish politics had departed the stage.

In yet a final twist, Haughey would again dominate the headlines in the '90s as revelations about money, donations, friends and affairs destroyed his reputation beyond repair. The grandeur and style that he exuded and was liked for was shown to be a mere facade for someone who had limited resources and was continually in enormous levels of debt. There was perhaps nothing that could have been further from the Lemass name that Haughey married into and to which he would provide a dynastic link. Money for high living would not have been something Lemass could have understood, even had he wanted to.

Sean Haughey, until the most recent election, continued to be the standard-bearer for both the Lemass and Haughey names in the Dáil. Having a grandfather and father of such national fame could be considered an unbearable weight on anyone's shoulders. Sean Haughey has grown accustomed to it, and handled the situation in admirable fashion. He was twenty-four when he became a Dublin City Councillor having studied Economics and Politics at Trinity College Dublin. He did not, though, find the Haughey name providing him with much electoral advantage while his father was leader of the party. He failed to get elected in 1987 and again in 1989. However, he served as Mayor of Dublin in 1989 to 1990, and this greatly helped to increase his profile. The Senate provided a springboard for his ambitions, where he served from 1987 to 1992. During the General Election of 1992 he had a better opportunity as his father stepped down from politics. He had little difficulty in securing the seat and his name did not harm his chances in the old family stamping ground of Dublin North Central. He was still only thirty-one.

There was little doubt that Haughey had to learn his trade, but revelations about his father's personal finances obviously created major difficulties for his career. Although he was considered bright and very able, Bertie Ahern did not offer him any position after the 1997 General Election. For many commentators this was understandable, in as much as it would have caused difficulties for both Fianna Fáil and put Sean Haughey under a particular spotlight.

Sean Haughey's amicable nature was respected around Leinster House regardless. People understood how difficult the period must have been for him, but Haughey showed remarkable fortitude. He did not seek to attack those who condemned his father for any base familial reasons. He did not condone what his father had done, and neither did he seek to distance himself from the controversy nor from his father, and this too gained him respect and sympathy.

After the 2002 Election, many people felt that he was one of the bright young lights of the party and should get an opportunity rather than be punished for the sins of his father. However, the call did not come. After the reshuffle of 2004 there was much surprise when Haughey was still not promoted, and some speculated that it was due to the fact that Bertie Ahern did not want to underline any links to the Haughey era with which people connected him so fervently. This rose to even greater levels in 2006 when yet again Haughey was overlooked for promotion. This was at a time when virtually every commentator in the country had tipped Sean Haughey for higher office.

The reasoning behind Ahern's decision is unclear, but certainly some personal rancour seems to have been involved. The decision by the Taoiseach caused Haughey to suggest that he was going to have to consider his future in politics. This was understandable. Now forty-six, Haughey knew that if his time was not going to come soon then he would not have much of a career to look forward to. A career lived out on the back benches was not appealing to man with his ability or lineage.

Haughey received enormous support, both from the media and from the Fianna Fáil organisation in his decision. The level of support was unexpected. Ahern had misjudged the popularity of Sean Haughey, and the willingness of the Irish people to see him forge a career separate to what might be attached to his father's name. Desperately, Ahern sought to fix the problem, and Síle De Valera, who had decided she was not going to seek re-election, was leaned upon to resign her junior ministry. Haughey himself was not at ease with this approach, although it received much support in the wider party as many felt that De Valera had been wrong to hold on to her post after her decision to step down from politics had been made.

De Valera seemed unwilling to bow to pressure at first, however the need for the party to be put above oneself was well understood and she relented, but waited until the following December to do so on her own timescale.

Haughey had finally made it into the junior ministerial ranks, and he was reappointed to this position in the wake of the 2007 General Election. Brian Cowen showed no desire to promote him further, but this may have as much to do with

Cowen's unwillingness to force any current Cabinet members to step down as any wish not to see Haughey promoted.

Whether Haughey could have gone further is undoubtable in terms of his potential. Unfortunately, time was against him. Haughey was, like so many others, unable to hold his seat for Fianna Fáil in the 2011 Election, and yet another dynasty came crashing to the ground. Sean Haughey had struggled long and hard to rebuild the family name, and had gone a considerable distance in doing this, which was no small achievement in itself. But a failure to attain a full cabinet post left him unable to fully rehabilitate the dynastic image. He has faced great adversity in his career, and rarely of his own making.

The future of the Lemass/Haughey dynasty would seem to be in considerable doubt. Seán Lemass remains one of the most respected figures of political history with former Taoisigh such as John Bruton and Albert Reynolds both citing him as an inspiration, despite their differing political views. Charles Haughey remains a divisive figure. There is little doubt that when Haughey was at his best he was a reformer and brilliant leader. Unfortunately, Haughey spent too much of his time at his worst. He could be truculent and destructive. For all of his undoubted achievements he will most likely be remembered for his shameful personal finances, which tarnished the dynastic name in a way that will be difficult to erase. Although Haughey married into the Lemass name, he proved that such a connection does not mean you have learned the morals or approach of the same family. Haughey seemed to take much of what he liked in terms of policy and reform from Lemass, but, sadly, he obviously disagreed strongly with Seán Lemass's approach to life and money.

Sean Haughey is in some ways remarkable. The ability to rise after such a mortal blow seemed to have been dealt to the Haughey name should not be underestimated. The support he gained from the media and the general public in relation to his promotion to a junior ministry suggests that he has indeed gone some way to repairing a little of the damage. He is well liked and, interestingly, it would seem that for the Irish people the sins of the father should not necessarily be the burden of the son.

There is little doubt but that Sean Haughey, as a blood relative of Seán Lemass, has shown more of his grandfather's style than his father's. It was remarkable that as Fianna Fáil tried to regroup after the mortal blow of the 2011 Election, most of the talk could be boiled down to a desire to move back to the ideals of Lemass and away from the ideals of Haughey. Sean Haughey must find himself in a very strange and often uncomfortable position when such a debate rages. Sean Haughey is unlikely to make any further forays into politics. Will we ever see this house rise again? Only time will tell.

The Irish Family Kitt

The Kitt family is unique in Irish politics, and proves the advantage a political name can confer on a politician. The family is also interesting in that it is debatable what the secret of their success actually is. Is it just the name? If so, how does it travel from one side of the country to the other despite a lack of high profile positions in government, and how does it work even when one sibling, Áine Brady, campaigns under her married name? If the family's success is indeed attributable to their name, then they prove a depth of influence on the Irish psyche of political names that is nothing short of gargantuan. Alternatively, is the success evidence that people who grow up in a political household learn and understand a game that puts them at a distinct advantage and gives them knowledge ahead of their rivals? Whatever way you look at it, the Kitt family provides one of the most intriguing dynasties in Irish politics, and yet the high office of a full cabinet ministry still eludes the family.

Michael F. Kitt was the founder of the dynasty. He had a difficult start to life in politics, taking a seat for Fianna Fáil in Galway North in 1948, but subsequently losing this seat again in 1951. He attempted to regain his seat at the following election in 1954, but was defeated again. However,

Michael Kitt was not the kind of man to give up, and showed the kind of tenacity and work ethic that has become synonymous with the name among those close to the dynasty. Continuing to work towards his ambition, Kitt finally regained his seat in 1957. From then, constituency changes were to benefit Kitt as he went to Galway East, where he made the seat his own right up till the time of his death.

Despite serving for twenty years as a TD, Kitt did not enjoy the benefits of high office. The high point of his career only came at the age of fifty-six in 1970, and this was in the wake of the upheaval caused by the arms crisis. As a result of changes to the Government Kitt was appointed Parliamentary Secretary (junior minister) at the Department of the Gaeltacht, and served in this position until 1973, when the Government lost the Election.

Failure to attain high office or gain accolades after such a long career is often seen as a fault in Irish politics. Although there can be many reasons this occurs, it tends to be harmful to a dynasty. Michael Kitt's death in 1974 while a serving TD opened the door for the dynasty to begin in earnest.

By-elections can be notoriously hard to win, occurring as they do both suddenly and unexpectedly. Getting a candidate in place is a difficult business, and building any kind of name or recognition for them is a particularly hard task. This is often made much easier if there is a family member willing to stand in place of the outgoing TD. The reason is simple. There is no need to establish a new reputation as the candidate can succeed on the back of what their predecessor has done, and is most likely to get many of those votes, and where someone has died there is likely to be a considerable sympathy vote in addition. By-elections, therefore, are a perfect breeding ground for dynastic candidates.

Michael Paschal Kitt was perfectly placed to assume his father's mantle. A teacher by profession, he was first co-opted to replace his father in the County Council, and in 1975 he took the Dáil seat with a clear majority at the by-

election. However, he would mirror his father's early tribulations by losing his seat in the 1977 General Election.
Considering this was such a good election for Fianna Fáil
generally, Kitt must have been tremendously disappointed.
But, not being from a family that would give up at such a
hurdle, he successfully got elected to the Senate, thereby
ensuring he could maintain his profile. In fact, it is abun-
dantly clear that the Senate is most often used by failed
election candidates as a way of keeping in the game in order
to regain a seat at a later election, and again, given the voting
system on a nationwide basis, it is safe to assume that a
strong and recognisable family name carries much weight in
securing a Senate seat. The move paid off for Kitt, who
managed to regain his Dáil seat in the 1981 General Election.
Despite the tribulations of the 1980s, and the many elections
that ensued, Kitt managed to secure his base and establish
what might be considered a safe seat for much of that time.

Michael Kitt suffered a similar fate to his father in more
respects than just his electoral misfortunes. Despite his long
service he struggled to gain a senior governmental appointment. It was a full decade later, in 1991, when a measure of
success came his way. Yet again the Kitt family was to be a
beneficiary of upheaval within Fianna Fáil. As Albert
Reynolds led the charge against Haughey in November 1991
there was a rush to secure favour with both sides. Those
who backed Reynolds were sacked or banished, and this
opened the way for new appointments. Michael Kitt would
be one of these, being made a junior minister at the Department of the Taoiseach. But the success was to be short lived,
for in just under three months Reynolds had returned and
taken over, and had little time for anyone who profited from
his earlier difficulties. Kitt was subsequently demoted.

That did not deter him from his task, however, and the
Kitt tenacity saw him hold on to fight another day. However,
perhaps a warning sign was on the horizon in the 1992 Election, as his percentage share of the vote began to drop. This

continued in 1997, which saw an alarming fall off in first preference votes, causing Kitt to take the third seat as opposed to the first or second to which he had become accustomed in previous elections. He seems to have been unable to arrest this pattern, and yet again, while 2002 was an election where Fianna Fáil enjoyed immense popularity, Kitt proved to be a victim, losing what had been a relatively safe seat. In 1997 Fianna Fáil had expected to win a third seat in the constituency, but narrowly failed, mainly thanks to a very disciplined performance from Fine Gael. This time Fianna Fáil tried even harder to balance the vote of their three candidates, but the surge of support for an independent candidate upset this plan. While it cost Fine Gael a seat, it also saw Kitt losing out to his running mate, Joe Callanan.

For many, losing a seat at fifty-two years of age, having had a long and perhaps undistinguished career, might be enough reason to hang up the gloves. Yet again, however, Kitt was fighting his way back in familiar style, being nominated by the Taoiseach to serve in the Senate. Maintaining his profile carefully, Kitt was perfectly positioned for the 2007 General Election, and determined not to make the same mistake again. The Fianna Fáil vote in the constituency was down, and was also far less evenly balanced between the candidates. Kitt topped the poll and regained his seat yet again, a full thirty-two years after he had first won it.

Following the Election, Kitt was to see his many years of hard work and determination pay off as he was appointed Junior Minister with responsibility for overseas development. A year later, in 2008, Brian Cowen came to power and, being a man who placed much stock in age and experience, he didn't want to make wholesale changes. Kitt moved departments to Environment with responsibility for local services and served there for another year. However, the axe fell again in 2009 when the Taoiseach, under pressure to cut the number of junior ministers, dropped Kitt. At sixty years of age the game certainly appeared over for him. Politics, though, can be a strange mistress. As the 2011 whirlwind of change blasted Fianna Fáil, Michael Kitt was one of the few survivors, and the sole representative of this dynasty to return to the Dáil. In a Fianna Fáil of only 20 TDs, Kitt was to secure a position on the front bench at last. Despite a very long Oireachtas career he has thus far failed to make a lasting impression on the Government. For the dynasty this has implications, because if voters and supporters usually follow a name based on the assumption that they will get a similar return from each successive candidate, then it often follows that dynasties need big appointments and senior positions to survive. The role on the front bench gives Michael one last chance to claim the limelight and provide some significant achievements for the dynasty at last.

The Kitt family story has other twists. Michael's brother, Tom, was a TD for the Dublin South constituency. Tom Kitt is also a teacher by profession, which brought him to Dublin. Here he became involved in politics, and carried with him a wealth of family experience. He was elected to Dublin City Council in 1979 and quickly began to establish a platform for himself as a General Election candidate. The opportunity came his way in 1987 when he took a seat in Dublin South for the party aged thirty-five. Tom Kitt was a perfect picture of what many expected a politician to be: he was considered good-looking, calm and intelligent. Many tipped him for great things. Tom was also to break a family tradition in that he would not lose his seat. In fact he grew his base and showed considerable acumen in building it in Dublin among an electorate that is considered far less loyal. For the Kitt dynasty, Tom was certainly, even at this early stage, becoming a standard-bearer. On his shoulders rested much of the familial hope of high office.

While his brother Michael lost out when Reynolds came to power, Tom, being considered a bright politician with potential, would benefit. Reynolds made sweeping changes, bringing in many new younger and fresher faces to the political centre stage. The Kitt family would be split by this turn of events, as while Michael had been rewarded by Haughey and dumped by Reynolds, Tom was presented with his first real opportunity under Reynolds. He was made Minister of State at the Department of the Taoiseach with responsibility for arts, culture and women's affairs. A year later he moved to the slightly more glamorous position of Minister of State at the Taoiseach and shared with Foreign Affairs, giving him a particularly interesting role as the peace process began under Reynolds.

The collapse of the Government in 1994 brought a halt to Tom Kitt's progress for the time being. However, he was now well established in Fianna Fáil, and considered by many to be a future key figure and prime candidate for promotion. While in opposition Kitt took on the mantle of Fianna Fáil spokesperson for Labour Affairs until the 1997 General Election.

If Tom Kitt had one difficulty at this point, it was that he shared a constituency with Seamus Brennan, who was an indispensable figure within Fianna Fáil, and indeed within the Cabinet. Therefore geographic concerns conspired against him in that having two senior ministers in one constituency is always a rarity in Irish politics.

When Fianna Fáil returned to power under Bertie Ahern, Seamus Brennan did indeed get a full cabinet portfolio while Tom Kitt had to be happy with another junior ministry at the Department of Enterprise, Trade and Employment. However, this added to the breadth of Kitt's experience, and many believed it was only a matter of time before he was called to the Cabinet. But he was to be disappointed yet again following the 2002 General Election when Bertie Ahern played things cautiously and opted not to make any great changes to the Cabinet. He found himself back at Foreign Affairs with responsibility this time for overseas development – a role that his brother Michael would fill some five years later.

It must have been a frustrating time for Tom Kitt. Despite high hopes, he had now been fifteen years as a TD, and his career had pretty much stalled for the last ten as he was no further on than he was when Reynolds gave him his break. But fate would intervene. After the 2002 Election, Charlie McCreevy, the Finance Minister, began to worry about a global slowdown caused by the September 11 terrorist attacks in New York and its effects on the Irish economy. Despite promises made during the 2002 Election, McCreevy maintained that not all of these could be fulfilled, as to do so might risk Ireland's new-found prosperity. He introduced a series of spending cuts, or 'adjustments' as they became known, and several key targets on public service numbers, such as Gardai and staffing levels, were put on hold. This was highly unpopular. Fianna Fáil took a pasting both in the media and in the public at large for what was seen as a series of broken promises. While the exchequer was still buoyant there was an insatiable demand among the public for more services and investment, particularly capital investment. This would over the following years lead to an overheating of the construction sector. The prices of construction projects rose completely out of proportion, and there was a scarcity of labour to carry out the work. The Government investment was to lead to a huge over-reliance on construction within the economy. This had a series of knock-on effects, such as increasing house prices and the cost of all associated works. The Ireland of this time, however, was a nation that had suffered for decades with inferior services and high taxes – the people, in their preferred view of matters, were simply demanding their just reward and share of the good times being experienced by the country. There were many calls for Ireland to borrow to fund capital development, and it had ample scope to do so, such was the health of the public coffers.

By the local elections of 2004 Fianna Fáil was in trouble. The party was savaged at the polls and its leadership was very worried. A party think-in at Inchydoney was central to changing things. The message was clear: the party needed to shift to the left and increase spending to provide the people with the services and facilities that they required. There was scope within the budget to do this, particularly with a buoyant property sector. Charlie McCreevy was seen as a block to this, and his 'adjustments' had cost the party heavily as its opponents made hay. The result was simple, Bertie Ahern declared himself a socialist and Charlie McCreevy was shipped off to Brussels.

This reshuffle presented Tom Kitt with the opportunity he had been waiting for. He found himself promoted to the role of Chief Whip. This was a step in the right direction, but may still have been tinged with disappointment for him. Chief Whip is effectively a junior ministry, however the whip is entitled to sit at cabinet meetings, but cannot vote in them. Therefore it was still one stop short of a full cabinet portfolio that was hoped for and very much needed for the dynasty. He also knew that, at fifty-four, he was no longer considered a bright young thing and time was running out. Regardless, the appointment represented the highest achievement to date for the Kitt family, and of that he could be rightly proud.

Kitt served in the role of Chief Whip under Bertie Ahern with some merit, handling the Fianna Fáil/Progressive Democrat coalition and the subsequent agreement between Fianna Fáil, the disintegrating Progressive Democrats and the Green Party with the support of a number of independents. This was a considerable task.

While Kitt must surely have harboured further ambitions, his career was dealt a hammer blow in 2008. Brian Cowen ascended to the position of Taoiseach, and he placed a high value on age, experience and continuity. He brought little change to the face of the Fianna Fáil machine at the top. There would be no raft of losers under his stewardship as happened under Albert Reynolds. In fact, Cowen would not sack any of Ahern's junior ministerial team bar one: Tom Kitt. For whatever reason – and it has never been fully explained – the new Taoiseach did not want Kitt as part of the team, and the fact that he was singled out so spectacularly must have hurt. At fifty-eight, Tom Kitt could see no future in politics, and the chance of a full cabinet portfolio had passed forever. There was no willingness to fight on this time and Kitt almost immediately announced that he would not be contesting the next general election, bringing the curtain down on a career that had promised so much and yet had failed to deliver the coveted ministerial post for the dynasty.

Tom Kitt continued to be a strong voice for his remaining days as a TD, and was among the first of a small group of back benchers that saw the writing on the wall and appealed to Brian Cowen to resign for the good of the party and the country as confidence had fallen so low. Kitt argued strongly during these months but was continually dismissed as holding a grudge due to his demotion. He was, however, true to his word and did not stand in the 2011 Election.

But the story is still far from over. Tom's younger sister, Áine Brady, continues to fly the flag and has now assumed the mantle of the dynasty's highest hope. Aine was involved at a high level internally in Fianna Fáil and, like other members of the family, she found early outings in electoral politics difficult. She stood in the 1981 Seanad Election but was unable to take a seat. In the family tradition she was also a teacher, and it seemed that her defeat at this Seanad election was perhaps the end of her ambitions.

In another interesting dynastic twist she married Gerry Brady, who was the Fianna Fáil TD for Kildare North. Gerry Brady first took his seat in 1982 but, in a story that would be all too familiar to his in-laws in the Kitt family, he lost the seat again in the November Election of the same year. A further defeat at the 1987 General Election marked the end of Gerry Brady's Dáil ambitions, although he continued on in council politics in Kildare.

The story took a turn, however, in 2005. A full twenty-four years after her unsuccessful bid to join the Seanad, Aine's political ambitions resurfaced. The change in Fianna Fáil thinking and the posting of Charlie McCreevey to Brussels may have given an opportunity to her brother Tom, but it also presented her with a chance to revive a political career as it caused a by-election in Kildare North. She took up the challenge and contested the by-election on behalf of Fianna Fáil. It was never going to be easy, with Fianna Fáil still highly unpopular among the electorate, and this was evidenced in the election result where Brady lost out and the seat went to an independent candidate of a hard left persuasion.

Typically, Brady, like her brothers and father, was not willing to give up, and had a good platform for the 2007 General Election. She duly won the seat, topping the poll and romping home on the first count. This gave the Kitt dynasty something very unusual in that it had now succeeded in having TDs elected in completely different geographic regions: Galway, Dublin South and Kildare. It is difficult to suggest that the voters in each of these regions were swung simply by the dynastic connection or feelings of any loyalty or affinity to it, particularly due to the fact that it still lacked a strong national figure to carry the name. Instead, it is far more likely that the reason behind this success was that each of the individuals had obtained a keen insight and understanding of politics and elections due to their family connections, and that it was this knowledge that offered them a distinct advantage.

As we have seen earlier, the Kitt family has endured divisions due to the choices of various leaders of Fianna Fáil. It is clear that successive leaders do not somehow see the family as a particular bloc or as sharing one particular view. This came to the fore yet again under Brian Cowen. While Cowen created some bad feeling letting the axe fall on Tom Kitt, and in 2009 ended the ambitions of his brother Michael Kitt, in that very same reshuffle he also identified Áine

Brady as a new voice and promoted her to a junior ministry with responsibility for older people and health promotion.

Áine Brady had significant potential, however, aged fifty-six, she typified many of the promotions that Brian Cowen made, adding to the belief that he favoured age over youth. Her appointment rekindled some hopes of a full ministerial appointment in this generation of the dynasty. But such hopes were short lived as Brady was a faller in the 2011 General Election, and any further comeback now seems unlikely, unless perhaps some of her family has caught the dynastic bug.

The Kitt family have been long and loyal servants to Irish politics. There is little doubt but that they have taken many knocks along the way, and yet have held firm and resilient. It is interesting to suggest that some of the electoral difficulties experienced by the dynasty are connected to its lack of high achievement in government. But yet Tom Kitt had an impeccable electoral record. It was perhaps his sharing of a constituency with such a figure as Seamus Brennan that denied him an opportunity for higher office, which seems very unfair. But politicians know that politics often isn't fair. Ultimately, Tom Kitt should have been well positioned for promotion under Brian Cowen, and yet the opposite happened. Whatever personal dislike was there cost him dearly.

The Kitt family is a perfect example of how a political bug can spread through a family, how ambition can be mirrored and how knowledge of the political process and the life can be the most valuable attribute of all. No doubt a political name can travel, and certainly assists its owner, but the electoral difficulties experienced by the family indicate that it is not a pass to guaranteed success, particularly in the absence of a dynasty member who has made it to the top of the game. A strong name will gain you a certain respect in politics, but it is only when one of the family has attained high office and is seen to have a series of strong achievements, preferably while avoiding any disgrace, that it will pack a true electoral punch. The Kitt family certainly used an accumulated knowledge that was of great advantage to them, but the lack of a senior figure to enhance and shape the name meant that it entered something of a political wilderness. Only a family with a strong figurehead can really ensure that a name carries enough weight for the electorate and other politicians to sit up and take note.

Blaney Faith in Donegal

Certain names are known the length and breadth of Ireland. They evoke an image that is shared by all people who hear it. There is little doubt but that the name 'Blaney' is one of these. Neil T. Blaney was a powerful figure who commanded the attention of all who encountered him. He not only continued a dynasty established by his father, but for a long period of time forged a completely separate political movement – one that in his home patch in County Donegal was followed with unquestioning dedication – and formed a stronghold where opponents feared to tread.

The Blaney dynasty in Donegal began with Neal Blaney, who took the seat in 1927. He had been a leader of the IRA in Donegal during the War of Independence and the Civil War and was a man who commanded huge respect locally. However, during a long career he struggled to make a lasting impression on politics. He lost the seat in 1938 and took solace in the Senate.

It was 1943 before he returned to the Dáil aged fifty, where he held the seat through further elections in 1944 and 1948. Although he firmly established the Blaney name as a political force in Donegal, it was his son Neil T. Blaney who would make it a household name for generations.

Neal senior died in 1948 and his son took the seat in the resulting by-election.

The Blaney power base in Fanad in Donegal was a rural heartland; a strongly republican territory and deeply affected by partition. It shaped and moulded almost every aspect of Neil T. Blaney's character. When he took his father's seat, he became the youngest member of the Dáil at twenty-six. In an age when politicians were older, and generally viewed as needing to have long years of experience, Blaney was never going to have a short rise to the top. However, his involvement with Lemass's reorganisation of the party gave him an unparalled insight into the Fianna Fáil organisation across the country and how it thought. He was keenly aware of the hunger for attention felt by the grassroots of the party, as well as their need for greater political involvement . His running of by-election campaigns for Fianna Fáil quickly became the stuff of legend, and this was were the original phrase 'the Donegal mafia' was coined, although it was later applied to other elements of party organisation across the country.

There was little doubt that Blaney was a brilliant strategist. In later years the likes of Albert Reynolds and others would ascribe much of their knowledge of campaigning to working with him. He was a tough taskmaster for any election team, and worked canvass groups for long hours and left no stone unturned. He was a charismatic figure, and his teams of supporters followed his direction with unquestioning faith, even enjoying doing his bidding. For many, Blaney was also the first to introduce a real razzmatazz to Irish politics: barnstorming speeches, bonfires, enormous gatherings and celebration rallies all helped to keep the party members motivated and feeling part of something.

Jackie Healy Rae has recounted by-elections in the past run by Blaney, particularly the election of Maire Geoghegan-Quinn, and pointed to a particular attention to detail that he believes has become lost to all parties in the modern age. He still keeps a picture of Blaney in his Dáil office.

After nine years of hard graft on the back benches and diligent service to his party, Blaney got his reward in the wake of the 1957 General Election when he was appointed to the Cabinet as Minister for Posts and Telegraphs. This was a significant step; Blaney had achieved national recognition for the name and moved the dynasty on to a whole new platform. He was also the first minister appointed from Donegal, and this would cement his power base long into the future. A Cabinet reshuffle caused by the death of Sean Moylan saw Blaney move to the Environment portfolio.

Blaney was responsible for one of the few attempts to reform the Irish electoral system. He proposed the scrapping of proportional representation and its replacement by a 'first past the post' system similar to that of the UK. For its time this was both a daring and innovative proposal. It had a firm basis, which was that one of the main problems with proportional representation was the difficulty for any group or party to gain a clear majority. This meant that governments tended to struggle for votes, and in difficult times this could lead to populism and an excess of compromises. Where coalitions were formed they were usually viewed as the small party dominating the policy of the larger one.

While the argument made much sense on the surface, it hid a reality that many found uncomfortable. That was that while the straight vote would certainly lead to strong government, such was the popularity of the Fianna Fáil machine, and so strong was its organisation, that such a change would effectively mean that Fianna Fáil would never be out of power, as it dwarfed its opponents. Many people felt that for this reason it was an attempt by Fianna Fáil to secure its position, and the referendum was rejected, but only by a narrow majority of 51.8% to 48.2%.

Blaney's backing of the measure was a case in point for the study of the referendum. The Blaney dynasty had become so powerful locally and so well loved that it would be almost impossible to imagine any kind of situation where he would be outpolled in a straight vote. Such a system places a high value on the ability to get lots of first preference votes, and there is little doubt but that many popular dynastic names could have benefited from it. Smaller parties and new entrants to politics normally get elected to the 4th or 5th seat in a constituency. For example, the five-seat constituencies invariably proved themselves a breeding ground for the likes of the Green Party and independents. The reason for this is quite simple. A voter will cast their first preference for a party or individual that they think will have the most impact. Established names and parties have a significant advantage in this regard. However, as a voter continues their preference they are more likely to take some 'risks' and to vote 2, 3 or 4 for a less well-known party or candidate. In a 'first past the post' system made up of single seat constituencies it is very difficult to break this mould, and almost impossible to outpoll well-known parties. A prime example is the relatively rigid nature of UK politics (3 parties) compared to the multi-party (and independents) system that Ireland has. First past the post would benefit the large parties and would likely kill off the smaller ones, who would not be able to compete effectively. Conversely, though, one must also bear in mind that some figures from Irish dynasties were not poll toppers, and in a first past the post system would never have been elected under such a system in a single-seat constituency.

Blaney proved himself a forward thinker in other aspects of his portfolio. He introduced legislation to allow non-nationals to vote in local elections, he completely overhauled planning regulations, introduced driving tests, and perhaps in one of his most significant achievements, and one that spoke to his own experience, he oversaw the provision of piped water to rural homes. These were all achievements that Fianna Fáil would be proud to identify itself with in the future.

When Seán Lemass resigned as leader Blaney was not a fan of either Colley or Haughey and considered running for the position himself, however the emergence of Jack Lynch solved the dilemma and Blaney held on to his cabinet position, moving to Agriculture and Fisheries.

Blaney was a powerful orator and a man of principled and uncompromising beliefs. He had little time for small talk or side issues and was a man concerned with the principles of the republic at all times. It was no surprise when he found himself on the side of those who believed in a firm stance on the northern question, one that involved sacrifice and one that involved intervention.

The central question of the arms crisis has been looked at elsewhere in this book and in more depth in other publications. The important thing to establish here is that Blaney himself was determined to stand by nationalists in the North, and this was an unflinching principle on his part, central to his dynasty and to the vote on which he depended.

The arms crisis was a seminal moment in Blaney's career. The allegation was that Blaney and Haughey had both been part of a plot to use £100,000 of public money set aside to assist nationalists to buy arms for the IRA. Blaney and Haughey were among those sacked by Lynch over the allegations. They were both prosecuted but found not guilty by the courts.

Blaney now found himself devoid of the ministerial post he had fought so hard to win. For a man so grounded in the ethos of loyalty and service it was difficult to take. He also knew that this was an episode that would mark his name and dynasty irrespective of what the courts had said regarding his innocence. Politics is a game of perception. A return to the Cabinet was always unlikely given that all such appointments are at the discretion of the Taoiseach and, after such a deep personal falling out, it was highly unlikely Lynch would ever reconsider Blaney for the Cabinet. Equally, political parties often feel a need to move on quickly, and the last thing Fianna Fáil needed was to have the crisis dragged up again.

At the 1971 Fianna Fáil Ard Fheis Blaney was defeated in an attempt to become honorary treasurer of the party, sending a clear signal that those at the top were moving against him and no longer wanted to be affiliated with him – in particular Jack Lynch. This was compounded by the fact that in the Cabinet re-shuffle Liam Cunningham, Blaney's Donegal running mate, had been promoted to parliamentary secretary, signalling that Blaney was not seen as top dog in Donegal any more by the hierarchy.

Blaney's abstention in a vote of no confidence in Minister Jim Gibbons signalled his intent, and the irreconcilable nature of the differences that had occurred. He was expelled from the parliamentary party as a result, and was later to be expelled from the Fianna Fáil organisation. Unsurprisingly this came as a result of his followers in Donegal backing him and arranging a financial collection independently of Fianna Fáil headquarters, which was against the party's rules and provided sufficient excuse for his expulsion.

The contrast between Haughey and Blaney in this regard is striking. Haughey endured much the same difficulties, however he had a longer term ambition in mind. Haughey was happy to hunker down and take the abuse and return to the grassroots. Blaney, on the other hand, found such action impossible: his pride and principles would not allow him to accept Lynch's actions. He felt duty bound to stand up for himself and face this fight, but with a Fianna Fáil organisation eager to move on, it was one he was never going to win.

When Blaney left Fianna Fáil it is clear that he believed that the party had now in some way betrayed itself, and indeed that he still believed in his vision of Fianna Fáil even if that was no longer the same vision the party itself shared. This is most evident in his choice not to stand as an independent candidate but rather as 'Independent Fianna Fáil'. Where many individuals jump at an opportunity to establish themselves as independents and drop the party flag, Blaney on the other hand accepted his new role, but in typical principled fashion was determined to show everyone that the party had left him and not the other way around, and that the things he said he stood for had not changed.

Independent Fianna Fáil was established by Blaney in Donegal. He would contest all future elections under this banner. He took with him a band of supporters who had an unwavering loyalty to him personally. The move hurt Fianna Fáil in Donegal badly. Indeed, it ensured that as the bitterness of elections rolled on there was little support from those who remained loyal to Fianna Fáil to ever allow Blaney to return to the party, even as its leaders changed.

The idea of Independent Fianna Fáil briefly fluttered as a flame but never caught on in any way in a national sense. It was, however, a powerful force in Donegal, with a number of councillors securing election under the banner. Of course Paddy Lenihan, brother of Brian Lenihan and Mary O'Rourke, carried the flag of Independent Fianna Fáil in Roscommon when he defected from Fianna Fáil itself.

In another dynastic twist, Paddy Keaveney, father of former Fianna Fáil Senator and TD Cecelia Keaveney, was elected as an Independent Fianna Fáil TD in 1976.

Neil T. Blaney remained a powerful figure in Irish politics for the rest of his life. But it was only a type of moral power – he would never again attain high office. In the 1979 European Elections he romped home in the Connaught Ulster constituency. Considering how isolated his home territory of Donegal is in that constituency this was impressive, and indicated both that he still had not lost his campaigning ability, and also the sheer strength of his position in Donegal. He lost out narrowly for re-election in 1984, but was reinstated once again in 1989.

Blaney was a colossus of Irish politics admired by many. His contributions to Dáil debates were engaging and often insightful. Having once been the youngest member of the Dáil he finished up being its oldest member. There was one battle that even such a powerful man was not able to win, and Neil T. Blaney lost his life to cancer in 1995. His loss was mourned by friend and opponent alike.

It was perhaps to be expected that Fianna Fáil would win the resulting by-election in Donegal. The county, whatever about Blaney's personal heartland, was still very much Fianna Fáil country. The loss of Neil himself even saw some voters return to the party. Although Neil's brother, Harry, contested the Election, he was not able to hold the seat.

But dynasties do not die easily. A strong organisation of Independent Fianna Fáil persisted, and while it was caught still mourning its loss in 1996, it was well positioned for the 1997 General Election. Harry Blaney was perhaps a surprising choice at sixty-nine years of age, although he had long been an Independent Fianna Fáil councillor. It was clear that the decision to run could not be seen as anything but an attempt to take the seat for the dynasty and hold it for the future. Harry Blaney clearly had little future in politics, and would be unable to add to the achievements of the name, but he did manage to take a seat at the expense of Fine Gael. This situation would greatly assist the delicate Dáil arithmetic for Fianna Fáil and Bertie Ahern. More importantly, however, it was a means of preserving the name and the seat for the Blaney dynasty and ensuring its ongoing connection to the people on the ground.

After an unremarkable five years in the Dáil, Harry Blaney decided not to stand in the 2002 General Election. In his stead came his twenty-eight-year-old son, Niall. In the intervening years, Niall had established himself in politics by gaining a council seat in 1999. In the 2002 Election Niall held the seat, although he did see a fall in first preferences from his father's vote. But winning the seat was what mattered most, and the Blaney dynasty now had what was seen as a young, energetic and talented face to represent it.

Following the Election, Niall Blaney was a strong supporter of the Fianna Fáil/Progressive Democrat Government. There was little doubt that he was young and ambitious. And while Neil T. Blaney could reside on the back benches and point to achievements of the past and be seen as a father figure, there is little to attract a young politician to such a life. Politics is about taking decisions and making changes. Niall Blaney knew this. He also knew that the dynasty would struggle into the future if it remained independent, for while it might succeed in one election or another, eventually the memory of his uncle's achievements would fade, and later generations would be seen as no more than constituency politicians.

Fianna Fáil and Niall Blaney entered talks in 2006. It was clear that all the original reasons for the thirty-five year rift had long since evaporated. However, other members of the Blaney family were deeply opposed to any merger with Fianna Fáil – indeed the family of Neil T. Blaney himself opposed the move – but the decision was taken and Niall Blaney decided to rejoin Fianna Fáil, effectively ending the Independent Fianna Fáil movement. Of course, if Fianna Fáil's current levels of unpopularity persist then it is entirely possible that we will see its re-emergence.

In the 2007 General Election Blaney was re-elected under the Fianna Fáil banner. However, Fine Gael took a seat too, and Blaney's return to the party saw him narrowly nudge ahead of Cecelia Keaveney, who lost her seat. It was perhaps strange that the children of two former Independent Fianna Fáil TDs found themselves battling against each other, now both back under the Fianna Fáil banner. Niall Blaney was seen as a young face of Fianna Fáil with strong potential, and his decision in advance of the 2011 General Election to quit politics for personal reasons came as a shock to many. It certainly brought an end to the dynasty's involvement in politics for the short term.

The Blaney name remains one of the most instantly recognisable ones in politics today. It remains, though, dominated by Neil T. Blaney himself. It has been devoid of high office for nearly thirty years. Unless a new face emerges to carry the flag of the dynasty into the future it is destined to matter less in national terms, and limit itself to being yet another constituency-based phenomenon. It is much too early to rule them out, however. If Fianna Fáil does not find a worthy successor, and continues to struggle to find electoral support, a local resurgence of Independent Fianna Fáil could find a very willing audience. Either way, this name remains synonymous with Donegal politics – whether it has a future at a national level remains to be seen.

The Fabulous Bruton Boys

Most of the families in this book have had several generations of TDs. Of course, many siblings enter the Dáil too. What makes John and Richard Bruton so unique is the level of impact they have had upon Fine Gael, how close they came to securing two Taoisigh in the family, and how they have dominated and shaped everything that has happened in opposition terms for twenty years in Ireland.

John Bruton was considered a typical member of a Fine Gael elite, born to a relatively wealthy family and privately educated at Clongowes Wood. He was a barrister by profession, but never practised law because politics beckoned, and he was duly elected to the Dáil in 1969 at the tender age of just twenty-two. This was quite an achievement in a time when politics was still dominated by older figures. Bruton was no slouch, and knew how to work the ground. By the time the 1973 Election came around he was in a much stronger position and increased his vote significantly. Despite his still relatively young age, his potential was identified and Liam Cosgrave appointed him as a junior minister in the coalition Government formed after 1973.

Fine Gael's loss of the 1977 Election caused big changes in the party. When Garret Fitzgerald assumed the leadership it was a signal that a new breed of politician, younger and more reforming, was now in control of Fine Gael. Bruton was particularly well suited to the new regime, and gained instant favour with its new leader. He was first appointed front bench spokesperson on Agriculture before being promoted to the critical role of Finance spokesperson.

Bruton's performance in this role won him many fans, and he proved himself to be an able parliamentarian. He was crucial to the new image of Fine Gael and, when the party formed another coalition with Labour in 1981, he secured the role of Finance Minister. He was still only thirty-four, and this was a substantial vote of confidence in his ability. But Bruton was faced with a huge problem. It was no secret that ever since the seventies the Irish economy was struggling. The debate was raging within all parties about the need to control spending. The problem was essentially that there was little political willingness on any side to take unpopular decisions.

Fine Gael had come to power with a manifesto full of promises that were every bit as unachievable and irresponsible as what Fianna Fáil had offered in 1977. As soon as the new Government took over, they quickly realised that they would have to renege on most of them. It is difficult to see how Fine Gael could have truly believed that large-scale tax cuts were achievable, and far more likely that they and Fianna Fáil were in the realm of electioneering, where once the election was won they would deal with the consequences after.

Inevitably, Bruton found himself in a difficult position. His first budget would be nothing like what people had been led to expect. Bruton needed to raise revenue, and had decided to impose VAT on children's shoes. The main problem was not so much the measure itself, but the fact that it was so far from what some of the Government's supporters expected, leading to a fear of losing seats. It was Bruton's first budget, and the first major setback to his career as he failed to get it through the Dáil. The loss of independent support for the Government caused it to fall, thus causing another general election to be called.

Fianna Fáil returned to power, and Bruton found himself on the opposition benches again – and taking much of the blame from some of his colleagues. He was not forced to endure this for long, as the Fianna Fáil Government itself collapsed during the following November. Fine Gael and Labour returned to power, this time knowing that they had to make the Government last.

Unfortunately for Bruton, it seemed that his star was no longer on the rise. He was given the role of Minister for Industry, Trade, Commerce and Tourism, and must have been disappointed with his loss of the pivotal Finance position. However, the important thing was that he was still in the Cabinet and had time on his side. In 1983 he seemed to be demoted further as the roles of Trade and Tourism were removed from his portfolio. But Bruton continued to focus on the task in hand, and remained a loyal and strong minister within the coalition. In 1986 he got his chance again, regaining the coveted and prestigious Finance portfolio. At that point, John Bruton seemed older, wiser, and, having faced down the challenges, he was now seen as one of the key figures in Fine Gael.

But fate was to deal him another blow. Yet again Bruton failed to get agreement on his budget proposals and the Government collapsed. This was a serious dent in his reputation, and one that would be used against him throughout his career. Finance ministers take great pride in getting budgets through the house, and it is seen as the single most important task in government. Bruton now held the unenviable distinction of being the only person to have been Minister for Finance twice and yet still never having successfully introduced a budget. Bad timing played as much of a role in this regard as did Bruton's abilities or decisions. The fact remains, though, that he was the one in the position of responsibility at the crucial times, so he was the one who would be held to account for the fortunes of Fine Gael on both occasions. The decisions he made had an enormous impact upon the party at this time.

The election that followed in 1987 was not kind to Fine Gael, and a heavy defeat saw Garret Fitzgerald resign as leader. Bruton was one of those to whom many members looked as a new leader, but there is little doubt that his performance in the Finance role continued to cause some doubts. Peter Barry and Alan Dukes were the other candidates for the leadership. Barry was very much the favourite, with most of the party old guard supporting him. Dukes was ultimately successful, and his success seemed to indicate yet another shift in Fine Gael's political outlook. Bruton was somewhat more conservative than Dukes, and at that point many thought that his opportunity for success had passed him by. Dukes was young and popular among the Fine Gael party, and they had high hopes that he could continue with Fitzgerald's approach and in the meantime reform Fine Gael. Dukes came to power on the back of some talented and energetic deputies like Ivan Yates, Alan Shatter and Gay Mitchell. But Dukes made his first error as soon as he became leader. In attempting to appease the old guard he did not make sufficient changes, and none of the young guns who had backed him received a front bench position. It was the first step toward destabilising his power base. Bruton became deputy leader of the party and, to his credit, he showed no nerves or doubts throughout this period. Bruton clearly had his eye on a longer game. He knew that he retained significant support within the party, and that time remained on his side.

The period in opposition did little to help Fine Gael. Fianna Fáil were popular even when making cuts, and returned to power in 1989 in a coalition with the Progressive Democrats. In 1987 Ireland had been a country in a dire situation, with little hope of light at the end of the tunnel. When Fianna Fáil finally decided that it had to start taking tough decisions, and backed Ray MacSharry's austerity plans, there were serious doubts about its ability to succeed. However, Alan Dukes's introduction of 'the Tallaght Strategy' of cooperation clearly helped them. Dukes had good reasoning behind his strategy. He knew it achieved three crucial aims. Firstly, it was in his view what the country needed, and he was aware that political point-scoring was killing the economy. Secondly, Dukes wanted to avoid elections while Fine Gael remained particularly unpopular and could face implosion. Thirdly, in a very long-term gain, it allowed Fine Gael to be a policy-based party – dictating what it supported and establishing what it stood for. The problem before this was that with Fianna Fáil's electoral dominance, Fine Gael only stood for being anti-Fianna Fáil, which meant that Fianna Fáil always dictated the agenda and debate putting Fine Gael at a significant disadvantage where their argument was always reactive.

Such a policy did not go down well with the Fine Gael grassroots, who were predictably upset at this non-partisan approach. Dukes also failed to inspire as a leader, and seemed somewhat charmless to the public. He was capable of withering attacks on Fianna Fáil personnel, but inspired little confidence in his ability to be more than that.

The 1990 Presidential Election would cause serious problems. While Robinson defeated Lenihan, it was no happy day for Fine Gael. They had been forced to suffer the ignominy of playing a poor support role to Labour. Their candidate, Austin Currie, was never in the running. Fine Gael achieved only two things: to have questions raised about their actions during the Lenihan tape affair, and to see their candidate get just about enough votes to help Robinson overtake Lenihan. For a party like Fine Gael this was too much and Dukes had to go.

John Bruton's time had finally come. The grassroots had much more faith in Bruton's ability to represent Fine Gael and its views, in addition to endeavouring to remove

Fianna Fáil from office. Bruton was unopposed for the leadership, and this signalled his ultimate hold on the party at this point. However Bruton would not enjoy a quick return to glory.

Fine Gael still failed to secure favour from the public, while Fianna Fáil continued to enjoy healthy if declining levels of support. When Albert Reynolds became Fianna Fáil leader, it seemed in the early months as if Fine Gael were in serious trouble. Reynolds presented a far more acceptable face of Fianna Fáil than Haughey. He was also capitalising on much positive comment about his actions as Minister for Finance. In the first six months of his leadership Reynolds enjoyed a honeymoon, garnering enormous levels of public support in the polls.

Bruton suffered in the comparisons during this period. Reynolds was a businessman, decisive and hungry, while Bruton seemed grey and was often derided as boring. Reynolds's background and political success seemed to put Bruton very much in the shade as regards achievement. The media were hard on Bruton and this didn't help.

However, honeymoons always end, and Reynolds soon came crashing down from the heights. The beef tribunal became a political battleground with the debate focussed on reputations, trust and honesty. O'Malley accused Reynolds of being 'untruthful', and Reynolds responded by saying O'Malley was being 'dishonest'. The public began to doubt Reynolds, he lost the favour of the media and took the blame for the spat with O'Malley. His ratings plunged, and people began to view Reynolds not as a new face of Fianna Fáil, but as more of the same. Reynolds did not like such accusations, and was particularly temperamental during the period, which did nothing to help his cause.

Bruton on the other hand was calmness personified. Even so, in the election that followed the spat in 1992 Bruton failed miserably to connect with the people and capitalise on Reynolds's difficulties.

Alan Dukes had a vision for Fine Gael based on solid foundations. One was the reality that Fine Gael was not doing well in elections and needed to avoid facing the public for a prolonged period of time. The Tallaght Strategy could be argued to have served this end well, frustrating attempts by some within Fianna Fáil to have an election on a big issue of public finances that could have seen poll predictions of clear majorities realised.

Another was Dukes's ability to think in the long term. He realised that for any party to survive it must have positive policies, and cannot allow itself to be stuck in the position where its political adversaries get to set the agenda, to which it can only react. This was a major issue for Fine Gael. In order to come to power it relied not on its own strength, but instead on Fianna Fáil being unpopular, which had proved to be a shaky foundation. Dukes's strategy could have changed this by suggesting strong policies and, if Fianna Fáil agreed with them, then so be it. The problem with such an approach is that while it may prove to benefit a party's long-term future over, say, twenty years, the party will miss the opportunity to capitalise on an opponent's weakness in the short term. This proved too much to take for many members of Fine Gael. They knew that many people disliked Fianna Fáil's cuts whether or not they were in the national interest, and they knew that by opposing them they would benefit from an immediate upswing that some considered more important than the pursuit of a long-term national level objective. That longer-term problems would inevitably come was considered a necessary price to pay for removing Fianna Fáil from office, and John Bruton became a champion for many in this camp. Bruton was not seen as an opportunist, but he was viewed as unlikely to give Fianna Fáil the kind of easy time that they had come to expect from Dukes.

Bruton never enjoyed a strong public image. His failures as Minister for Finance haunted him, and he was just not seen as Taoiseach material by the public or commentators.

He was viewed as a very straight and even honest man, but his lack of charisma or natural ease was crippling.

The 1992 General Election should have been tailor made for Fine Gael. It was true that Fianna Fáil had enjoyed much support and popularity for their efforts to rescue the economy since 1987, and Reynolds had enjoyed a honeymoon period of early support. But they had somehow succeeded in throwing all this away, or at least in losing the argument for supporting them.

The Reynolds-O'Malley spat was a storm in a tea cup by two men who didn't like each other very much. Unfortunately for Reynolds, he took the most of the blame for this. Once Reynolds became Taoiseach he had an uneasy relationship with the media. While they noted his practical ability, his lack of education was often scorned and his pragmatic approach often derided as not being sufficiently well-read. He also suffered from the debilitating flaw of not being Haughey, whom – whether loved or hated – the media generally found to be infinitely more interesting.

Bruton was just not what the public or most commentators wanted as the alternative. So, despite Fianna Fáil facing huge losses of over ten seats, it was apparent from an early stage that the losses would be mirrored by Fine Gael, leaving both main parties set to lose ground. The public were making a conscious decision that they had swapped between both parties for long enough and now wanted a newer alternative. For some this was seen as a firm indicator that so-called 'Civil War politics' was dying. However, this assessment failed to take account of two central facts. For one thing, a swing vote always exists in any election – it had gone to Fianna Fáil, Fine Gael and the Progressive Democrats in previous elections, and there was no reason why it should not go to Labour in this one. For another, to assume that politics in Ireland is dominated still by the Civil War division is overly simplistic. Irish politics has no great ideological divide, except on certain policies, in which it is more similar to the US than anything else. In the US there is an allergy to being described as a socialist or left-wing. While some might point to the Democrats being more to the left than Republicans, it is a tenuous difference when viewed from a European perspective. Both parties value free enterprise and capitalism above all else. Power in the US sways between both parties as an electorate choses in the main on a question of an individual they trust for president. Personality, and the ability to sell a message, particularly on TV, is often the critical deciding factor in US politics. The Irish electorate has always been driven by personality, and put their trust in particular individuals to take decisions guided by a set of principles and policies away from which they can be trusted not to move.

For Burton, the '92 Election was a severe disappointment, as they failed to make any impact on Fianna Fáil despite having their best opportunity in years. Bruton had singularly failed to resonate with the public, despite its obvious antipathy towards Reynolds. For the leader of the main opposition party, this was not good news. But Bruton was not overly concerned – the result still meant that his proposed alternative 'rainbow coalition' of Fine Gael, Labour and the Progressive Democrats was in pole position to form a Government of which he would be Taoiseach.

With the stage set, Bruton proceeded to make the biggest error of his career. He knew that Labour had attacked Reynolds throughout the election, and he assumed that any alternative was better to Fianna Fáil and that they would agree with this assessment. Unfortunately, he underestimated how strong ideology could be in Labour, and that for a significant portion of the party this was more important than personality. Labour, and Dick Spring in particular, found Bruton's position difficult to stomach and somewhat arrogant. Spring had serious misgivings about the Progressive Democrats and his ability to work with them in Government. However, for Bruton this should be no issue – a central ground would be worked out once the primary objective of ensuring a change of government was complete. Spring made a counter-proposal to include Democratic Left. Democratic Left were not an alternative to the Progressive Democrats as the three parties did not have the numbers required to form a government, however Democratic Left could strengthen the position and numbers of the left in what they saw as a battle with a Fine Gael disposed to right-wing policy, along with many within the Progressive Democrats. The proposal met with serious opposition, unnerving Spring, who in turn upset Bruton by taking so much time to agree.

However, Fianna Fáil under Reynolds was a very different animal than under Haughey. Bruton underestimated Reynolds's ability and desire to strike a deal, which had been his hallmark. When Fianna Fáil responded to Labour's proposals it put Spring in a bind. As someone coming to politics with a view of openness and fairness, he quickly realised that to turn down Fianna Fáil flatly would be a PR disaster, and go against everything they said they stood for. A sense of fair play demanded that they talk to the party that had, after all, secured the largest vote. So, Spring agreed to discuss the ideas with Reynolds. It is safe to assume that this was probably just seen as an exercise in good PR by Labour – they never expected Bruton's reaction, and he opened the door for Reynolds to make his move.

Bruton broke off negotiations with Spring and said he would not discuss matters further until he stopped talking to Fianna Fáil. Spring could not do so, and it quickly became apparent that whatever was on offer from Fianna Fáil as regards a programme for government and cabinet positions would be superior as he could still threaten to walk away from them, and therefore Fianna Fáil needed to give Labour something attractive. However, if he closed the door on Fianna Fáil then he would be forced to accept whatever Bruton offered if he wanted to avoid another election that would have spelt disaster for Labour.

Fianna Fáil and Labour entered their first coalition and Fine Gael found themselves in opposition again. This was a disaster for Bruton, causing serious reservations to be expressed in Fine Gael, leading many of the grassroots to doubt Bruton's leadership ability. In the end he had been thoroughly outwitted and outmaneuvered, and found himself at a loss to explain this to his party.

Rumors of dissatisfaction among the Fine Gael party with his leadership abounded, eventually culminating in his having to face down opponents in a leadership challenge in 1994. At this point there was a general feeling of inevitability about Bruton's political demise – he was just hanging on, and it was not a matter of if but when he would fall. He reshuffled his front bench and, while careful not to cause all-out war, Bruton felt it necessary to reprimand some front benchers and reward those who had been loyal. But for those who said Bruton's time was at an end, it proved to be a serious underestimation of Bruton's ability and determination, and of course made no allowance for a twist of fate that would prove his saviour.

As Bruton languished in opposition he watched the new Government take centre stage. It seemed an ideal mix on paper: Reynolds and Fianna Fáil were pragmatic and knew how to get things through, they were efficient and brokered deals and handled realities of everyday politics with great efficiency, and this practicality would be balanced by Labour's strong idealistic and reforming proposals – something that was often missing from Fianna Fáil. However, while it was strong on policy and work rate, the Government was incredibly weak in terms of personal relationships. Members of the different parties generally got along well enough but they never really trusted each other, and both leaders fought elements within their own parties who were opposed to the coalition itself, making things difficult, to say the least. With no great friendships or genuine trust to back it up, what was a powerful working relationship could only be a temporary arrangement based on convenience, and never truly a functioning marriage. In a matter of months after it secured its particular high point of bringing peace to Northern Ireland, the Government collapsed over the appointment of the President of the High Court.

Bruton had learned from his time in opposition. He showed that he had grown as a politician and accepted the errors he had made. His efforts during this period were a masterclass in how to help sow the seeds of division. He attacked Fianna Fáil, but was careful never to tar Labour with the same brush, instead implying that while they were well-meaning they were perhaps misguided and being played for fools. Bruton was grimly hanging on to power within his own party, but got the lifeline he needed in 1994. Only a few years earlier it would have been easy to imagine Bruton being principled and demanding an election, but he was not going to be caught out this time. Instead, he held out the olive branch to Labour. Two recent by-elections had changed the Dáil arithmetic and allowed them to offer a Fine Gael /Labour/Democratic Left Government – and one that Bruton proposed would be reforming and left-wing at that.

The temptation proved too much for Labour. Working with Fianna Fáil had its rewards, but it was hard work where every day brought more political battles and struggles to be fought with their partners in Government. They were beginning to question whether life might be easier elsewhere, and Bruton, by bringing in Democratic Left, was effectively offering them *carte blanche* policy wise. The move secured the position of Taoiseach for Bruton, and cemented his name in the history books. He now had complete control of Fine Gael, as well as the respect of all who observed his talented leadership of the Government.

Bruton's reputation improved dramatically once he became Taoiseach. He became far more measured, and took on a lot more of the gravitas that many in later years would recall. Bruton was a strong chair of Cabinet meetings, and enjoyed the discursive nature of politics. With Reynolds, such meetings had been kept brief and to the point – they were a place for taking decisions, and discussion should precede this and implementation follow. Reynolds took this approach from business, and saw little value in wasting time on debating. Bruton, though, liked far longer meetings, and almost enjoyed the intellectual challenges that political decisions involved. Both approaches have their merits, but Bruton's was more effective in making friends and building relationships. Reynolds did not leave much room for this, and as a result meetings, while productive, could be wearing and were considered hard work.

Bruton was proud of his achievements in government and had a number of strong successes. However, he suffered a serious setback with the collapse of the IRA ceasefire. Bruton did not enjoy the trust of many in the North, who clearly preferred Reynolds's high-energy no-nonsense approach. In the North, Bruton's methods of encouraging discussion and debate were not welcomed by groups who were used to acting, often with deadly intent.

Bruton showed himself to have a composed character, and this was appreciated by the public and the media. He was not hot-headed in the face of provocation, and showed resilience on many issues that gained him huge credit.

Bruton enjoyed the new image that being Taoiseach gave him. There was little doubt that he viewed himself as a reformer and forward thinker. He took a brave step in holding a referendum to introduce divorce into Ireland, and managed to have it successfully passed, although with a slender majority. Even so, the scale of this achievement should not be underestimated as it was one of the most divisive topics in Ireland at the time. He was aided by the fact that Fianna Fáil did not oppose the referendum.

Bruton was also more than a little lucky in his timing. His coalition partner Dick Spring was very much aware of this. The financial decisions taken in 1987, and the huge tax-cut incentives, had begun working their way through the Irish economy, as had quantities of money from the EU, whose importance to Ireland was growing larger with each passing year. Spring was, as Foreign Minister, very aware of this importance. Thus, the two and a half years when the rainbow coalition was in place saw much growth and development in the Irish economy. Later, Bertie Ahern would benefit even further from this. However, it would be glib to credit either the rainbow coalition or the Fianna Fáil/Progressive Democrat coalition from 1997 onwards with the creation of this boom. It certainly did not happen overnight, and had its roots further back in decisions taken by Ray McSharry, Alan Dukes, Albert Reynolds and indeed by Dick Spring and the Labour party when they first came to power in 1992.

But it is also unfair not to credit Bruton and the coalition Government with sound, prudent and strong management of the economy. Luck may have been on their side, but they were far from reckless and did much to help in the development of growth at the time. This period with Bruton as Taoiseach and Ruairi Quinn as Finance Minister did much to put to rest the old ghosts that had haunted Fine Gael and Labour from the eighties over their handling of economic issues, and Bruton deserves much credit for this change. Bruton also excelled on the international stage, overseeing Ireland's presidency of the EU in 1996, and was one of the few figures to have addressed a joint session of the United States Congress.

The Government was also responsible for one of the most important drives against organised crime in Ireland. The murder of journalist Veronica Guerin had caused outrage in the country and the Government was quick to act. The establishment of the Criminal Assets Bureau was one of the most effective weapons the State has ever introduced, and is a lasting testimony to strong action.

It was not all plain sailing. Throughout his tenure, Bruton still suffered from a sometimes unfair accusation that he was somehow anti-nationalist or was too eager to appease unionists. Bruton had taken many strong stands on behalf of nationalism, but he abhorred the IRA – with good reason – and this distrust soured relations. The collapse of the IRA ceasefire was seen as clear evidence of the republican movement's loss of faith. Bruton did himself no favours in this regard when Prince Charles became the first member of the Royal Family to visit Ireland since independence. Bruton in his speech was at pains to establish this as a seminal moment in Irish history and the high point of his career. The media and public viewed the speech negatively and as 'embarrassingly effusive' according to *The Times*. Bruton stood over his assertions, but there is little doubt that most Irish people found his treatment of Prince Charles to be too fawning and subserviant.

Bruton's Government also lost a high-profile minister in Michael Lowry, which was a blow to the party. Lowry was one of the few Fine Gael politicians who carried the charisma and drive of his Fianna Fáil counterparts. He was highly popular among the grassroots and was seen as the toughest fighter the party had at the time. But Lowry was forced to resign over a scandal involving payments to his business from a millionaire tycoon, Ben Dunne. This scandal would go on to rock Irish politics for years with several high profile politicians, particularly in Fianna Fáil, facing questions. At the time, Bruton did not appear to grasp the gravity of the situation, and as Lowry resigned Bruton was visibly upset, declaring him 'my best friend forever'. As allegations continued to mount, Bruton beat a hasty retreat from this and was forced to abandon his links with Lowry.

He soon faced a new threat from Fianna Fáil. Bertie Ahern's rise to power had united the party, and Ahern was seen as a likeable politician at ease with people. However, Bruton held a trump card in that many still found it difficult to see Ahern as Taoiseach, whereas they had by now overcome all such doubts about Bruton. An election had to be faced and in 1997 Bruton hoped that he had done enough to be the first Fine Gael Taoiseach to be re-elected for a successive term.

There is a school of thought that argued that the Labour party was punished in 1997 by the electorate for entering Government with Fianna Fáil. This has to be viewed as one of the many great myths of Irish politics. Bruton as head of the rainbow coalition knew that if the Government was to be re-elected it was imperative that any Labour losses were limited. The three parties put on a strong united front against the Fianna Fáil/Progressive Democrat option from opposition. The theory goes that the electorate voted Labour in order to remove Fianna Fáil from power in 1992, and were annoyed when they subsequently entered a Government with Fianna Fáil. This in itself is a tremendous leap. There is no doubt this was the case for a vocal few, but the fact remains that in 1992 more people were voting Fianna Fáil than were voting Fine Gael, so to suggest that these people actually wanted Fine Gael at that point over Fianna Fáil is difficult to sustain. Even if this is somehow accepted to be true, the theory would have us believe that the public were so annoyed that they entirely overlooked the fact that Labour were now in Government with Fine Gael and Democratic Left. Were the electorate so annoyed with Labour for putting Fianna Fáil into Government in 1992 that they decided to punish Labour and their preferred partners Fine Gael in 1997? Were they really so angry with Labour for putting Fianna Fáil into Government in 1992 that they decided to punish them by voting them out of Government and putting Fianna Fáil in? This is abject nonsense, however you look at it.

Rather, the problem for Labour was that people swung to them not gradually over time but in a sudden move. The people expected dramatic change and difference. While Labour could point to many policy successes, though, the fact was still that everyday life for the man on the street had not changed dramatically and politics looked no different. This is always the problem for any party going into government, expectation is always too high. Sudden swings that bring you to power are likely to evaporate just as quickly, and this was always likely to happen to Labour in 1997. A second factor that may also have been in play was general anger surrounding the situation in 1994. It is every bit as likely that the public were annoyed at being denied an election in such extreme circumstances than they were about the events of 1992. Equally, the Democratic Left option had not been chosen by the people as an option in 1992, but only became one as a result of two by-elections and Labour's facilitation of that may have played a part. Most likely of all, though, is that the swing vote simply left Labour as easily as it came because politics hadn't changed dramatically and the voters who wanted change moved to the next stop.

The loss of the Election hurt Bruton. It was a close thing. Fianna Fáil and the Progressive Democrats needed the support of independents to form a Government, but Bruton was keenly aware that it was another electoral failure for the party and he was yet again faced with the accusation that he had been rejected by the public, even though Fine Gael had recovered most of the seats it lost in 1992. But it was in no way good enough to stem the flow of seats away from Labour. Interestingly, the Progressive Democrats struggled, and Fianna Fáil only achieved a fractionally higher vote than in 1992. The difference was that Fianna Fáil used its vote better this time, and managed it far better to ensure a higher return of seats.

John Bruton began to settle into life as leader of the opposition, but he was determined that he could return to government, and indeed there was every reason to expect that this new Government would fall. Bruton had shaped and molded Fine Gael into a party that was primed for continual attack. He had succeeded in eradicating any remnants of the old Dukes approach, replacing it with a party which was setting its stall on particular policies as well as being the clear alternative to Fianna Fáil.

The new Fianna Fáil/Progressive Democrat Government enjoyed much success, and, despite ongoing revelations, it managed to stick together and became the first Fianna Fáil coalition to serve its full term. The economy was on an upward trajectory and improvements year on year were dramatic. As the popularity of Fianna Fáil was increasing, Bruton took his eye off the ball internally in Fine Gael. He had become complacent in his belief that Fine Gael was now very much a party under his control. The polls, however, were highly damaging. It was becoming increasingly apparent that Bertie Ahern was winning the popularity contest, and also that the old doubts about Bruton's abilities were resurfacing in the media and within Fine Gael.

Michael Noonan and Jim Mitchell were key figures in Fine Gael. They knew that the party was panicking as the polls had begun to suggest electoral disaster. Bruton's calm approach was being interpreted as sleepwalking into political oblivion. They made their move against Bruton, and it was quick and ignominious. The party dumped its leader and hoisted Noonan's flag, with Enda Kenny being one of the few voices that stood out in defiance in support of Bruton.

John Bruton has come to the end of his time as a major figure in Irish politics. He could certainly claim to have many dynastic elements in his approach, with which he generally successfully infused his party. But in the end John Bruton was something of an enigma. He would go on to serve the EU as Ambassador to the US and earn much international recognition, yet his record was a series of question marks and qualified successes. He was one of the youngest Ministers for Finance, yet he did not succeed in passing a budget. He took over Fine Gael in the wake of a disastrous Presidential Election and had the task of reforming a very weak organisation, yet after two years at the helm he led it to electoral disaster in 1992. He was outwitted by Reynolds in the negotiations for government, yet he learned from this and earlier experiences and was a brilliant operative in undermining that Government. He became Taoiseach, but not of a Government that had been chosen in the General Election, but still he handled the role well and gained huge respect during this period despite his numerous detractors. He made significant strides in reaching out to unionists in the North, but completely lost the faith of nationalists. He recovered the seats Fine Gael had lost and increased its vote in 1997, but yet the party lost power. He found the Government led by Bertie Ahern a much more difficult animal to undermine. He was deposed in a *coup d'état* but his successors did not avert disaster and may even have accelerated it. There is much merit in the argument that Bruton was a better debater, and in 2002 would have been a more amenable choice to the public, than Noonan or indeed in later years, Enda Kenny. There is little doubt, however, that Bruton had left his mark on Fine Gael. He had been pivotal to every major event in the party's history for over twenty years and was a stabilising force. By the time he had departed, Fine Gael was much more a machine of his making than it was linked with any other leader from its past.

However, John Bruton's demise would not mark the end of the Bruton name's influence. His brother, Richard, stepped forward and was to become one of the best-known and most central figures to Fine Gael over the next decade. Hence the Brutons are important in terms of dynasty because both John and Richard have been so central and the driving force behind so many events. Few dynasties can claim to have had such a controlling effect on their political party, effectively deciding its course over a thirty year period.

Richard Bruton enjoyed a similarly strong education to his brother, John. He went on to study economics, and worked in the private sector as a research economist for a number of years. But like his brother he was destined for an early entry into politics, securing a seat on Meath County Council in 1979 aged twenty-six. He followed this up quickly with election to the Seanad in 1981. The General Election of February 1982 provided him with the perfect opportunity to continue his meteoric rise, and he secured his Dáil seat in that Election.

In the Fine Gael/Labour Coalition from '82 to '86, Bruton was rewarded with a junior ministerial post in the Department of Industry and Commerce. Although he was a more quiet and demure character than his brother, his ability was much respected and he was making a name for himself in his own right. His strong grasp of economic issues was a particular advantage at this time.

Bruton also served in opposition as the front bench spokesperson on Enterprise and Employment. There was a strong view within Fine Gael that John Bruton as leader relied heavily on his younger brother for support and direction. Richard was certainly to the fore in the negotiations for the rainbow Government in 1994. But even so, when the Government took over there were more than a few eyebrows raised when John Bruton appointed him to the most high profile ministry that Fine Gael had in the new Government: Enterprise, Trade and Employment. There was much to recommend Richard for the post, however the reality was that, unlike in opposition, John Bruton had to share the front bench positions on offer with other parties, and this left far fewer places for Fine Gael. In a party that still had highly experienced personnel like Michael Noonan, Alan Dukes, Nora Owen and the Mitchell brothers, the elevation of his own brother to the plum job seemed like nepotism. Much of this also came from the fact that, unlike Noonan or Lowry, Richard Bruton's quiet character did not lend itself to the tough street fighting image that Fine Gael wanted in the media. He seemed almost too nice. The accusation is somewhat unfair. Richard Bruton was clearly identified as a man with huge potential long before John Bruton came to lead the party. He had served ably, and was perfectly suited in terms of his own background for the post.

Bruton handled the portfolio well. He faced some difficult challenges such as some high profile job losses at the
likes of Hewlett Packard. Yet he oversaw a strong period of
growth and, while failing to ignite his profile on the national
stage, he rarely got into any problems. It was perhaps indica-
tive of this personality when in 1997 the *Sunday Tribune*
'Guide to Politics' described him as 'articulate' and an 'excel-
lent minister,' but 'not enjoying a high national profile'.

In opposition, Bruton was appointed spokesperson on
Education and Science. This was a difficult time to be in
opposition, but little occurred that could raise Bruton's personal profile. However, when Michael Noonan and Jim
Mitchell staged their coup, things looked to have gone from
bad to worse for Richard Bruton. But, once his brother
resigned, he decided to keep his feelings on the matter far
more low-key. Whereas Enda Kenny would openly challenge Noonan and Mitchell, Bruton played his cards close
to his chest and seemed content to continue working under
Noonan. At first this policy seemed to pay dividends as,
despite his obvious loyalty to his brother, Noonan retained
Richard on the front bench, perhaps hoping to mend some
of the wounds. On the other hand, Kenny found himself
in the political wilderness and *persona non grata* in the new
Fine Gael set-up.

But electoral disaster was not averted by Noonan, indeed
if anything it seemed to make matters worse, and Fine Gael
plummeted further. Although, like all in Fine Gael, Bruton
saw his personal vote fall in 2002, he still comfortably held
on to his seat. The defeat was on such a scale that Michael
Noonan could not possibly remain as leader having removed
John Bruton with the express aim of averting this very crisis.
It was also an absolute rejection of Noonan by the people.
His resignation seemed to spell opportunity for Richard Bruton. Some began to look to him as the inheritor of his
brother's mantle. This was natural – he was one of the
brightest figures in Fine Gael, though not the most

charismatic. He had also been its most senior minister in recent times, and was a natural choice.

Anger with Noonan was becoming palpable within Fine Gael. Many sought revenge, and those he had offended the most were now ready to take up the challenge. Among these was Enda Kenny who, despite having an even lower profile than Bruton when in Government, had become something of a standard-bearer due to his opposition to Noonan and his treatment at his hands. Enda Kenny was also a very experienced TD and knew the Fine Gael organisation on the ground inside out. This was something with which Richard Bruton could not compete. In the end, the Fine Gael party opted for Kenny because his profile had been enhanced by his opposing of Noonan, and also because, with the party broken and in disarray, it was necessary to install a leader who could fix its internal workings. For the first time in about fifteen years the party looked like it might not be heavily influenced by the Bruton family.

However, fate had another hand in these events. Kenny was quick to realise that with his party so weak he could afford no divisions. He appointed Richard Bruton deputy leader and spokesperson on finance, so while Bruton did not have the top job he was now in the key position within Fine Gael, the role that would shape and mold its policy going forward.

In this role Bruton ensured that Fine Gael remained a 'Bruton' party. He was always seen as stronger than Enda Kenny on economic and financial matters, and this often caused Kenny to defer to Bruton's opinions. It is always difficult to assess opposition spokespeople as regards their policies, but some things are clear about Bruton during this period. He deserves credit in particular with regard to two main policy areas which he strenuously opposed. Firstly, he argued strongly against benchmarking, saying that the rises for public servants were not connected to productivity and therefore represented poor value for money for the taxpayer. In hindsight, Bruton was correct. At the time, however, he made many enemies in the Trade Union movement for stating this. He was seen as anything but a friend to public servants. This was harsh, in as much as Bruton was simply pointing to an obvious failing in the benchmarking system, one that would haunt the Government when the economy collapsed in 2008.

Secondly, he opposed decentralisation, and this too was not easy for Fine Gael. Undoubtedly there are sound arguments for decentralisation in order to ensure balanced regional development, however the Government's plan was too sudden and proved unworkable.

Despite these, there is nothing to suggest in Bruton's record that he was any more aware of the impending doom for the Irish economy than his Government counterparts. He showed little policy disagreement outside of those two areas that would suggest he would have been more frugal. In essence, this was not a failing. The demands of the electorate were enormous, Ireland had suffered from a lack of investment for many years and now was playing catch up while there was a general acceptance among the body politic that spending was necessary to advance the country. Bruton did point to dangers in the property market, and in that context it should be remembered that in the course of several budgets Ministers for Finance had alluded to dangers in that market but suggested that even if property were to collapse the economy would not enter recession. What none saw was the enormity of what would happen internationally to compound the disaster.

While Bruton favoured more and more efforts to get value for money, and was critical of Governmental waste, he at no point suggested that any of the major capital developments should not go ahead. He criticised Government spending before the 2007 Election, but only criticised its timing, and never suggested that the raft of projects or expenditure should not happen at all.

Fine Gael's election promises were very much in line with those of Labour and Fianna Fáil, and no party suggested that if they came to power in 2007 they would cut spending in any way. Indeed, Richard Bruton was a major critic of the cuts Charlie McCreevy had imposed from 2002 to 2004, and his argument against them was so successful that McCreevey ended up being moved to Europe and Fianna Fáil began to reverse the cuts.

What this pointed to in the Irish political system was the fact that all parties guided their country to its doom by uncritically following what the electorate wanted during this period. They were also, it should in all fairness be said, all guided by the reports given by the likes of central banks and regulators, and while each one took criticism from their opponents and asked questions, not one actually foresaw the crisis, or if they did then the election manifestos of 2007 were a dangerous and dishonest exercise. This is highly unlikely. Things did not go wrong because of any one individual's failure of judgment – there was a deeper, systemic error in how politicians and the Government received information, assessed it and evaluated it.

Richard Bruton's stand on benchmarking, had he been in government and still been willing to do it, could have saved a considerable amount of money for the exchequer and much political pain. However, once the economic crisis hit, it was clear that Bruton had a firm appreciation of the problems. While his banking proposals met with stern opposition from many economists, he still showed the ability to formulate such alternatives, something that was considered to be badly lacking in the body politic.

In 2009 a by-election in Dublin South saw Fine Gael romp home with a celebrity candidate. Of course, George Lee had an immense advantage. He had been on every TV screen in the country for over a decade, he had presented numerous documentaries and reports on the economy, and this gave him the image of being the ultimate authority on the subject. Some also suggested that Kenny had been eager to bring Lee on board as a counterweight to Bruton's stranglehold on Fine Gael's economic policy.

While the move seemed an initial success, it quickly turned to disaster. Many colleagues in RTÉ were wary of Lee's entry into politics, believing him to have little understanding of the political game itself. As it turned out, Lee was eminently unsuited to politics. In debates, Fine Gael feared how the public might perceive him, as he was often abrasive and came across as threatening on TV. He needed time to soften his image. However, Lee was an ambitious man and eager to rise quickly to the top, and was frustrated by what he saw as inferior people gaining influence ahead of him. Lee also turned out to be a powerful weapon while attacking the Government, but in a number of interviews seemed to falter in terms of what he believed should be done in future, which was perhaps an early indicator that the did not entirely agree with Fine Gael policy.

Nine months later, George Lee resigned from Fine Gael in acrimonious conditions. In particular, he seemed upset by Bruton, who he said had never called him to discuss policy or economics. Bruton, in typical understated fashion, shrugged off the remarks, suggesting that it was open to anyone to propose a policy and he had not seen any from Lee. The row threatened both Kenny and Bruton as regards the esteem in which they were held by the public. The Fine Gael faithful were clearly incensed by Lee, but the public at large seemed to blame Bruton for treating him badly, and accusations were levelled that he was threatened by Lee. However, given Bruton's political and economic experience, this is unlikely to have been true.

As 2010 trundled on, it became increasingly clear that Fine Gael faced two major issues. Firstly, while the party was at record highs in the polls, its leader Enda Kenny was getting consistently poor ratings, only a few percent above the disastrous Brian Cowen, who took the brunt of the criticism and blame in relation to the economy. Secondly, Fine Gael were not reaping the reward that they hoped from Fianna Fáil's demise – in fact they now found themselves locked in a battle with Labour to be the most popular party, and Labour's leader Eamon Gilmore was the most popular of all party leaders.

Richard Bruton held the respect of many commentators, and he was the public's choice it seemed as the real voice of Fine Gael. Pressure mounted, with many feeling that if Bruton was leading Fine Gael then far more of the electorate would be amenable to voting for them. The Bruton name and his record suggested that he could act as a counterbalance to Gilmore's popularity surge. As the polls mounted and media pressure built a breaking point was finally reached. Bruton was encouraged by many of the youngest and most able deputies that Fine Gael possessed, and was also backed by a clear amount of city-based candidates who perhaps feared Labour more that their rural counterparts – people like Leo Varadkar, Lucinda Creighton and Simon Coveney to name a few. At first, it seemed to spell the end for Kenny. With such high levels of unpopularity it was assumed by some commentators and much of the public that the leader would not be able to face down the momentum building behind Bruton.

But things started to go wrong, and Bruton's supporters showed every ounce of their inexperience as they were totally outwitted by Kenny's seasoned backers. Bruton dithered for days, failing to exploit the advantage while he had it. Instead, he wanted to take a gentleman's approach and face Kenny in the parliamentary party. But once Kenny overcame the initial shock of the move he was in no mood to let Bruton continue to set the pace. He had to act, and if he did he knew that a decisive show of muscle with Bruton would deter a rush from back benchers to get caught offside with the leader. He sacked Bruton after a phone call in which Bruton refused to say he would support him. Now the initiative was with Kenny, in fact it was still not clear if Bruton even intended to challenge him. The attempted coup was a farce in the end with little or no real strategy behind it. If Richard had discussed the move with his experienced brother, John, then it certainly did not show. However, while the result was not officially announced, sources within Fine Gael suggest it was at most six votes with some believing it as close as three. This is not a lot in terms of a party. But, yet again, Bruton showed he lacked a certain ruthlessness and desire and still preferred to be a gentleman and indeed a good loser – a mood that infected his entire camp. The reality was that Fine Gael was split pretty evenly down the centre. In 1991, Albert Reynolds had led a much smaller percentage of his party to defeat, and yet by standing by his principles there was little doubt that the end had come for Haughey, even though he won the vote.

If Bruton and many of the leading young voices who followed him had been true to their word and refused to serve under Kenny, then it is difficult to see how Kenny could have survived for any longer than a couple of months to the next opinion poll. For it would be clear to the six or seven voters who made the difference that the only way for the party to move on now would be to remove Kenny. Instead, panicking at the thought of being consigned to the wilderness as Fine Gael was about to enter government, the conspirators ate humble pie and agreed to accept positions, and even in some cases, in particular Bruton himself, demotions. This action allowed Enda Kenny to survive, and it damaged Bruton's own reputation immeasurably.

In a somewhat ironic move, Kenny promoted Michael Noonan to Finance to replace Bruton, extending perhaps another hand of forgiveness to shore up his position. During the 2011 General Election, Bruton handled the enterprise and employment questions for Fine Gael with some ease. He preformed confidently in an Election that Fine Gael simply could not lose. Interestingly, it was also a campaign marked by the avoidance of the media by Enda Kenny. The strategy paid off, however, and Fine Gael romped home. As was widely expected, they formed a coalition with the Labour party, but Fine Gael managed to secure most of the key economic roles and even the health portfolio that may yet determine the perception of this Government. Richard Bruton was appointed Minister for Enterprise and Employment, and his performance here will do much to define the Bruton dynasty. In the early days of the Government he has shown a strong belief in public pay that is in line with his previous utterances on benchmarking. It also seems that he is unafraid of the Labour party in this regard and feels that he can count on their support for his stance.

Should Ireland begin to recover in the next few years then Richard Bruton may well play a key role in this. His abilities are unquestioned, but he will also need timing, judgement and courage on a level that has not been required of him before. Questions still hang over Enda Kenny even though his term as Taoiseach got off to a good start. The local elections in 2014 will provide a test for the Government, and an uphill task given that Fianna Fáil is starting from such a low base that some form of advance could reasonably be expected. Any sign of a Fianna Fáil recovery, no matter how slight, will scare many Government backbenchers, who know that, while there is every chance this Government may be re-elected, it will be almost impossible for them to retain the sheer number of seats that they won in 2011. This can make for some nervous figures on the back benches. Should Fine Gael face any kind of crisis, and should any doubts emerge about Enda Kenny's handling of an issue, Richard Bruton may yet follow his brother to the Taoiseach's office. There are certainly pages left to be written in this particular story.

The Ahern Web

Bertie Ahern was one of Ireland's most popular and best-loved politicians. He was a man who sacrificed much due to his love of politics. There is little doubt but that he saw himself as a hard working and dedicated public servant. He established an intricate network of loyal supporters in key positions. More importantly, his brothers established strong footholds in politics too, and the bedrock of a powerful dynasty was set. However, it is a classic example of how a dynasty can unravel almost overnight. In the years immediately following Bertie Ahern's resignation as Taoiseach, his once unassailable popularity took a battering. He was blamed for many of the problems in the Irish economy, and without the position of Taoiseach he seemed helpless to stop this view of events despite his repeated media efforts. Proof of just how low the dynasty had fallen was evident in the by-election in his home patch of Dublin Central when the dynasty took nothing short of a savaging.

Bertie Ahern was a man who came to politics with no pedigree or advantage of family name to endorse him. Much of his story has passed into political legend. What made Ahern different was the fact that he knew how to turn his lack of an established name to his advantage, and that he could use people's frequent underestimation of him to drive his career further still.

Ahern certainly hoped to write the family name into history, and there is no doubt that, as proven by the selection of his brother, Maurice, to stand in a by-election, he would wish that a dynasty could continue. But what Ahern lacked in terms of family or party connections he more than made up with the vast personal network he cultivated. A number of other books and assessments have been written detailing this network and the powerful political machine it created, and Ahern and his brothers were at the centre of this. It is easy to overestimate the Ahern political machine too. While it was no doubt a perfect example of how it should be done, and of hard work and diligent cultivation of the grassroots, some of the hyperbole used to describe it are excessive. What Ahern did was nothing new in Irish politics, and his tactics have been the stock in trade of most of the highly successful vote-getters in one form or another. Some commentators who stood back in amazement and shock when describing its efficiency and intelligence-gathering methods perhaps mirrored the overall misunderstanding of politics that caused so many to underestimate Ahern. Many of those who have described Ahern's methods do so from a point of view of never having been close to a well run political machine before. It was nothing new, but it was how things are done by those of all parties who have reached the top.

Bertie Ahern was more than a little lucky in his early career. He was first elected in 1977: an election that saw a massive swing to Fianna Fáil. When he was added to the ticket there was a widespread suspicion that the reason was really to split the Fianna Fáil vote, thus ensuring that the top dog in the constituency, Jim Tunney, was not effectively threatened by his running mate. The famous 'tullymander', which we spoke about in connection with Liam Cosgrave, backfired, leading Fianna Fáil to cruise to victory with Bertie taking his seat and, for the first of many times, surprising all those who looked on.

What few had realised was that Ahern, when joining the cumann, was encouraging a huge number of friends to sign up too out of a personal affiliation to him. He was gradually changing the grassroots into an organisation that was loyal to him. Building such a machine is important if you wish to forge a successful dynasty: their loyalty must be to your name first and the party second. Such voters can be counted upon to then support your chosen successor.

He was no stranger to the problems of changing constituency boundaries. Following the Election he was moved to Dublin Central, where he faced the difficult situation of having nine TDs fighting over just five seats. Yet again, many underestimated Ahern, and as the new boy they expected him to lose out. That was never in Ahern's plans however.

During this period he found himself in the same constituency as the Finance Minister, and for many the Taoiseach in waiting, George Colley. The story goes that Colley's estimation of Ahern was that 'he won't amount to much'. Whether or not this is true we cannot tell, but it would fit a pattern on Colley's part of being completely unable to appreciate new talent or sense the mood for change, both within Fianna Fáil and in the country at large. He was a man who was not at ease with the more affable, friendly nature of politics either. He had worked hard to get to his position and expected respect as a result. Ahern was expected to back Colley, but as Ahern later described, this wasn't likely. For the most basic and usually most common reason in politics: he simply didn't know Colley, who was aloof and distant. Instead, Haughey was a man who made it his business to get to know Ahern and many other new young TDs.

Ahern continued to back Haughey throughout his leadership. Even so, he displayed an amazing talent for staying friendly with all sides in this acrimonious period of Fianna Fáil history. Ahern was not the type to take big stands or mount a heroic policy argument – instead, as he often said himself, he 'kept his head down'. While no one doubted his loyalty to Haughey, those on the other side believed him a decent guy, and not entirely beyond redemption.

When Fianna Fáil found themselves back in opposition, Bertie Ahern was the Chief Whip. It was a role he relished, one that gave him a keen understanding of parliamentary procedure, and also acquainted him with every TD in the party. Bertie Ahern knew exactly how to use such a role. His popularity was on the rise within Fianna Fáil, and while still not a well-known figure nationally he was becoming popular with the grassroots of the party. In 1986 he got the opportunity to raise his profile considerably and take his career to the next level by becoming Lord Mayor of Dublin.

This increased profile served him well both locally and nationally and, by the time of the 1987 General Election, it was clear that Ahern had the power to be much more than just another politician. His ability to win an impressive vote while assisting two running mates to secure their seats hinted at the powerful organisation he had behind him, something that is vital for the foundation of a dynasty. At just thirty-five years of age, Ahern would become a full Cabinet Minister in the new Government, handling Labour Affairs.

It was a portfolio well suited to Ahern who had a definite gift when it came to getting around people and reaching consensus. Ahern was also popular among the trade unions and seen as sympathetic to their cause. By using this trust and relationship he played a central role in the formation of the early social partnership agreements.

Ahern was now firmly on the national map and, due to his youth, was clearly seen as the future of Fianna Fáil. He retained his Cabinet post after the 1989 General Election, and was again involved the next social partnership deal. Bertie Ahern sat comfortably with most of the Fianna Fáil membership who, despite any policy arguments, liked to view themselves as slightly left of centre. Fianna Fáil had always seen itself as a friend to public servants, an ally of trade unions and the semi-state sector. Ahern fitted that image well, and his man-in-the-street approach to politics was welcomed by all. Ahern was careful never to put himself above others or suggest he was more powerful or had more valid opinions than the next person.

Ahern's electoral prowess was one of the reasons that he was chosen as Director of Elections for Brian Lenihan's presidential campaign. This campaign was a difficult one from Ahern's perspective. While he could not be faulted for his strategy, he ended up caught in the middle of the crisis. On one hand he was defending Lenihan, but on the other he was also doing the bidding of his leader Charles Haughey when it became apparent that Lenihan would either have to resign or be sacked. It was of course an unenviable position, yet it is remarkable again that he came through it relatively unscathed. He did so by not taking a strong vocal position either way, successfully portraying himself as the hapless figure just caught in the middle. While other relationships floundered during this time, all of Ahern's seemed to remain particularly solid.

Ahern was famed for positioning his own people where they could effectively control the Fianna Fáil organisation from the ground up. This had been accomplished within his own constituency, and now increasingly could be seen to spread out as his brother Noel took a council seat, another brother Maurice would later follow, and so Ahern ensured that he had a stranglehold on politics across the city. Where some political dynasties have developed in an organic fashion over time, Ahern's was entirely deliberate, planned and executed with great political skill. Across the county, the principal players in constituency level politics were being replaced, gradually, by people whose primary loyalty was neither to their party nor to any particular political ideals, but rather to their political benefactor: Bertie Ahern. Meanwhile, on the national stage, Ahern saw to it that he was central to Haughey's plans, making himself indispensable to the political well being of the party. The combination of the local

and the national ensured that Ahern would be in an unassailable position from which to take control when the time
was right. It was around this time when most Haughey supporters began to see Ahern as the next leader. Indeed, it was
in the wake of a tough renegotiation of the programme for
government with the Progressive Democrats that Charlie
made the comment: 'He's the man. He's the best, the most
skilful, the most devious and the most cunning of them all.'

Fate gave him yet another promotion, and clearly put the
issue of Haughey's chosen successor to rest. When Albert
Reynolds chose to back a motion of no confidence in
Haughey in November 1991, his sacking became the
inevitable consequence. Haughey moved quickly to shore up
his victory, and knew the value of establishing a clear successor to watch his back during this period. It was clear that
Haughey's time was coming to an end, but he was not willing
to go just yet. Haughey needed to remove people from a
sympathetic position to Reynolds and direct them towards a
view of a new life after Charlie but without Albert. This
came in the form of Bertie Ahern, whom he promoted to
Minister for Finance.

Ahern did not get much opportunity to enjoy this rise to
the position of heir apparent. Firstly, he had to face the difficult personal tragedy of the breakdown of his marriage,
which all took place within the public eye. When he presented
his first budget, and it was well received, it was noted that he
had only been in the job for such a short time that to all out-
siders and commentators this was still essentially Reynolds's
budget. Haughey was dealt a final blow by Sean Doherty's
revelation that Haughey had known about the tapping of
journalists' phones in the early 1980s. The end had come, and
come far more quickly than Ahern might have anticipated.

The leadership contest that ensued was short and bloody.
Reynolds already had a clear cadre of loyal supporters.
Those in Haughey's gang rushed to Ahern's banner, but not
out of personal loyalty but rather a belief that he was the

only one who might be able to defeat Reynolds, of whom many in the party were afraid, and with good reason. Ahern knew he had little to fear from Albert, and that his own position was very much safe unless he decided to offend Reynolds badly, and this would probably only happen if he entered into a bitter contest against him. Ahern was twenty years younger than Reynolds, and he knew that time was on his side. He would pick a fight only if victory was sure.

Ahern did not decide quickly. As was his fashion, he took his time, consulting with his organisation and friends. By contrast, Reynolds had a forceful and decisive style. This made the early stage of the campaign awkward for many TDs. Despite the ruthless efficiency of the Ahern political machine, the fact was that Reynolds had been around, gathering support, for a much longer time, and would not be easy to remove. Although Reynolds's crew were pushing them for an answer, and if it didn't come quickly they could be in trouble, this was a political judgment that Bertie Ahern could not afford to get wrong, and he knew it.

Number-crunching is a difficult business in politics. Most agree now that Ahern was probably short on the numbers, although some have argued he could still have won. It must be remembered, however, that Reynolds's team were canvassing openly in the field and knew the lie of the land better. Reynolds's team also contained several veterans of earlier heaves on both sides of the Haughey divide, and were very well acquainted with the numbers game. From their side, there is little doubt that they believed they would win even if Ahern ran, but only at significant political cost, as the resulting fight would be sure to divide and the party – and Raynolds and his team knew that Ahern would not want to inflict great damage upon his own future political prospects. It was thus with some confidence that Reynolds met Ahern, and the two struck a deal with Reynolds essentially pointing out that he would win any contest, but that he wanted a more united party and that his tenure would not be overly long. As a result, Ahern backed Reynolds, and a flood of supporters came to Reynolds's side in what must be seen as a late skin-saving exercise that didn't entirely work out for many.

Bertie Ahern could now settle into his role as Minister for Finance with some confidence. Ahern would never be part of Reynolds's inner circle, nor did he show any desire to be. With the political deal he had made with Reynolds he had given up hopes of taking the leadership immediately in exchange for greatly enhanced future political prospects, keeping his powder dry until he was ready to move. He had not allowed himself to be bullied into a fight whose outcome was not sure. He kept faith with many of those banished to the back benches, and remained their standard-bearer. He did serve loyally for the most part, though, and never showed any open hostility or unwillingness to work in the new regime. It was clear that Reynolds would have liked Máire Geoghegan-Quinn as his successor should he last long enough to ensure she could be established, but Ahern, by biding his time, had made that hope appear distant.

It was during this period that Ahern received a number of donations that would later prove his undoing, and the mystery surrounding his personal finances would later engulf him. At this point in time, however, it was far from apparent, and he continued to enjoy the support of the party at large. He often had to walk a fine line, and this was particularly apparent in 1993 when the tax amnesty was introduced. At this stage Labour were the Fianna Fáil's partners in Government. Albert Reynolds had a very pragmatic view on the issue. As he saw it, there was an enormous amount of 'hot money' that had been deposited elsewhere to avoid tax. Reynolds was leading a Government that had an ambitious social programme, much of it based on policies of social change proposed by the Labour party. Reynolds saw no issue with their arguments. Instead, he saw it as his end of the bargain to find ways to fund the delivery of the programme and make sure it happened. Reynolds had heard for years, even as Minister for Finance, about Revenue attempts to catch tax evaders, but still the results never came. While Revenue could estimate how much money it was losing out on and could run investigations, promises of seizing it never materialised. As Reynolds saw it there was a choice: the Government could continue to wait for years in the hope that Revenue might eventually catch up with the tax evaders, and this in itself would require extra resources, or they could accept a large settlement of cash right now and start from scratch. He believed that an amnesty could deliver a serious injection of cash into the economy that could then be used to fund various programmes – yes, it meant letting the evaders off the hook, but in his view they were getting away with it anyway. It would also tidy up the process now that Ireland was moving away from excessively high tax rates, and the penalty would be even greater for those who did not come clean at this opportunity.

The Labour party was opposed to the idea. No matter how much money the tax amnesty might deliver it still infringed on a key policy for Labour: that tax evasion was wrong and should never be accepted. The amnesty suggested that there was a level of forgiveness for those who had evaded tax up to this point, and it set a bad precedent by letting them off in any way. What was to stop a tax evader doing the same again in the future in the belief that another amnesty would be offered later? In compromise, the proposal had to contain serious consequences for anyone who availed of the amnesty but did not use it as an opportunity to get all of their tax affairs completely in order.

Bertie Ahern also opposed the idea, saying that he wanted 'non-compliant taxpayers to go to jail'. However, in a surprising turnaround, so many in the Cabinet seemed sure that someone else would oppose it and did not want to oppose it themselves that Reynolds got it through in typical single-minded fashion. The move would always remain controversial. It certainly brought in significant and immediate cash to the exchequer, but it was viewed by many as morally questionable. Ahern insisted that he had never liked the idea for the remainder of his career.

In late 1994, Ahern got the chance he had been waiting for. Albert Reynolds had gambled once too often and, in a bizarre and politically pointless argument in relation to cases before the Attorney General's office, Reynolds was to lose power. John Waters in his recent book *Feckers* lists Reynolds as one of the men who destroyed Ireland, contending that Reynolds did not put up enough of a fight during this period, and, had he done so, Ahern might never have been able to get into power.. It is difficult to say if Reynolds could have fought on. Had he done so it looks highly unlikely that he could have defeated Ahern, and it would certainly have ensured a long and bitter split within Fianna Fáil. This split may indeed have weakened Ahern, and could have placed an even bigger question mark over his leadership. In the end, it is a question which will forever remain in the 'what if?' section of history.

Another bizarre incident occurred during this period, where Reynolds was speaking in the Dáil and awaiting a definitive answer from the new Attorney General, Eoghan Fitzsimons, who possessed relevant information. The issue was complex, but it surrounded the appointment of Harry Whelehan, the former Attorney General, as President of the High Court. As Attorney General, Whelehan had advised that a delay had occurred in the extradition of paedophile priest Brendan Smyth due to the fact that it was the first time a case occurred where a particular section of the law regarding 'delay' had occurred. Eoghan Fitzsimons was appointed as the new Attorney General, and suggested that he thought this was not correct, although there was serious disagreement on the issue within the Attorney General's office. Reynolds asked Fitzsimons to come to a decisive conclusion and advise him in writing. Fitzsimons wrote a reply overnight, but the Taoiseach was already addressing the Dáil when he made it to his office, so the note was passed to the chamber, then down from one TD to the next, eventually reaching Ahern, who appeared to look at it then put it in his pocket. The letter later turned up in the file and Albert sought to change his reply on that basis. Later argument would lean towards the conclusion that Fitzsimons's reply was not correct itself and that his senior civil servants disagreed with his position, nonetheless the timing of the events and the failure of the letter to reach Reynolds remains one of the great mysteries of Irish politics. The fact that the letter stopped its journey with Ahern is of course interesting in itself. In any event, Reynolds revised his speech and Dick Spring chose to continue in Government. Then, only a few hours later, he got a call to say that the Attorney General had informed Reynolds of the situation long before the letter. This happened at a very long meeting of Fianna Fáil ministers where Fitzsimons mentioned that he felt there was another case that changed things, but that there was disagreement regarding its validity. Reynolds argued that at this point he asked the new Attorney General to get him a definitive answer but, until the question was resolved, he had to go ahead on the basis of facts as they were currently understood. Pressure was building up from a cadre of advisers in the Labour party who were ill at ease with Fianna Fáil and were battling a core of Ministers who felt things were still in reasonable shape.

Spring asked Reynolds if he could speak with Fitzsimons, and Reynolds agreed he could, fully believing that there was nothing that Fitzsimons could say that would alter the facts. In fact, Reynolds believed that Fitzsimons would completely verify what had happened. To his credit, Dick Spring seems to have known he was about to face an impossible problem. He prefaced his question to Fitzsimons by telling him that he had no obligation to answer it and that it could be seen as confidential between the Attorney General and Taoiseach, and Spring would accept that. He then asked Fitzsimons when he had first informed the Taoiseach of the second case. Fitzsimons considered, and then said he had a duty to the Tánaiste as a member of the Government and that it was first made clear before Reynolds's speech to the Dáil in a conversation. Dick Spring, in a reference to both men's occupations as barristers, simply replied 'Oh lord Eoghan, you will have us all back in the Four Courts.'

After Reynolds's resignation the way was clear for Ahern to assume the leadership. Máire Geoghegan-Quinn briefly toyed with the idea of opposing him, but this came to nothing. Ahern was hugely popular within Fianna Fáil. His negotiations with the Labour Party to form a government were scuppered by more confusing stories of events leading up to the Reynolds speech. Dick Spring, the Labour leader, had agreed to work with the new Fianna Fáil leadership but then withdrew this, saying he now believed that most of the Fianna Fáil Cabinet had known of Fitzsimons's advice before Reynolds's speech. Labour crossed the floor and formed a Government with Fine Gael and Democratic Left.

Ahern was deeply hurt by this episode, and annoyed at the way it had been handled. But he had no choice but to settle into opposition where he showed great talent in appeasing all sides of the Fianna Fáil fraternity and, for the first time in decades, uniting the entire party to a common purpose. For many, one of his most surprising moves was reinstating Ray Burke on the front bench. By doing so he risked offending Reynolds's supporters and seemed to cause himself an unnecessary difficulty.

Ray Burke was a heavy hitter in politics. There was, however, no love lost between him and Reynolds. Indeed, in his autobiography Reynolds recounts that when appointments were being made to the Cabinet in the late eighties he wanted an economic portfolio that suited his talents. When Haughey offered another post, Reynolds asked, 'Who got Industry and Commerce?' and was told 'Ray Burke'. Reynolds's reaction was to turn down the opportunity of serving in the Cabinet and to tell Haughey he had a business to run at home. A few days later, Haughey changed his mind and appointed Reynolds to Industry and Commerce.

As Taoiseach Reynolds sacked Burke, who then remained the biggest thorn in his side throughout his tenure as Taoiseach. He was a malcontent, and worked the back benches at every opportunity to stir up trouble for the new leadership. Ahern knew this, and knew also that he was Burke's preferred alternative as leader. Albert Reynolds maintained that questions abounded even at this stage about Burke's *modus operandi* and, while no proof existed about his financial dealings with business, it was one of the reasons Reynolds sacked him. This is perhaps borne out by Ahern's move to ask Dermot Ahern to find out if there was any truth to such rumours. This investigation turned up nothing, and Ahern stuck with Burke.

Opposition proved difficult for Bertie Ahern, and many people struggled to see him as a Taoiseach. He used the time effectively, though, changing the way Fianna Fáil did business and making it a far more media savvy organisation, as well as changing the approach to candidate selection, which made its return of seats far more efficient. All of this helped usher him in as Taoiseach in 1997.

Ahern was to enjoy much success as Taoiseach. His ability to get people to trust him was invaluable in Northern Ireland, and he played a major part in the second IRA ceasefire. Indeed, the peace process in the North will remain Ahern's biggest achievement. Despite the efforts of those who dislike him or his politics to try and rewrite this and airbrush his role, the fact remains that he was a committed and central player in the process, and a key part of bringing peace. For that alone Ireland owes him a debt of gratitude and, similar to his mentor Charles Haughey, it would be churlish to try to deny Ahern's achievements because of other failures.

Tribunals would dog his time as Taoiseach, however. Ray Burke was found out early on in the new Government, and the episode was highly embarrassing for Ahern. The Government from 1997-2002 presided over unprecedented growth in the economy. This boom was handled relatively well during this period, and in a similar vein and pattern as the rainbow coalition had acted. Although it was generally seen as a good government, the same thing must be said here as was said of the rainbow Government, namely that the increase in prosperity happened largely despite the Government rather than because of it. The roots of this boom were planted in the late eighties and early nineties, and Ahern's Government had come to power at a time when this was reaching its zenith.

Ahern also delivered for Fianna Fáil a working coalition that went the distance, something its opponents had said was impossible due to the nature of the party regarding compromise. But Ahern could find compromise and consensus like no other politician, and in this he was a very different style of Fianna Fáil politician.

In 2002, Ahern had a stranglehold on Fianna Fáil. It had become very much 'his party'. He came within a whisker of an overall majority in 2002, but things soon began to change. The global economy suffered a shock in the wake of the 9/11 terrorist attacks and on top of this Ireland's boom was beginning to level out. Charlie McCreevy quickly started to cut programmes in response. Election promises on the numbers of Gardai, nurses and teachers, as well as promises and regarding new buildings, services and infrastructure were all cast into doubt. McCreevey saw no problem with this. The public, however, had different ideas. Five or six years of high spending had still gone only a little way to repairing the damage to an economy that had been on the rack for nearly thirty years. Chronic under-investment that was forced on the economy through lack of resources had left a long legacy, and people wanted it addressed. Exchequer figures still looked healthy enough, and there were many calls for Ireland to borrow heavily at this point to fund the deficit.

McCreevy refused to bow to the pressure, and as a result Fianna Fáil lost the 2004 Local Elections heavily. After this a change occurred within Fianna Fáil, and for Ahern in particular. He led the party to the now famous 'think in' at Inchydoney and, in its aftermath, he declared himself a socialist, moved McCreevy to Brussels and installed Brian Cowen as Finance Minister with instructions to find the money to deliver the programme as promised, to show a more caring side to Fianna Fáil, and to do it before the next general election.

This resulted in the Government taking a gamble on the economy. It was predicated on the belief that even if the property market collapsed, Ireland would still have a strong economy in other areas. But, more importantly, it also gambled that property could be gradually wound down to a 'soft landing'. The banking sector in particular showed immense faith that this could be done, believing that it was the only sensible course of action to avoid a severe shock to the economy. So, property became the new engine of the economy and kept tax receipts buoyant.

In the meantime, revelations about Ahern's personal finances continued to dog him, and issues at tribunals were mounting. Some of the explanations that Ahern gave seemed to grow more fantastic and less defensible as time went on. By 2007, Ahern had delivered on many public promises and therefore remained highly popular. His closeness to trade unions had sealed a deal on public service benchmarking, cementing Fianna Fáil's image as the friend of public sector workers. Fine Gael were the only ones to oppose it.

The property market had already stalled suddenly in 2006 due to an ill-advised statement by new Progressive Democrat leader, Michael McDowell, in relation to the abolition of stamp duty. This brought an early shock to the Irish economy and had destroyed any chance of gradually managing the property boom in any event. But worse was to come. Ahern was embroiled in debate on his finances for much of the 2007 campaign, but it was Brian Cowen who won the election for Fianna Fáil. His press conferences, debating style and ability to convey an authoritative figure of leadership clearly impressed the public, although it was a skill he himself seemed to lose on becoming Taoiseach a year later.

Ahern got through the campaign, but in 2008 the revelations from the tribunal had simply done too much damage. Cowen's popularity had also increased far too much to be controlled. Ahern was forced to call it a day. Shortly after his departure, the world crisis would subsume Ireland, and its bad banking practices would be magnified by it. Banking would almost collapse completely, and the mistakes of the spending between 2004 and 2007 would be laid bare for all to see. The fallacy of trying to mange the property boom became apparent. Bertie Ahern had presided over the Government that took the blame for this, with most of that blame being fully merited. However, it is important to point out that there is little to suggest that anyone else would have done differently, except on issues like benchmarking, which had become a noose around the exchequer's neck by 2009. It is quite plausible that Ahern did believe he was doing the right things for the country. When governments spend money they do not spend it on themselves, or at least not very much! Although waste was prevalent during this period it is clear that the real spending occurred on major projects, infrastructure, pay and services: things people wanted.

To understand perhaps how the finances looked in 2004, and where the money was going, the following should be considered. From 1998 to 2004 the general government balance showed surpluses of €2.6 billion, €4.3 billion, €6.9 billion, €4.7 billion, €5.4 billion, €4.4 billion and finally in 2004 the surplus was €5.6 billion. These were astounding figures, and showed just the kind of profit the country was generating. This money was used to fund things like infrastructure which now saw investment of 5% of GNP, which was twice the EU average. While this could be explained due to Ireland's poor starting point, it remained a significant commitment. The capital side of the budget was now funded in the main from such surpluses. This seemed sensible in that it suggested the Government was not relying on surpluses but was using them for one-off investments. But it gave a lie to the current side of the budget. This seemed to be self-financing, but no one seemed able to gauge how much of this 'self-financed' portion was also due to boom income. The spending was based on the income rather than the other way around.

In other words, the presumption was that it was like a man who gets €200 in a pay packet. He then decides that in order to have all the things he wants to live for the day, in food etc, he must spend €100 and invests the other €100 in the long term. This seems like a very good and sensible plan. But what the man doesn't know is how much of that €200 he receives in pay is actually guaranteed. If the guaranteed amount is €100 then he is fine. But let's imagine that a few weeks later he gets a pay packet of €30 and is told by his employer that is all he is guaranteed, then he has a significant gap of €70 to sustain his lifestyle and this is going to be quite a shock, however prudent he formerly considered himself to be.

There is no doubt that significant waste occurred in Ireland. There is no doubt that there was a significant level of corruption that was allowed to become the norm in too many areas of society. However, bankrupting a country cannot be accomplished by these means alone. If Ireland is to learn a lesson from this period, it is important that we attempt to understand what actually happened.

The problem in Ireland was that the Government wanted to be popular. Their way to achieving this was populism: giving the people exactly what they wanted. This meant new schools were built, hospital wings, health spending increased beyond all recognition and in GNP terms was among the highest in Europe. Motorways were built, by-passes, transport was funded as never before. Supports were increased across the board, pay was increased year on year. Now if you are a politician do you think reducing the pupil-teacher ratio is a bad thing? Is building new public facilities a bad thing? Of course not, we all see the merit in this, and politicians can convince themselves that all of this is for the good of the people and entirely merited.

The problem was that all this spending was predicated on a gamble taken on the property market, and the belief that even if this collapsed the rest of the economy would pick up the slack. It made no allowance for a collapse in the domestic property market and a global downturn which destroyed the rest of the economy too. Nor did it make any allowance for the fact that the regulation of banks was still based largely on trust, with politicians believing whatever the banks chose to tell them regarding their liquidity and solvency. In short, the people were happy during the period as the spending kept the money rolling, and the politicians were happy because they convinced themselves they were doing very necessary things, but it was all based on a gamble, and one that went horribly wrong. It is in such large-scale spending sprees that countries go bankrupt.

Bertie Ahern had led a career that was hallmarked by being all things to all people, and it was rare for him to fall out with anyone. In the end, perhaps inevitably, he ended up being nothing to anyone. In a TV interview he suggested that he would have to question whether his career had been worth it. Perhaps in time someone will prove that his Government was indeed corrupt, but for now the facts simply point to a salutary lesson. Government is not about pleasing people. It is not always about consensus, or keeping people happy, and most of all it is certainly not about giving the people what they want. Bertie Ahern had a strong career with many solid and honourable achievements. If he had left office in 2002, history would judge him very differently. Unfortunately for him, politics is not a matter of longevity, but is more concerned with what you do with the time you have.

Ahern left an intricate web of councillors and committed party workers in his wake, all with a strong loyalty to the Ahern name. Ahern would have relished a chance at running for the presidency, but his sheer unpopularity, both in Ireland at large and within Fianna Fail, ensured that securing a nomination was impossible.

Few politicians consciously think of establishing a dynasty when they enter politics – it is more a matter of their actions and high level of control that sets them apart as having dynastic tendencies. In other words, they lay the ground for the name to carry on even if they do not fully realise it, and they facilitate the growth of the dynastic approach. Bertie Ahern certainly had every stamp of such an approach. His control within his constituency was nothing short of a stranglehold. He had risen to such heights within his party that his name would for ever more bring instant recognition. But for Bertie Ahern all this came at a price. In particular, his marriage and personal life all suffered. For Bertie Ahern the dynasty and name was to be perpetuated by his brothers, aided by his attempts to secure seats and positions for them at local and national level. He had little other option.

Bertie Ahern had two daughters and, understandably perhaps, having seen the effect politics had on their father and family, they had no interest in following in his footsteps. In fact they enjoyed far better lives elsewhere. In what might be considered a success for a Taoiseach, one daughter was married to a member of the most successful boy band in the world and the other was one of the biggest-selling international authors in the world. There was little that would attract either to a life in politics.

Noel Ahern was always destined to live in the shadow of his brother. However, his dynastic link to Bertie Ahern was certainly one of the reasons he got elected. It was also a typical dynastic move of extending coverage and links to firm up a powerbase.

He has always struggled under the accusation that his own success was purely down to nepotism and the strength of his brother's position. Noel was first elected in 1992, but when Bertie Ahern became leader he received a promotion to opposition spokesperson on the Environment. This was hardly a major posting, but it did hint that Bertie Ahern would not be afraid to promote his own brother. When Fianna Fáil came to power in 1997, Noel Ahern did not get a Government post, but he did secure a role as a committee chair. He never reached any level of recognition within Fianna Fáil. The party viewed him as little more than another set of eyes and ears for Bertie. He didn't possess any of his brother's charisma, and this held him back greatly.

In 2002, though, he received a promotion as a reward for his loyalty and work, and was made Junior Minister with responsibility for Housing and Urban Renewal. Unfortunately, there was little that set Noel Ahern apart in this role, and he remained largely unnoticed. He got embroiled in a number of arguments that often seemed unnecessary, and there was clearly little appetite within Fianna Fáil to see him go further. The move in 2002 frustrated some within Fianna Fáil. For many, Brian Lenihan Jnr was a brighter hope for the party, yet he did not make get a cabinet position, remaining a junior minister. This seemed to put Lenihan on a par with Noel Ahern career-wise, and this was something the majority of observers found it difficult to comprehend.

Despite an almost total lack of noteworthy achievements, the aftermath of the 2007 Election saw Noel Ahern again re-appointed as a junior minister, this time at the more prestigious Department of Finance, with responsibility for the Office of Public Works. This was a strong and quite meaningful portfolio, and could justifiably be interpreted as a promotion of sorts. However, when Brian Cowen became Taoiseach in 2008, Noel was moved again, this time to the Department of Transport with responsibility for Road Safety. This may have hinted that although Cowen did not want to lose Ahern he did not quite place the same emphasis on his abilities, and in the 2009 reshuffle Cowen chose to drop him from the junior ministerial ranks. The move effectively ended his career ambitions. Following the loss of the 2011 General Election, Noel Ahern was forced to call time on his career. If there is to be a continuation of the Ahern dynasty, it may well come from Noel's side of the family tree.

Another source of a potential successor may be the eldest of the Ahern brothers, Maurice. Maurice was elected to Dublin City Council in 1999 at the height of his brother's powers, and, at the age of sixty, he was certainly a latecomer to the political game. He had spent many years however as a key member of Bertie's backroom team and was a principal 'fixer' in the locality. Despite being new to the council his rise was quick, being installed as Lord Mayor of Dublin in 2000. This again points to the serious dynastic intention of the Ahern machine. Maurice Ahern was clearly promoted to serve as Lord Mayor, and it is obvious that he could not have achieved this so suddenly, if at all, without his dynastic connection.

However, Maurice is also one of the reasons that the study of the Ahern dynasty is important. After Bertie Ahern had left the office of Taoiseach the economy was in freefall and Fianna Fáil was highly unpopular. But the death of Independent TD Tony Gregory caused a by-election in 2009. It was perhaps the most naked display of a grab for power by the Ahern clan. There was no young family member in a position to run at this point, so, despite some strong internal opposition, Maurice Ahern was selected as the party candidate for the election. Maurice was now approaching seventy years of age. It was certainly a risky maneuvre, and the only explanation behind it is that the Ahern name still carried such weight in the constituency of Dublin Central. It was a chance for Bertie's famed organisation to flex its muscle and, even in such averse circumstances, grab a seat. The only reason Maurice winning the seat could matter was in order to hold it in similar fashion to the way Harry Blaney did in Donegal.

The result was damning. There are few instances in Irish politics where a dynastic name crumbles so suddenly and dramatically. In the by-election Maurice Ahern was fifth behind a plethora of candidates and parties who had spent years in fear of the fabled Ahern election machine. The rejection was total, and must have hurt profoundly. National rejection is one thing, but rejection by one's own people is always worse. Further ignominy was to come, as in the local elections Maurice failed to even hold his council seat, coming in well below the Ahern's Fianna Fáil constituency rival, Mary Fitzpatrick.

It was a picture of a dynasty that had once been all-consuming and all-powerful, but one that now lay in abject ruin. The Ahern name had suddenly become electoral poison. This, probably more than any other event, put Bertie Ahern's presidential ambitions in doubt. However, for all the faults associated with Bertie Ahern or his era in Government, there were also several considerable achievements. If the Ahern dynasty is ever to recover it will be a long and hard road back, but 'impossible' is a word that never sits well with Irish politics.

The Andrews Story:
One Party, One Country,
One Family

If there is such a thing as royalty in Irish politics, then the Andrews family are almost certainly candidates for it. In a typically Irish manner their story is of a family always close to the pulse of Irish history, and mirroring the country's evolution. Todd Andrews was never a politician, and yet was undoubtedly the founder of a dynasty, something that is remarkable in itself. He was also a man whose origns were far removed from wealth and success, yet he built a base that saw his family prosper. Linked to many of the great industrial and commercial achievements that were the hallmark of Ireland's growth, the family also gained a proud record on humanitarian issues.

Todd Andrews was typical of the men and women who provided the foundation of the Irish State. From the age of fifteen he served with the Irish Volunteers and the IRA. Imprisoned in 1920, he spent ten days on hunger strike before he was released. He backed the Anti-Treaty side in the Irish Civil War, and was in turn imprisoned until 1924 by the Free State Government. As a freedom fighter and a rebel he had quite a record, but pragmatism took hold at the end of the Civil War and he went on to study for a commerce degree.

His marriage to Mary Coyle was to prove a definite incubator for a political family. She herself was highly active politically being a founder member of both Cumann na mBan and Fianna Fáil.

Andrews never ran for political office, but would become a man of significant political influence when Fianna Fáil came to power in 1932. After a trip to the Soviet Union, Andrews saw how the communist regime had made use of specific natural resources and had tailored machinery and process to best deal with it. He put a huge plan into operation in 1946 to set up Bord na Móna, and served as its first managing director. The new body harnessed Irish peat resources with great efficiency, using machinery specifically designed for the purpose, and combined with the narrow-gauge railways formed something of a mini industrial revolution.

This success was widely recognised. In 1958 Andrews went on to become chair of CIÉ, the state-owned transport company. The company was struggling, and Andrews saw the need to rescue it. It had a large and outdated rail network that was simply not viable in economic terms, and he took the tough decision to close many lines to ensure the company could remain in existence. However, these decisions were not popular, and Andrews was blamed by many for the destruction of railway services in Ireland. The debate still rages today about the controversial decision. Certainly Ireland is drastically underserved by its railway system, and the company now in charge, Iarnród Éireann, is still faced with closing particular rail lines. It is difficult to judge Todd Andrews in light of that debate. Railways are an international problem with two very differing views.

Todd Andrews's brilliance in Bord na Móna was offset by the opposition to what he did in the railway system. Undoubtedly there has been a price to Ireland for those decisions, but it is still difficult to see many of those lines in operation, particularly in the current environment of financial constraints for the government which, in the end, has to subsidise the service. There is little doubt but that if Andrews had not taken the decision, it would have happened at a later date out of necessity. CIÉ would always struggle into the future against private bus companies and hauliers.

Andrews went on to serve as the Chairman of the RTÉ authority, where he was one of the most forceful and opinionated figures in Irish life. While he was not a politician, he gained a reputation for being an uncompromising, fearless and decisive character. Many politicians were heavily influenced by him, and his name gained such recognition that it would always be a political advantage to those who carried it.

Todd Andrews's eldest son, David, trained as a barrister. However, given his family background, politics was always a profession that would appeal. He was twenty-nine when he was first elected to the Dáil in 1965 in a constituency that would become so entwined with the Andrews name: Dun Laoghaire Rathdown. David Andrews quickly established himself as an intelligent and composed thinker on political issues, and in 1970 he achieved his first major break by being appointed Chief Whip for the Government.

Although Fianna Fáil lost the 1973 Election, their victory in 1977 saw Andrews back in government with a post as Junior Minister at the Department of Foreign Affairs. This was a role that suited Andrews. He was an avid studier of international politics and relations and was well at ease with international issues.

Andrews was sometimes accused of being aloof and not in touch with people, but there were few practical examples to back this up. He had a great interest in social issues and poverty and in particular developing countries. He was, however, what some would term 'a thinker', and this was not something many people appreciated in Irish politics at the time.

In 1979, Andrews took a fateful decision to support George Colley for the leadership of the party. This was perhaps to be expected – Colley went back a long way in Fianna

Fáil, he was also the favoured candidate of Jack Lynch the outgoing Taoiseach, and Andrews was loyal to such traditions. However, while some, like Ray Burke or Seamus Brennan, managed to rehabilitate themselves with Haughey after they voted aginst him as leader, the same could not be said for Andrews.

Haughey continued to dislike Andrews for the remainder of his career, and by all accounts the feeling was mutual. Andrews was seen as a back bench critic for most of the eighties, but although great change occurred during the period of heaves, such as the formation of the Progressive Democrats, Andrews's loyalty to tradition and belief in the party were stronger than any personal feelings towards Haughey. He stuck with his party and was determined to fight for its soul rather than walk away from it. That was perhaps something that was very much part of the dynastic thinking, feeling that they had contributed and had as much right to Fianna Fáil as Haughey or anyone else.

Andrews's interest in Human Rights was always to the fore, and he backed a number of high profile issues during the period, including those of the Birmingham six, Guildford four and Brian Keenan.

As the worm turned, Andrews was to have his chance again. When Albert Reynolds was banished to the back benches he found many TDs who he felt were capable of cabinet level appointment. Andrews said in his autobiography that he felt Reynolds's time had come. He wasn't opposed to Ahern, but felt that at that point in time he was still too closely linked to Haughey. It was Andrews who first floated the idea of a 'dream ticket' where Reynolds became leader with Ahern's support. On his appointment as Taoiseach, Reynolds promoted Andrews to the role of Minister for Foreign Affairs. This was a big step that made up for many years of wasted talent languishing on the back benches. Andrews was a strong ally of Reynolds, and this afforded Reynolds two things: a dynastic chain and imprimatur from the party's past, while also having at his side a man of very different personality to balance. Andrews's thoughtful yet strong character appealed to Reynolds.

Andrews did not get long to enjoy his new position, with the Government collapsing later that year. However, following the General Election, Fianna Fáil and Labour entered government together and Andrews was again chosen for the Cabinet despite Fianna Fáil having fewer jobs to offer. Dick Spring had wanted Foreign Affairs, so Andrews was moved to Defence and Marine, but it was a role in which he was again comfortable. There was little doubt but that his role in the Cabinet was something in which he took pride. Todd Andrews had laid a foundation for the dynasty, but it was David Andrews who first took it to high political office and made it a household name for a whole new generation.

The fall of the Government in 1994 was unexpected and tumultuous, but by then Andrews was a central figure in the party and his position was safe and respected. Indeed there were more than a few who believed he had leadership potential, although the sheer popularity of Bertie Ahern meant that this was just not going to happen.

Ahern understood Andrews's potential though, and was quick to appoint him to the Cabinet as Minister for Defence and the Marine on returning to Government in 1997. For some in the party, there was a surprise – Bertie Ahern had shored up his relations with all sides of the party, and bringing Ray Burke back to the Cabinet was a significant part of this. Burke, after all, was still an influential part of the Haughey faction. For the remaining Reynolds supporters, Burke's return was a bitter pill but one that had to be taken. However, the real surprise was in the fact that on returning to Government Ahern chose not only to award Burke a Cabinet position but to give him one of the most senior positions on offer: Foreign Affairs.

There were more than a few in Fianna Fáil who believed that Andrews was eminently more qualified for the post and had a stronger record. However, within months of Burke's appointment, shocking revelations came to the fore about his actions in the past, including the acceptance of money from big business. He was on the receiving end of a damning tribunal report, and was the only politician at whom it felt confident enough to describe as 'corrupt'. Burke would later serve time in Arbour Hill prison for tax evasion. He himself had been the son of a Fianna Fáil TD, and his actions brought his dynasty to an abrupt end.

Faced with the crisis that this caused for the new Government, and with a delicate situation in Northern Ireland, Ahern turned to Andrews to fill the role of Foreign Affairs Minister. This period would be dominated by Andrews's deep involvement in peace talks, culminating in the Good Friday Agreement of 1998 and its historic ratification in overwhelming numbers by the Irish people North and South of the border. Indeed, David Andrews's involvement in the Peace Process at this time is often forgotten and overshadowed by the part Bertie Ahern played, but as Minister he played a central role and deserves particular credit for his part.

David Andrews stepped down as minister in 2000 aged sixty-four. Despite the hiatus caused by his opposition to Haughey, he had left an impressive legacy. He went on to be involved with humanitarian issues, particularly the Irish Red Cross, of which he was Chair until 2009, and is widely respected by all sides of the political divide. His son Barry Andrews in 2006 recounted that he never remembered any animosity towards Fine Gael in the house growing up, in fact quite the opposite, and that David Andrews had many friends including the likes of Des O'Malley and Michael D. Higgins, with whom he was close.

Without doubt, David Andrews had ensured that the dynasty would be remembered, but he was not alone in this. His brother Niall Andrews also chose to enter politics. He first took a seat in the Fianna Fáil landslide of 1977 in Dublin South, and he held that seat through some tough elections. He was appointed a junior minister in 1982 and, while his time in the role was too short to have any real impact, it was yet another family achievement. It also pointed to a more favourable attitude towards Niall on Haughey's part as opposed to David. However, in 1984 the second European Elections for Ireland saw him move to this new arena. At this time the idea of MEPs was still new, and was held out as an exciting new prospect for existing TDs. Given the history of the dynasty it was perhaps fitting that the Andrews name should represent Ireland in Europe. It also was recognition of the limited opportunity that was on offer at home during the 1980s, and Niall Andrews saw little prospect of a further advancement of his career at home.

He took the decision to leave domestic politics behind and remained an MEP for the rest of his career, retiring at the 2004 European Elections. He was succeeded by a member of another strong dynasty: Eoin Ryan. Throughout his career he held his seat, and was a significant vote-getter and a committed politician. A former colleague in the parliament, Pat Cox, praised his service and described him as a 'consistent and passionate advocate of the rights and development needs of poorer peoples and countries'. He died two years after his retirement having given twenty-seven years of public service to his country.

Niall Andrews's son Chris caught the political bug too. He first contested a Dáil seat in Dublin South East in the 2002 Election. This was never an easy task, as the constituency has a history of being hostile towards Fianna Fáil and the sitting Fianna Fáil TD Eoin Ryan was a member himself of a well-established and highly respected political dynasty. Two seats were never likely for Fianna Fáil, but Andrews had a strong showing all the same.

However, the decision of his father to retire as an MEP saw Eoin Ryan elected to the parliament in 2004. That left a vacancy in Dublin South East, and by the 2007 General Election Chris Andrews was in prime position. Widely recognised both within Fianna Fáil and his constituency, he put in a particularly impressive showing, doubling the vote he had achieved in 2002 and topping the poll. At forty-three he was relatively late in taking a seat, but quickly established himself as an uncompromising voice, particularly on International and humanitarian issues, very much in keeping with his family roots.

He called for the Israeli ambassador to be expelled during the Israel-Gaza conflict of 2008, and was a harsh critic of what he saw as an over the top response by Israeli military to the threat that existed. He went so far as to describe Israel as a 'terror state', and this in itself was quite an unusual and strong departure for an Irish politician.

Along with Mark Daly and Aengus Ó Snodaigh he tried to travel with the ill-fated international flotilla that tried to get to Gaza, breaking the Israeli blockade. All three politicians were prevented from boarding the flotilla in Cyprus, but the later actions of the Israeli military on boarding one of the boats was roundly criticised by the international community.

Chris Andrews's career is still in its early days, though it is clear already that he has inherited his dynasty's interest in international affairs and the problems of poorer states. It is a career that has suffered a serious setback, however. Chris lost his seat in the 2011 General Election. He had been an out-spoken critic of the way Fianna Fáil was run and of how the organisation was neglected, but he was one of those who would suffer as a result of this and of the anger at Fianna Fáil in general. It will be interesting to see how his uncompromising approach is received in the years ahead. He has shown no desire to give up on politics, and continues to fight the Fianna Fáil cause on social media like twitter, and an attempt to regain his seat is surely likely. He is another of the voices that now exist outside the Fianna Fáil parliamentary party, but that hold considerable weight and influence on the direction the machine takes and its role, if any, in future political debate. Yet another page in the Andrews story must be written.

David Andrews's son Barry was a TD for Dun Laoghaire, inheriting the seat his father vacated in 2002. There is little doubt but that his name played a major role in inheriting the party machine that had been so loyal to his father. His election showings in both 2002 and 2007 were impressive. He shared the constituency from a Fianna Fáil perspective with a senior Minister, Mary Hanafin, who herself is from a political dynasty.

Between 2002 and 2007, Andrews served on the back benches, but was seen as one of the figures most likely for promotion. Although loyal at all times to the party, Andrews made no secret of the fact that he felt back-benchers and grassroots were being omitted for the party's decision-making process, and sought greater policy influence within the party for these groups. He was met with strong opposition from senior party figures in this regard.

In the aftermath of the 2007 Election, Andrews could be forgiven some disappointment in being overlooked for a junior ministerial post by Taoiseach Bertie Ahern. However, a year later, when Brian Cowen became Taoiseach, Andrews received his promotion and became Minister of State with responsibility for Children. This was an influential junior ministry with access to the Cabinet, and marked Andrews out as one of the key figures for the future of Fianna Fáil. Now aged forty-one, he represented a younger face than many at the Cabinet table. Some had hoped Cowen would promote such figures further and reduce the average age of the Cabinet, but this did not materialise.

On coming to office, Andrews had to deal with significant issues such as the Ryan and Murphy reports into clerical abuse of children. He had to walk a fine line on the issue, containing public anger while also trying to encourage positive change. He showed himself to be unafraid to criticise the Church and even its authorities in Rome, however he also maintained a composed and diplomatic stance on the issue.

It is still far too early to judge Barry Andrews's role in politics, or indeed his contribution to the Andrews dynasty. However, by holding such an important junior ministry he certainly continued the family tradition of achievement.

Although he backed Brian Cowen in the leadership contest of 2011, Barry Andrews was promoted to the Fianna Fáil front bench as Health spokesperson by Micheál Martin in advance of the 2011 Election. However, both Andrews and Hanafin felt strong links to the Dun Laoghaire constituency, and neither were willing to give way in a titanic struggle for a seat. Either candidate had the option to move to the neighbouring constituency of Dublin South where the death of Seamus Brennan and the retirement of Tom Kitt had left an opening filled only by the relatively unknown Maria Coirrigan. With the wind firmly in the face of Fianna Fáil, their unwillingness to move compounded the party's difficulties. When the votes were counted, neither Andrews nor Hanafin had enough to secure election. This defeat, combined with the loss of Chris's seat in Dublin South East, brought an end to the once mighty Andrews dynasty. However, both are well placed for political recovery should they wish to follow that road, and both would potentially be very helpful to any revival of Fianna Fáil. Like so many others, their name is synonymous with the party founded by their forefathers, and their future is inextricably linked to it.

There is little doubt that the Andrews name still carries significant weight and has the potential, given the high esteem in which it is held, to regain its position in Irish politics in the future.

The Kennys: A Dynasty for the Future?

Born in 1913, Henry Kenny grew into a young man with a sound career in teaching and a sporting prowess that most could only aspire to. Having qualified as a national school teacher from St. Patricks College in Drumcondra, Kenny went on to teach in Galway before returning to a post in Mayo in the village of Islandeady.

He was a GAA footballer of some repute, claiming a number of county championship medals, before entering Mayo folklore as one of the team that captured the All Ireland title for the county in 1936. The same team also won a hugely impressive six consecutive national league titles.

Little is known about Kenny's desire to be a politician in his early days, but he did not openly display any particular affiliation, although this would not have been unusual at the time for someone in a teaching post, or indeed for someone so focused on their GAA career. But there is little doubt that he provided the exact mix that any political party would have been eager to recruit. Sporting heroes are always popular with the electorate, and when added with a good education and a strong and respected profession it is irresistible to those who headhunt the candidates.

Opportunity knocked with the 1954 General Election, and Kenny duly secured a seat as a Fine Gael TD. Like so many TDs, Kenny did have to serve an apprenticeship in politics on the back benches, and was subsequently elected to Mayo County council, which shored up his position locally for the future.

Politics is a game that is all about timing and opportunity, but neither were kind to Kenny apart from his early election. Fine Gael lost the 1957 General Election and were destined to remain in opposition looking on as Fianna Fáil took one of their customarily long soujourns in power lasting sixteen years, and allowing Lemass to change the face of the country. Kenny showed a strong ability in constituency politics during those long years, and was returned without difficulty at every election.

In '54 and '57, Kenny comfortably took the last seat, and saw his vote rise substantially by 1961, coming second in the constituency with a full quota. This certainly indicated that Kenny had carefully built his machine and was now the top dog for Fine Gael in the constituency with no threat to his seat. His vote rose again in 1965, and he was able to bring in a running mate in the four-seater constituency. Indeed, he was only 200 votes behind the Fianna Fáil powerhouse in the constituency, Michael Moran, who topped the poll. In 1969, constituency revisions saw both Kenny and Moran move to the Mayo West constituency from Mayo South, and it created a battle royal in the three-seater. However, Kenny finally topped the poll 300 votes ahead of Moran. The victory, however, was purely a personal one as Fianna Fáil showed far superior vote management and took two seats while Kenny's running mate was well over 2,000 votes behind Kenny himself. This may have demonstrated a desire on Kenny's part to ensure he topped the poll, and may also have been the age old problem for parties where a popular candidate is determined to secure their own base first and foremost.

On a personal level, the achievement for Kenny of topping the poll did not go unnoticed, and he was rewarded by a front bench position as spokesperson on the board of works. Kenny now had the chance to create a national profile, and he held this post until 1972. With the wind at Fine Gael's back for the 1973 Election, Kenny approached it from a far shrewder position. In '69 both Fianna Fáil and Fine Gael had run three candidates each. In 1973 Fine Gael changed this to two candidates while Fianna Fáil persisted with three. This split the Fianna Fáil vote, and all three candidates came in lower than their Fine Gael rivals. Kenny also must have felt somewhat more secure as the vote breakdown favoured his running mate, Myles Staunton, who topped the poll with Kenny second, only taking the last seat on transfers. That meant that Fine Gael reversed the situation in Mayo West and took two seats while reducing Fianna Fáil to one.

Delivering such a prize put Kenny in the hunt for an appointment in the new Fine Gael led Government. He was not disappointed on this occasion, and was made parliamentary secretary (junior minister) in Finance with responsibility for the board of works. This would be the high point of Henry Kenny's political career. He had been a TD for nearly twenty years, and was now sixty years of age.

Opportunities to impress do not come quickly to junior ministers, but Kenny handled his portfolio competently. The Dáil debates do not give us much insight into his thinking, but they do show a man comfortable with the brief, if staying close to the advice of the Department. During his tenure, he was involved in one interesting spat surrounding Fota Island in Cork. At the time there was much support for it to be taken over by the State. However, Kenny was adamant that Fota Island was a great resource for the people of Cork, but could never be considered a national park like the Phoenix Park. He attracted the ire of Flor Crowley (father of Brian Crowley MEP) and Seán Lemass for taking this position. They felt it was wrong to suggest it was only of interest to Cork, and that it could be a national park. Kenny abided by the rules on the definition, however, and to the advice of his Department. He made clear that the State would not be intervening in Fota Island, and that if there were to be parks that would be raised to national status Fota would be 'well down the list of priorities'. Such comments may not have endeared him at the time to the people of Cork and Munster, but he stood over his position steadfastly.

Kenny was a competent manager, but had little time to make any real policy impact in the Government. Just two years after his appointment, Henry Kenny was diagnosed with cancer, and he passed away shortly after on 25 September 1975. His death was a sudden tragedy, and Dáil Éireann was robbed of a man who was liked by many across party lines in Leinster house.

As we have seen in previous chapters, even if you had no intention of creating a political dynasty in Ireland, there is one sure way of ending up with one, and that is through a by-election. It is this system more than any other that opens the door for family members to enter the fray. However, Enda Kenny was not the kind of man who had been closeted away from politics; he was exposed to it and involved in constituency clinics and work from an early age. There is another trait that is perhaps interesting in so many dynasties. As mentioned at the outset, it is not uncommon for children to follow their parents' chosen profession. This may be out of a form of respect or admiration or simply a life with which they are familiar. Many politicians enter the professions of their parents before going on to follow them into politics also. In this regard the Kenny family were no different: Enda Kenny qualified as a primary school teacher having studied at UCG and St. Patrick's College in Drumcondra in Dublin.

Enda Kenny was certainly involved and interested in politics, but he found the career suddenly and unexpectedly thrust upon him by the premature death of his father. He was still just twenty-four years of age, and it was an enormous task to take on. He was, however, the ideal candidate for Fine Gael. He had a recognisable name, there was an outpouring of sympathy for his father, he had a good education and was a confident man. The by-election itself was interesting in that it showed just how rooted in the main parties the Mayo constituency still was. There were only three candidates in the field: Kenny, Michael McGreal of Fianna Fáil and Basil Morohan, an independent.

If the lack of candidates indicated the strength of Fianna Fáil and Fine Gael, the vote itself underlined it even more with Morohan only mustering 1,481 (5%) votes by comparison with McGreal of Fianna Fáil attaining 12,448 (42%) and Kenny topping the poll with 15,584 votes (52%). Enda Kenny had taken the first step in his political career and was on his way to Leinster House.

But as we have seen, politics is not the kind of career you choose if you want a meteoric rise to the top, particularly within larger parties. Kenny had to serve his apprenticeship like everyone else, and set about building his own constituency profile in advance of future elections. Most of his Dáil work consisted of parliamentary questions on constituency and specific matters rather than any chance to shine on the national stage. Fine Gael had approached the 1977 Election with quiet confidence, but once it was called it quickly appeared that there was a major swing towards Fianna Fáil and that they were about to lose power. As we saw in earlier elections, Henry Kenny had secured his base and only when he was confident, and in a strong front bench position, did vote management really occur in Mayo to allow Fine Gael gain two seats.

In 1977, Enda Kenny could not have felt as confident as his father. Although Fine Gael stuck to a two-candidate strategy and Fianna Fáil still opted for three candidates, the split for Fianna Fáil was far more balanced. Enda Kenny topped the poll and was elected on the first count, but his running mate, Myles Staunton, was a full 4,000 votes behind him. This, allied to strong vote management for Fianna Fáil and the swing to them, allowed Fianna Fáil to regain two seats in Mayo West. One of these was another young candidate by the name of Padraig Flynn.

Enda Kenny remained focused on his constituency, and over the following years he tried to cement what was a dominant position for him within Fine Gael in Mayo. The General Election of 1981 saw Kenny top the poll again, but well ahead of his running mates, and Fianna Fáil still remained more popular in Mayo. Indeed, the Fianna Fáil vote was creeping upwards and Kenny's own vote was falling, along with that of Fine Gael generally, which may have dissuaded any suggestions of stronger vote management. February 1982 saw Kenny top the poll again, but only 500 votes ahead of Denis Gallagher of Fianna Fáil, and there was a certain pride at stake. Although the General Election in November 1982 was kinder to Fine Gael generally, Enda Kenny was unable to deliver an extra seat in Mayo West as the Fianna Fáil stranglehold continued, taking two seats. The Election saw Fine Gael with a two-candidate strategy, and the vote management was somewhat better with Kenny now just 2,000 votes ahead of his running mate, but the Fianna Fáil lead proved too much. Worse still, while Kenny topped the poll, he was under a quota, and Denis Gallagher of Fianna Fáil was the first to be elected.

In large parties, TDs are often rewarded for helping to deliver extra seats with strong strategies and good local machines. Enda Kenny's failure to stop Fianna Fáil taking two seats in Mayo West may have played a part in his being overlooked for promotion when Fine Gael took power again after the November 1982 Election. He was, however, a young man, and had time on his side.

In 1983 he was appointed by Fine Gael as a representative on the New Ireland forum, and this gave him his first taste of national exposure. Kenny was loyal and hardworking, and this was finally rewarded in 1986 by his appointment as a junior minister in the Department of Education.

For Kenny it was a welcome opportunity to prove his worth and match the achievements of his father. His abilities were finally being recognised, and at thirty-six years of age he was certainly considered one of the up-and-coming voices in Fine Gael, and part of a new breed who could ensure the party's survival through another generation.

Circumstance was not to be a friend, however, and Fine Gael would lose the 1987 Election heavily. Enda Kenny again topped the poll, but Fine Gael was a long way off taking a second seat. Indeed, the transfers meant that Kenny himself now took the third seat behind Denis Gallagher and Padraig Flynn of Fianna Fáil. Fianna Fáil's return to power signalled problems for Fine Gael. Some of these problems would, however, provide Enda Kenny with his opportunity. Fine Gael needed to regroup. They had to change their approach, and spent several years in soul searching. As part of this, the party was on the lookout for new voices, and Enda Kenny was perfectly placed to serve on the party front bench and increase his profile. However, Fianna Fáil remained highly popular and, after a period of strong economic management, were ready to go to the country again. The 1989 General Election saw new Mayo star, Padraig Flynn, top the poll ahead of Kenny. Although Kenny was the first to be elected after his running mate was eliminated, it was small consolation, as the constituency now looked an impregnable fortress for Fianna Fáil and their hold on two of the three seats.

Enda Kenny served as party spokesperson on Education and also on Arts, Heritage and the Gaeltacht. Having been elected so young, Kenny grew up within the environs of Lenister House, and it was there that he met his wife, Fionnuala Kelly. As it happened, she was actually working for the Fianna Fáil press office when they met. The situation posed no difficulty for the couple, however, and she later moved on to work for RTÉ. In 1992 they were married, and this coincided with Kenny's increased prominence within Fine Gael. While other young men such as the Bruton brothers may have outshined him politically, Kenny was slowly and steadily building his profile.

The 1992 General Election was sudden and unexpected. Enda Kenny had a new running mate in the charismatic Michel Ring. Fianna Fáil ran three candidates, but were lucky that the third candidate polled so poorly, while Padraig Flynn, who was now a senior minister with a strong national profile, romped home, and Fianna Fáil took two seats. It was clear that Fine Gael might just be able to change that if the circumstances fell their way.

Fine Gael did not manage to return to government, but Enda Kenny became more prominent in debates in Leinster house, and was a key figure in the Fine Gael front bench. As Chief Whip he had performed well, and had built a strong base of support – as seen elsewhere, the role of Chief Whip is a laborious task, but used correctly it offers a politician the chance to get close to every member of a parliamentary party, and that is invaluable in a large party. Kenny played a pivotal role in the fall of the Fianna Fáil/Labour coalition, although he did not realise it at the time. However, Padraig Flynn had left to become a European Commissioner, which caused one of two by-elections to take place in 1994. However, the one in Mayo West was one that Fianna Fáil could have expected to win, particularly with Beverley Flynn standing in her father's stead. Kenny played a key role in delivering the vote for the Fine Gael candidate, Michael Ring, and in doing so the Dáil arithmetic changed and allowed the possibility of a Fine Gael /Labour/Democratic Left Government to become a reality. When Albert Reynolds's Government collapsed, Fine Gael finally had their long awaited opportunity, and Enda Kenny could finally get his reward for long years of loyalty and service. Kenny was one of the team that negotiated the new programme for government, and it was clear that he was going to be appointed to ministerial office and take the Kenny name one step higher in Irish politics.

He was assigned the role of Minister for Tourism and Trade and, while the post might be considered junior to that received by Richard Bruton and a number of other rivals, Kenny put his head down as was his nature and made the most of the ministry. With the boom already beginning it was a good time to be in Government. Kenny oversaw the bringing of a stage of the Tour de France to Ireland, and tourism in general was expanding and growing. Enda Kenny deserves credit for his work in this role: he took the job seriously and his enthusasim was plainly evident. He displayed a strong work ethic in his efforts to promote Ireland, and one of the highlights of his term was chairing a round of the World Trade Talks.

It is difficult to assess his long-term impact as minister from this period. The role did not lend itself to major policy initiatives, or to explicit original thinking on the part of the minister. It did suit Enda Kenny's style in many respects as a result of this. It could be argued that his approach to ministerial office was not that dissimilar to his rival of later years, Brian Cowen. Both men shared a view that advice should be listened to and heeded, and both in the performance of their offices demonstrated a belief that politicians should not interfere where they lack expertise, but instead should listen to advice and see themselves as managers and facilitators who can allow plans be put into action rather than devising original plans themselves.

As things turned out, Enda Kenny did not have much time in his office in any event, with Fine Gael unable to maintain power and losing the 1997 General Election. This meant that Enda Kenny was yet again forced to take to opposition, focusing on profile building as opposed to policy. The 1997 Election held mixed messages for him. Mayo was changed from two three-seater constituencies to one five-seater, and there was a battle royal between Fianna Fáil and Fine Gael to try and become the dominant force. In the end, the constituency revision was to prove the very thing

Fine Gael needed to tip things in their favour in Mayo, where they took three of the five seats on offer while Fianna Fáil had to settle for two. Enda Kenny showed much stronger vote management skills, but Michael Ring began a certain in-party rivalry by shooting ahead of his colleagues to top the poll. It was a day Fine Gael could celebrate, but Michael Ring had given Enda Kenny pause for thought in that he was not going to be the laid back team player that they might have hoped.

Greater turbulence lay ahead for Fine Gael, and indeed for Enda Kenny. With the economy forging ahead, Fianna Fáil and the Progressive Democrats were popular over the years that followed. The best the opposition could do was highlight problems in capacity and demand more spending, although the fact was that more was now being spent than ever before. The idea of someone calling for less spending was not really a runner at this time, with the public feeling that there was much ground to make up. So Fine Gael was caught, and could do little more than look on. Enda Kenny served the party ably, but his impact was muted as he turned his attentions back to his base.

It was in 2001 that Enda Kenny would perhaps become a household name. The opinion polls showed Fine Gael was set for an implosion. Michael Noonan made his grab for power. It was without doubt a sudden and unexpected stab in the back for John Bruton. Enda Kenny, a man who had spent much of his life keeping his head down and showing great loyalty found the move repulsive. While many expected Richard Bruton to lead the opposition to Noonan's attempt to become leader, this did not transpire. Bruton, afraid perhaps of the repercussions, kept his head down. Instead, it was Enda Kenny who led the charge, and his promise to Fine Gael members that he would 'electrify the party' went into political folklore. Noonan was, however, too much of a heavyweight for Kenny at this point, and he was pushed aside as Noonan swept into the leadership.

While Noonan then proceeded to keep Richard Bruton on the front bench due to his acceptance of the new reality, there was to be no forgiveness for Kenny, who was immediately dismissed to the back benches. Kenny said that Noonan was sending a 'dangerous message', but he was now a voice in the wilderness. But a crucial change had happened. Suddenly the general public were very aware of Enda Kenny, and he became a focus for those who believed in a principled stand and who opposed Noonan. If Richard Bruton had hoped that the extra profile might aid him subsequently he was badly mistaken. As is so often the case in politics, it is the man willing to take the stand and who suffers the consequence who reaps the reward when opinion changes.

Instead of Noonan saving Fine Gael, he drove them even further into an abyss. The 2002 Election was not pretty, and the blame was laid at Noonan's feet. A party desperate for salvation looked for a new leader and turned to the one man who had been a solid voice against the Noonan regime. Instead of turning to the brother of the stabbed John Bruton, they turned to the highest profile victim of the new regime, and Enda Kenny became leader of Fine Gael at a time when many said the party had no future.

Even in Mayo, Fine Gael had been reduced to two seats with Independent Jerry Cowley taking a seat. Indeed, but for this, Fianna Fáil might have secured three seats and been on the verge of an overall majority. Fine Gael vote management was poor, but it was not something that could be blamed on Kenny. Michael Ring topped the poll, but he had almost twice Enda Kenny's vote as the next Fine Gael candidate. Ring had demonstrated that if there was to be a high profile casualty in Mayo it would not be him, and that the party would come second. Enda Kenny knew he had a fight on his hands within Mayo if vote management was ever to work and if he was to be truly safe. He suffered hugely in the media with many dismissing his ability. Enda Kenny was never comfortable with the media, often looking awkward and unable to relax, but this was very different to the man whom many people knew personally. Most importantly, Kenny knew the Fine Gael organisation inside out and he knew exactly what was required to reinvigorate the grassroots.

A side helping of luck also came the way of Fine Gael. After the attacks on the World Trade Centre the world had suffered some economic setbacks. Ireland was insulated from most of this, but Finance Minister Charlie McCreevy quickly moved to change the Government's tack in the budget of December 2002. McCreevy instigated a number of cuts, and it became clear that some Election promises would be reneged upon. The idea of broken promises and a hood-winked electorate that had been lied to was manna from heaven for Fine Gael. The line was pushed that Fianna Fáil had duped everyone, and McCreevy quickly found himself isolated as people became angry with his talk of reining in spending. Enda Kenny used the opportunity to the full as he went around the country. While his front bench now lacked experience, they more than made up for it by looking youth-ful and eager. By the time of the 2004 Local Elections, Fine Gael were well set for a comeback, and an angry electorate kicked Fianna Fáil hard for not delivering on spending prom-ises. Fine Gael also elected more MEPs than Fianna Fáil, and this was a huge victory for Enda Kenny. Fine Gael had not beaten Fianna Fáil in a national election since the early years of the State, and this was a portent of things to come.

The result, however, would backfire for the country. The Fianna Fáil response was to pack McCreevy off to Brussels and to try and retrieve the situation by living up to all com-mitments. Money that had been promised would have to be found, come what may, and the spectre of these spending commitments was to haunt Fianna Fáil. It was during the following years that many of the economic woes that haunt Ireland now began to take form as spending increased hugely and a national gamble was taken on the future of the property market.

Kenny remained highly popular within Fine Gael, and was noted for always being willing to do whatever it took to improve the image. He climbed Mount Kilamajaro for charity in 2003, and it was efforts like this that began to win him some friends. His poor media performances continued, however, and the general public showed no appetite to see him as Taoiseach with poor personal ratings always following him.

Kenny did not support the 'Shell to Sea' protesters in Mayo, saying that the rule of law had to be upheld. Slowly, he earned respect for seeming calm and not jumping on each bandwagon that came his way.

But if Enda Kenny had won Fine Gael over, he still had a long way to go with the public. Ironically, while the party ratings improved, and much of this was down to Kenny's organisational skill, his own qualities in the sphere of leadership were creating doubts. Kenny was certainly a good manager, and he professed that to be his approach, but there was a feeling that something more was needed if people were to trust a leader. In the run up to the 2007 General Election, Kenny knew that he had a genuine chance of becoming Taoiseach as Fianna Fáil continued to slide in the polls.

All parties favoured increased spending and lower taxes, rendering the 'choices' before the electorate highly populist with very little to distinguish them. In such a situation, approach and personality became all important. Enda Kenny signed a pre-election pact with Labour called the 'Mullingar Accord'. It surprised many, as previous election results clearly showed that when a small party agrees to a pact with a larger one before an election it is the smaller party that suffers. On the surface, Kenny sold it as a need to present a clear alternative, but in reality many were underestimating Kenny's political astuteness on behalf of Fine Gael.

With the agreement in place, he had closed off any danger from the Labour flank, who now supported him steadfastly for the role of Taoiseach. This even extended to

Labour leader Pat Rabbitte addressing a Fine Gael National Conference. Kenny had also spotted a key weakness in Labour's approach. Pat Rabbitte as leader was a very different man to his predecessors, Ruairi Quinn or Dick Spring. While both of these opposed Fianna Fáil, both had also worked with them. The Labour party was, for them, the vehicle, and all other parties were separate entities over which they had no control. Rabbitte, though, was deeply opposed to Fianna Fáil. The principal aim became the removal of Fianna Fáil over any particular gains or the immediate needs of the Labour party. Kenny was therefore able to ensure Labour were tied into Fine Gael policy in the common interest of stopping Fianna Fáil, and this allowed him to ensure that it was a two way debate, and a straight choice between Enda Kenny and Bertie Ahern.

In terms of planning and approach, Kenny had reason to be confident. His poor media handling and some gaffes aside, Kenny knew Fine Gael was now well placed for major gains and Fianna Fáil was stumbling. He could not legislate, however, for what happened during the campaign. Towards the final week it became evident that the economic tide was changing and that there would be troubled waters ahead. No one appreciated just how bad it was going to get, but Brian Cowen as Finance Minister single-handedly deconstructed the opposition promises. The fact that the opposition manifesto promised even higher levels of spending than Fianna Fáil's played directly into Fianna Fáil's hands as people began to realise that the situation may mean that there was much that would not be delivered. Fianna Fáil made a virtue out of their stance, and asked people not to risk prosperity for such promises. The people began to feel that change would be a risk and opted to stick with Fianna Fáil. It was ironic that when the full scale of the problem emerged in the following years and the errors became apparent that the same public would be forced to rush to Fine Gael.

While Kenny did not succeed in bringing Fine Gael into government in 2007, the impact of his strategy could clearly be seen in a huge gain of seats for Fine Gael, making them a force to be reckoned with once again. On the other hand, Labour stagnated and failed to make any gains, largely because the public had essentially been offered a choice of two competing Taoisigh.

Doubts soon emerged over Enda Kenny's leadership again, but were quickly forgotten as Fianna Fáil proceeded to lead the country straight into economic oblivion. In December 2007, the Government attempted a stimulus package to improve Irish growth, but it failed, Ireland's small economy remaining ultimately driven by external factors. Unlike the UK or US, Ireland cannot just decide to implement a stimulus – it must do so only when the time is right and there is a sign that consumer confidence will increase. The situation became so serious that a series of cuts were made in mid-2008. Bertie Ahern departed the office of Taoiseach, and Brian Cowen took over. There was no respite, however, and the country moved further into crisis. So too did Fianna Fáil's ratings. The budget in December 2008 saw a stronger series of cuts in an effort to rein in spending, but it still did not go far enough and the Government rowed backwards on certain issues. By mid-2009, Brian Lenihan introduced a mini-budget that was perhaps the first real attempt to control the situation, but it was much too little, much too late.

Electorally, Enda Kenny had more good news with the 2009 Local Elections: the Fianna Fáil vote collapsed and Fine Gael became the largest party at local government level. Kenny had now brought them to a historic situation. He also enticed RTÉ presenter George Lee to stand in the Dublin South by-election and, while this caused him grief only nine months later, it was seen as yet another victory.

Enda Kenny had done very little wrong, but the plague of poor poll ratings and a lack of ease in front of cameras still left the public dubious. Kenny is not a strong orator, or a man given to decisive strength – his talents lay elsewhere, but they just did not seem to be what people were looking for. However, in June 2010 Kenny would have his mettle tested, and would take his first steps towards a new image.

The collapse in the Fianna Fáil vote created a vacuum in Irish politics. Fianna Fáil had been the 'default setting' for many voters for decades – many voted Fianna Fáil continuously, and others might change for a time but knew that Fianna Fáil was always an option, and could be relied on to keep patterns and systems steady. For the first time in living memory, Ireland was faced with the implosion of the political structure. Where voters would go was very much open to question. By mid-2010, the Labour party appeard to be gaining significant ground, and one opinion poll indicated that they had overtaken Fine Gael. Even though Fine Gael themselves were doing very well, many felt that a golden opportunity was about to be lost and it was all because of Enda Kenny. His low ratings indicated that the public liked Fine Gael but not their leader. In this situation a party has a choice of either telling the public they are mistaken and wrong, or to try give the public what they want.

A core of Fine Gael front bench members decided the time was right for change. Richard Bruton, as we saw earlier in this book, was the man that the rebels felt could best fly the flag. The move seemed disastrous for Enda Kenny. He turned to his most trusted aide in Government, Phil Hogan, to try and salvage something from the situation. Although he was firmly on the back foot, there were a couple of things worth noting. Kenny and Hogan were both skillful organisers and both had a broad network to call upon. Their main disadvantage was media image. Once word of the rebellion got out they were playing catch up as a host of others ran to position themselves with the new order, including the likes of Simon Coveney, Denis Naughten, Olwyn Enright, Olivia Mitchell, Fergus O'Dowd, Michael Creed,

Billy Timmins, Leo Varadkar and Brian Hayes. It was a formidable line up.

The rebels made the fatal mistake of waiting and procrastinating, in particular Richard Bruton, who took several days before admitting that something was actually afoot. This was the break that Enda Kenny needed. It afforded him the time to organise while everyone else was in doubt about what the rebels were doing. It allowed him to plan, and with Phil Hogan ably assisting, Kenny was suddenly back in the game. The rebels were inexperienced and failed to build on early momentum.

By the time the weekend papers had laid the scheme bare, Kenny was ready to act. He took the initiative and tabled a motion of confidence in himself, then asked Richard Bruton to back him. Bruton was now forced into the open, and when unable to give Kenny an undertaking to support him, Kenny sacked him. This was a major turning point in his career. For the first time Enda Kenny seemed a man of anger, of conviction and decisiveness. He made his opponents look like ditherers being dragged this way and that and unable to speak their minds.

The results of the vote were not released, but it was believed to be close, some say as few as four or six votes. Kenny, who only a week earlier seemed finished, had come out stronger than ever. But it was in the aftermath of this victory that Kenny illustrated his true tactical brilliance and appreciation of the political game. Enda Kenny knew there may be more bad personal polls for him, and knew that the media would always have a question mark over him. He knew that the reason he was leader today was because Michael Noonan had sacked him.

As his opponent Brian Cowen would find out a year later, leaving a potential leader on the back benches can be a fatal error. Kenny had one luxury that Brian Cowen did not, however. He knew that those who had formed the rebel grouping were not willing to risk everything for their beliefs, the prize of being a minister would be just too great. Having taught them a lesson, Kenny offered most of the main players alternative positions in his new front bench. He knew that once they agreed, his position would be safe, and there would be no more talk of rebellion. Had he left them on the back benches, there was always a chance that the problem would resurface. He did not have to worry – his olive branch was gratefully accepted and the matter was closed.

Enda Kenny took a major step in reforming his image with this. For the first time the wider public and the media began to respect his political muscle and character. He was now clear to plan his election, while across the divide of Dáil Éireann attentions began to shift to the leadership of Brian Cowen, but this was to be a long, drawn out affair.

Fine Gael began to creep up again in the polls. From a Fine Gael perspective, natural order was restored when they overtook Labour in the ratings once again. Throughout the summer of 2010, Enda Kenny must have thought that things could not get any better from the point of view of his party. The Irish economy remained in serious trouble, and any hope of a Fianna Fáil revival had faded completely by October as the party failed to get any kind of strategy in place and was organisationally paralysed.

But Fine Gael were set for a bonanza. The pressure on the Government was incessant. Despite some figures showing signs of stabilisation, it was far too little for the Government, who saw that the debt from the banks was an ever increasing mountain. The budget was improved, but only in terms of the disasters that had been the previous two years – getting out of this mess was going to take the Irish economy the best part of a decade, and the Government had only months to go.

When the IMF/EU agreed a loan package for Ireland it was curtains for the Government, and any remaining hopes of Fianna Fáil holding back the flood were dashed. Yet still Fianna Fáil prevaricated, and in the aftermath of a tough budget the people might have expected an act such as a resignation or a gesture of acceptance of responsibility, but it was not forthcoming. Some in Fianna Fáil hoped Brian Cowen would fall on his sword at this point, but he was in no mood to take a hit for the team. Fine Gael had already won the Election by January 2011.

The fall of the Government was sloppy and badly handled, and only served to allow Fine Gael an even stronger opportunity. Enda Kenny had in reality two problems, and neither was anything to do with the Government. The first was how to manage expectation while at the same time striving for a record breaking victory. The second was what Fine Gael might face in the future, given that a perfect storm was now hitting politically there was never a more fertile ground for radicalism in Irish politics. There was a real danger that in the 2011 Election, parties of the extreme left such as Sinn Féin or the ULA would make enormous gains and change the face of politics to a far more uncertain future. If it was ever going to happen then this would be the time, as circumstances so bad were unlikely to be repeated. For Fine Gael as a centre-right party this presented a problem with planning.

Enda Kenny himself avoided media contact during the Election, and challenges from Micheál Martin for debates were ignored in the early stages. The Election was Kenny's to lose and he knew it, and reasoned that the less time he spent in front of the camera the less risk there was. Particularly, he was mindful of ensuring that Labour would not gain ground at his expense. As the campaign wore on, though, Kenny's popularity rose. On the campaign trail people liked him, moreover the people became protective of him. When he did take part in debates people seemed surprised at how well he did, simply because the hype about how bad it could be had reached epic proportions.

Enda Kenny's brother Henry is also a schoolteacher, and also involved in the family trade of politics, being a local councillor and former chair of Mayo County Council. He, with Kenny's team, kept a close eye on the home patch of Mayo where Kenny needed to win big. Similar to Bertie Ahern's approach in Dublin, Enda Kenny knew the value of having a family member guarding the home turf when you are ascending the political ladder.

Mayo was not to let Enda Kenny down, seeing him not only top the poll on over 17,000 votes, but also delivering an unprecedented four out of five seats for Fine Gael in the constituency, with Dara Calleary of Fianna Fáil being the only other voice in the county. The result was the icing on the cake for Kenny. Delivering so forcefully on home turf emphasised the strength of his position and reasserted the dominance of the Kenny name. Since Enda Kenny became leader he had comfortably overtaken Michel Ring on their home patch, and left the Kenny name the prevailing political force.

While in terms of the percentage share of the vote the result was not as good as Garret Fitzgerald delivered in 1982 in terms of seats, it was an even stronger result. 75 was the final haul, and never before had a Fine Gael leader looked at so many chips on the table. A host of new faces gave Fine Gael vitality and a clear expression of the confidence of the electorate. Enda Kenny had been vindicated, his critics silenced and many of the public forced to admit that they had perhaps got him wrong.

Kenny quickly sealed a deal with the Labour party to become Taoiseach and elevate the Kenny name to the highest level. In many ways his style was similar to Bertie Ahern. The public became protective of him, they began to resent the criticism of him, they began to see him as an ordinary bloke just trying his best. No great orator or charisma, but probably the type of guy you could relate to and might even share a drink with. A very ordinary guy. Whether or not that image will eventually catch up to Kenny the way it did to Ahern is open to question, but in his early days of office he received much support and rising popularity ratings.

There are problems on the horizon for Kenny. The economy is still in a delicate state. He also chose the option of a record victory over that of managing expectations of what the new Government could realistically accomplish. Early flirtations with changes on banking policy were quickly dispensed with when the reality set in. He set a priority on renegotiationg the EU/IMF deal, saying it was a 'bad deal for Ireland', but while Ireland did get a reduction in interest rates there was no major renegotiation on other terms. However, if the Euro remains in peril, Europe may be forced to rethink its entire strategy and approach to the markets and, in this respect, Kenny may yet have a chance to negotiate with his European partners.

The early days of the Government saw at least some acceptance of the reality and some relief at the stability the new Government gave. Its enormous majority means that in effect there is little or no opposition in a parliamentary sense. That will be on one hand a great comfort to Kenny, but he will know it also brings pressures. A government in that position is expected to implement any policy it likes, but knows that it alone will be answerable for things done. It faces pressure continually from every group wondering why one issue or another is not simply addressed and pushed through.

Enda Kenny has also promised dramatic political reform, such as the abolition of the Seanad and constitutional reform. The proposal to reduce the number of Dáil seats is also a promise, while electorally appealing, as likely to benefit both Fine Gael and Labour as the two largest parties unless Fianna Fáil have a dramatic change in fortune before the next general election. Larger constituencies, particularly five-seat constituencies, benefit smaller parties. The Dáil used to be only 144 seats, and was increased by 20 after the 1977 Election. However, it is clear that in the smaller Dáil, Fianna Fáil, Fine Gael and Labour had much greater power. Larger constituencies started to break this hold. If the number of seats in the Dáil is reduced again then it will increase the ratio of constituents per TD, making the typical constituency comparatively larger. Fianna Fáil, as a much smaller party, could be a victim in this, and Fine Gael and Labour could benefit hugely, although it must be remembered that, in the past, when the electorate has sensed any government working the Dáil numbers or voting system to its advantage it has reacted negatively to the move.

Amidst all this, however, are several potential pitfalls. The public may get angry at what they see as a continuance of policy when such change was expected. Referenda can be notoriously hard for governments to win if the issues are complex, no matter how well intentioned they might have been. There is a long way to go before we know the destination of the Enda Kenny story. But he has confounded his critics at every opportunity, and it's likely that he may continue to do so. Given the depth of family involvement and the dominance of the Kenny name in Mayo it is also likely that it is not going to disappear from the Irish political map whenever Enda does call it a day. The Kennys built this dynasty brick by brick with much family support, and a Mayo ballot paper might just not seem right without the Kenny name on it.

Fathers, Mothers, Sons and Daughters

While this book covers a select number of examples from families in the Oireachtas, there are of course many more. In fact there are a multitude of families that have a history of public service, siblings, parents, cousins and more. While there are also a couple of examples of politicians who seemed to have every ingredient possible for the basis of a dynasty and yet it never happened, these are as interesting perhaps in the study of dynasties as the successful ones.

The following is a list of just some of the other recent dynastic connections in Irish politics:

Former Fianna Fáil TD Bobby Aylward is son of Liam Aylward, who previously served the Carlow Kilkenny constituency and is currently an MEP for the Ireland East Constituency. Bobby's grandfather, Bob, was also a Fianna Fáil senator in the mid-seventies.

The Barrys of 'Barry's Tea' fame are another political dynasty. Richard Barry was a Fine Gael TD for nearly thirty years, and was succeeded by his son, Peter, who was a major figure in Fine Gael throughout the eighties and nineties. His daughter, Deirdre Clune, currently flies the flag for the dynasty in Cork as a TD.

Fianna Fáil TD John Browne served since 1982 as a TD, and was the inheritor of his uncle Sean Browne's seat in Wexford.

In Mayo, the promotion of Dara Calleary to a junior ministry and now the Fianna Fáil front bench will have come as little surprise. Often seen as one of the TDs with most potential within the party, he comes from a strong bloodline. His father, Sean, was a Fianna Fáil TD for Mayo for some twenty years, and his father before him served the same constituency from 1952 to 1969.

Joe Carey is currently a Fine Gael TD for Clare, which continues another family tradition, his father having held the same seat between 1982 and 2002.

In Limerick, the Collins name has always held particular weight. Niall Collins is the current carrier of the dynastic flag. His father, Michael Collins, served as a TD before him, and his uncle, Gerry Collins, was a well known Fianna Fáil minister and later MEP. His grandfather, James, served as a TD for almost twenty years.

Former Tánaiste Mary Coughlan was first elected in 1987, and lost her seat in the 2011 Election. Her father, Cathal Coughlan, held the same seat for a period of three years before he died suddenly in 1986. He had won the seat in a by-election caused by the death of his brother, Clement, in a road accident. Clement himself had just won the seat three years previously in 1980.

Simon Coveney is one of those often cited as being the future of Fine Gael. He was elected in 1998 in a by-election caused by the tragic death of his father, who had been a TD since 1981.

The sudden death in 1984 of long-standing Fianna Fáil TD Ber Cowen caused a by-election that saw his son, Brian, elected to the Dáil with one of the largest victories on record. In the 2011 Election, Brian's brother Barry took over the seat.

Fine Gael TD Michael Creed is the son of former Fine Gael TD, and MEP, Donal Creed.

Michael W. D'Arcy was elected a Fine Gael TD for the first time in 2007, continuing the tradition of his father, also Michael, who also served the Wexford constituency on a number of occasions.

In nearby Waterford, Fine Gael's John Deasy occupied the seat vacated by his father, Austin, in 2002, after twenty-five years of service as a TD.

As an example of how a dynasty can disappear, reappear and disappear again, Jimmy Devins was a Fianna Fáil TD for Sligo/North Leitrim until 2011, and is a grandson of James Devins, who served in the 1921/22 Dáil.

Michael Ahern is a well-known figure in Fianna Fáil, having served in a number of junior ministries. His father, Liam, was a Fianna Fáil senator and TD in the mid-seventies, and Liam in turn is a nephew of John Dineen, who served as a Farmers Party TD between 1922 and 1927.

Laois/Offaly TD Olwyn Enright stepped down at the 2011 Election. She is married to another Fine Gael TD, Joe McHugh, as well as being the daughter of the long-standing Fine Gael TD and Senator, Tom Enright.

Also in the Laois/Offaly constituency is Charles Flanagan, who took over his seat from his father, Oliver J. Flanagan, a colourful and popular TD for nearly thirty-five years.

Beverley Flynn in Mayo stepped down at the 2011 Election having followed in the footsteps of her father, the former minister and EU Commissioner, Padraig Flynn.

Mary Hanafin lost her seat in the 2011 Election, and was a high profile loss for Fianna Fáil, but also the leading light in the family dynasty. Her brother, John, was a Fianna Fáil Senator, while her father, Des Hanafin, was a long serving senator for Fianna Fáil and pro-life campaigner.

Even newer parties can have dynastic connections. Former Green Party TD Ciaran Cuffe is a grandnephew of former Fianna Fáil TD for Waterford, Patrick Little.

Kathleen Lynch serves Cork North Central as a Labour TD, and she is also a sister-in-law of Ciaran Lynch, the Labour TD for Cork South Central.

In Kerry, the McEllestrim dynasty is well known. Tom is the current standard-bearer for this deeply Fianna Fáil family, but lost his seat in 2011. He follows in his father's and grandfather's footsteps as a TD in a tradition going back to 1923. Incidentally, all were called Tom.

John O'Donoghue married outside of the party, so to speak, being the son-in-law of former Labour TD, Michael Pat Murphy.

Denis Naughten keeps the Naughten tradition going for Fine Gael in Roscommon, following in the footsteps of his father, who was a TD and then Senator until his tragic death in a car accident.

M. J. Nolan also followed in his father's footsteps. Tom Nolan was a TD for Carlow/Kilkenny, and also served as an MEP between 1973 and 1979.

Another one of the new faces for Fine Gael is Kieran O'Donnell. The Limerick TD is a nephew of Tom O'Donnell, a former Fine Gael TD and MEP, who in turn was a nephew of Richard O'Connell, who served the first Cumann na nGaedheal Government from 1923 to 1932.

Former Fianna Fáil TD Sean Power is of course the son of Paddy Power, who served as a TD for twenty years and was a former Government Minister.

Ruairi Quinn is a long standing Labour TD and Minister, and is also a first cousin of the Independent Senator and former supermarket tycoon, Feargal Quinn.

Sean Sherlock was a new face for the Labour party in the 2007 Election, but his father, Joe, was a well known TD and Senator for the Workers Party/Democratic Left and finally Labour.

In 1997, Fine Gael TD Billy Timmins took the seat held by his father in Wicklow for over thirty years.

Mary Upton stood down in the 2011 Election, having taken her seat in 1999 for the Labour party in a by-election caused by the death of her brother, Pat.

There are of course many dynasties on hiatus, waiting to enter the Dáil or with members serving in the Senate, and some that have died out. Some of the other famous dynastic names include the Ryans in Dublin, where Eoin Ryan lost his MEP seat in 2009, but there remains a talented younger generation willing to fill the role of a dynasty going back to 1918. When Gerry Reynolds lost the Fine Gael seat in Sligo/Leitrim in 1997 it brought an end to a ninety year dynasty. The O'Malleys in Limerick have a long tradition of ministerial service, through Tim O'Malley, Des O'Malley and Donogh O'Malley. Kevin O'Higgins, who was assassinated in 1927, left behind a dynasty that could still be traced in the high levels of Fine Gael as late as 1989, when Chris O'Malley finished his term as an MEP, and the O'Higgins name still represented the constituency of Laois/Offaly in the Dáil into the mid-seventies.

The wife of Terence McSwiney, who died after seventy-four days on hunger strike in 1920, served as TD until the 1927 Election, and the couple had a son-in-law, Fianna Fáil TD Ruairi Bruga, in the Dáil in the mid-seventies.

Former Finance Minister Ray McSharry was a powerful figure in Sligo, and his son Marc is currently a Fianna Fáil Senator.

Sir Thomas Esmonde founded a political dynasty back in 1885 that could still trace its lineage to Sir John Grattan Esmonde, who served as a Fine Gael TD for Wexford from 1973 to1977.

Perhaps a name that has no current connection to politics, but one that can only be a matter of time, is that of Michael Collins. His cousin and his sister both served as TDs in the thirties, and his two grandnieces, Nora Owen and Mary Banotti, served as a Fine Gael Minister and MEP respectively.

Sir Maurice Dockrell was the last member of the Irish Unionist Alliance to be elected an MP for Dublin in 1918. His son, Henry, served Cumann na nGaedheal and later Fine Gael from 1932 to 1948. Henry's son, Percy, also served as a Fine Gael TD between 1954 and 1977, while another son, Maurice, served as a Fine Gael TD until 1977. Indeed, Percy's sons also served as councillors in Dun Laoghaire.

There are many others. They all serve to prove what value a name can have in politics, but also demonstrate the value of the accumulated knowledge and experience that has been handed down through generations.

Of course, there are always exceptions, and sometimes dynasties do not seem to take root where you might expect them to. There are two very notable exceptions from the pages of this book. It has only occurred twice in Irish history that a Taoiseach has not had a blood relative to carry on their name or dynasty subsequent to their tenure in office. Yet those two exceptions are, on paper, surprising, for both would have seemed well established. The first is Jack Lynch. Of course, Jack Lynch had no children so this perhaps explains the lack of any continuing dynasty in his case, however for a man with such a reputation in Cork, and one of the most popular politicians and sportsmen in Irish history, it is perhaps surprising that there was not even some more distant relative to continue the line. But several factors might go some way towards explaining this. The manner of Lynch's departure, and his apparent animosity towards Fianna Fáil, both make his a difficult dynasty to continue, as does the fact that his reign was effectively ended when two by-elections in Cork were both lost. Picking up the mantle of a popular politician with a loyal powerbase in a constituency is one thing, but carrying the weight of an unpopular political predecessor is quite another.

The other exception is Albert Reynolds. On paper he had all the ingredients for a powerful dynasty. He came from a small county, and was an enormously powerful figure with a well-oiled machine and electoral support, even in his last election. He also had a large family, who were well liked at home with plenty of supporters. However, while his son Philip considered running for some time, it was perhaps another trait of the Reynolds name that caused him not to run: pragmatism and hard-nosed business sense. For Reynolds, it was never about power or the trappings of office, it was about business, deals and extreme pragmatism. The result was always what was important. Therefore politics was never the ultimate goal. Philip was as committed to the family firm, C&D pet foods, which he now runs, as he was to the ideals of politics. His loyalty to firm and family led him to decide against running. It is still not ruled out locally that he may yet change his mind. But political dynasties tend to thrive on the political game and its importance. This was one ingredient lacked by the Reynolds core, for it seemed to be just a means to an end, and there was often the impression that there was much to dislike about politics.

It should also be remembered that this book deals purely with the dynastic element of politics. If a book were to be written focusing on the people who have made it in politics without any family heritage then it would probably well exceed those who have had family connections. After all, every dynasty had to start somewhere. New dynasties will be formed in the future on the back of people who will get elected in the next general election, who today have no relatives or history of family service in the Dáil.

Conclusion

Politics can be a brutal game. Observers of it generally fall into two camps: those who look on but know little of it, and those who are close to it and through this closeness gain a deep respect for all those who run for election and serve in public office. The former usually dismiss politicians as something close to parasites and view their life as an easy one, but only open to particular 'insiders'. The latter see it as tough, unforgiving and often unrewarding, and while they understand the bug that drives politicians, they often struggle to fathom why they do it at all.

Political families are a natural breeding ground for candidates. They understand the life better than most and know exactly what is required of them. They have an enormous advantage of insight and experience that proves invaluable. Then they have the ability to rely on support even from their first election due to their name, and a loyalty that is perceived as being owed to that name rather than to any particular individual who may bear it.

It is difficult to see this ever changing in Irish politics. Roman politics was dominated by families and their clients, and for over a thousand years subsequently Europe was dominated by monarchs and tribal systems that were based on families in control with the support of those who either owed them or believed in them. But such systems were from a culture that was based on an elite 'class politique', whose members, one way or another, saw it as their natural position in the world that they should govern the rest of the population. In Ireland, politicians come from varied backgrounds: farmers, teachers, trade unionists, professionals, public sector and private sector. Many have seldom if ever spent any time with their would-be colleagues before entry into Leinster House. This is not evidence of a closed culture.

However, perhaps we all still retain some genetic imprint from the thousands of years where such cultures did exist. Names in politics are something akin to a security blanket for a voter. You know what you are going to get, in theory at least. To this day, right across the world, families from the Kennedys and Bushes to the Lenihans or Kitts occur in many political spheres. In Ireland there is a particularly high prevalence of dynasties, but there is also a much smaller population from which to select.

There is also clear evidence to support the idea that a family in the political sphere does indeed accumulate knowledge and experience. Growing up in a political household could be compared to a prolonged internship that must lead to a better knowledge of the system. Hence, it is possible to argue that dynastic candidates may perform better.

But if the experiences of Irish political families show that there are certainly advantages in having a candidate from a political family in terms of knowledge, the jury may be out in terms of the consistency of approach. It is a key feature that votes and support continue seamlessly to another family member because supporters believe they are going to get something very similar. But this is not always the case, and as we have seen, families, while holding to certain traits, can often change policy approach radically and be very different people to their predecessors or relations. Liam Cosgrave Jnr was a much different man to either his father or grandfather. None of the De Valera clan ever managed to recreate the sheer force and brilliant strategic political brain of Éamon De Valera. Bertie Ahern's brothers had little in common with his own approach and ability. Richard Bruton was unable to sway party support that had belonged to his brother, John.

However, for all that some striking patterns exist. The electoral record in the Kitt family is fascinating in terms of its own struggles and similarities at the polls. The ability of those with a strong political name to attain Senate seats is also interesting. Should a Dáil seat be lost, it would appear that a family name can be instrumental in keeping a career alive through the Senate, even seeing you elevated by your peers during your time there. The current debate around the future of the Seanad could have a huge impact upon this. The Government has promised to abolish the Seanad, subject to a referendum. If this happens, then there is a serious implication for political dynasties. Throughout the pages of this book we have seen how a family name can be supported and aided by securing a Seanad seat. The electoral system used for the Seanad favours well-known names too. Therefore, many dynasties have used it, whether as a stepping stone or a safety net, in a way that might not be open to other candidates with fewer contacts or less famous names. Whether we see a reformed Seanad, or its abolition, it will certainly impact greatly upon many of the family names we have become used to, and also on the ability of new dynasties to establish themselves.

Following a parent's profession is not unusual for any child. It is an approach familiar to many walks of life. However, in politics it would seem that it is crucial to have a powerful local party organisation and machinery. Name alone cannot guarantee you success. Hence we can see the difficulties experienced by people like Síle De Valera in her early career. Liam T. Cosgrave is another example. If too long a period of time has elapsed or there is no party organisation where you are the candidate, then the name alone will most certainly not guarantee you success at the polls. However, where a politician has a strong and dominant local organisation behind them, if they stand down that organisation can transfer directly to another family member. It is in this scenario that dynasties are at their most powerful. A local party structure and a long list of voters who feel they owe something to your predecessor makes a combination that is difficult to beat in any election.

A common enough occurrence in Irish politics is the story of a TD who, for whatever reason, disagrees with their party HQ. Party HQ tries to impose a rule or an order, but the TD easily sways the local organisation to back them against the oppressive and unfair hand of central control. In many instances where a TD is expelled from a party they take a large swathe of the local organisation with them, as for example Neil T. Blaney did. This points to the highly personalised nature of politics on the ground. With such a low population it is relatively easy for anyone in Ireland to gain access to a TD and to become friendly with them – in short, all Irish politics is essentially local politics. While other electoral systems have been put forward, almost all are based on countries with much larger populations. The difficulty in Ireland is that, whatever system is used, in all likelihood the majority of the population rate to be at no more than one or two degrees of separation from personal contact with the politician, and therefore action and assistance is expected. Personal loyalty and relationships count for a lot and, while there is sometimes a perception that Ireland's political processes and divisions occur at the national level, the reality is that the national parties form at most a loose amalgamation of what can often be widely differing views. It is in effect more like a collaboration of fiefdoms and personal units that come together under a party banner rather than enormous party organisations that support the party no matter what. No party of any duration has been immune to this effect, and therefore they have reacted to protect their vote, and one way of achieving this is through recognisable names or candidates with strong links within the party. When faced with an election the most important thing in the first instance is finding a candidate who can deliver the local troops on the ground for canvassing and organisation, whatever their views on national level politics, which is way down on the list when it comes to candidate selection processes. A candidate without a well kitted out local unit is as effective as a general without an army. The old adage that 'all politics is local' was never more true than it is in Ireland. Knowledge of communities, personal contacts and a long list of local achievements is a recipe for success in electoral terms. A dynasty that can count on generations of such contacts and favours knows that this system and approach is crucial to maintaining its supremacy.

Another pattern that has an enormous effect on the role of dynastic politics is that of the by-election. In some electoral systems it is preferable to simply replace a TD by nomination. Indeed, at local council level in Ireland if a councillor dies or has to step down, they can simply co-opt a replacement and there is no need for a by-election. At first, this sounds undemocratic. However, as we know, the case is different at national level. A general election is, in democratic terms, an opportunity for all the people to speak at a set time. It would be unacceptable to hold a general election over a number of days of polling and have different constituencies voting on different days as information changes daily. It would be equally unacceptable to publish an opinion poll where some of the respondents were asked their voting intentions six months before others.

However, if a TD dies or is otherwise unable to continue we hold a by-election. In effect, this does mean that the make up of the Dáil is now formed by people speaking at different times and with different information, and this itself could be argued to be undemocratic. In the normal course of events it presents no problem – as we saw, such by-elections may have saved John Bruton's career, for a Government that was not possible in the wake of the 1992 General Election suddenly found itself with the numbers in late 1994. The argument is academic, however, but necessary to show the idea that in politics there is almost always a contrary argument that can be equally based upon principle.

By-elections in Ireland have been vital to the dynastic tradition. Such elections usually occur suddenly and unexpectedly. While governments can wait, sometimes an unacceptable length of time, to hold them, it is still difficult for parties to prepare for them adequately. A new candidate has little time to build any kind of recognition with the public at large. Internal party jostling for superiority makes it incredibly difficult for any one candidate to deliver the entire party organisation in a constituency. However, if a family member decides to run, then most problems are solved. The party organisation will usually accept this person as they will be the outgoing candidate's choice and they have all worked for that predecessor and will accept that a family member will have the knowledge to handle the role. The public in by-elections are prone to sympathy votes, particularly if an outgoing TD has died or resigned due to illness. Most important of all, however, is that in the tight period of time where it is difficult to make an impact, the voters can still look at the ballot paper and see a name they recognise, a name perhaps that they have scratched that invaluable '1' beside on a previous occasion. This again is a hint of the security blanket approach. The only way for an opposing party to combat this is to effectively put up a celebrity candidate, and by-elections are equally notorious for parties' efforts to find such instantly recognisable name to stand.

For some, the existence of dynasties is also part of a lack of ideological divide in Irish politics, however there is nothing to suggest that a family can't be equally attached to a party with a strong ideological leaning than one without.

Because Fianna Fáil and Fine Gael both came out of the ashes of the Civil War, it has always been argued that ideology is lacking in politics. But the ideological divide that exists between both centre-right parties in the US is small. Recent governments in the UK have shown very little meaningful policy difference between Labour and the Conservatives. The key difference is on the question of trust, and who people have faith in to take decisions. Ironically, many commentators criticise some voters for voting Fianna Fáil, Fine Gael, Labour or Sinn Féin regardless of what they hear about them or what is said about them. Yet this is the essence of voting on a basis of trust, personality and personal assessment. If you believe in an ideology it is unlikely you will ever vote any other way than your party, and most of the reasons given to stop supporting a party centre around assessing the individuals at the head of the party and their personal morals or approaches.

Differences between the main parties in Ireland are small, but perhaps no smaller than most parties who are in and out of government in other countries. Sinn Féin and the Socialist party represent the hard left in Ireland, Labour occupies the softer left, which is as a result of its experience of being in government. It is a left-wing approach that accepts certain realities about what is possible. Fine Gael occupy a centre-right position where there is much greater emphasis on the private sector, as was evidenced by Richard Bruton's opposition to benchmarking and the scepticism that exists within Fine Gael for trade unions and semi-state sector. Fianna Fáil occupies the centre ground, with a membership made up of some who feel close to Labour and some who feel close to Fine Gael. It is the need to bring all this together that has led to its overriding pragmatism. In the end it is the centre ground that is crowded, but that is not dissimilar to any other modern western country. What makes Ireland different is our electoral system, which ensures that any one party coming to power alone is a very tall order. Therefore we have a series of coalition governments. Fianna Fáil has shown that it is swayed by the party with which it shares power. In coalition with Labour, those who are on the left of the Fianna Fáil spectrum were in the ascendancy, while when it shared power with the Progressive Democrats those who were on the right of the spectrum came to have more influence. Fine Gael has always shared power with Labour, however the party has never had the huge levels of support it currently enjoys, and there is little doubt but that some of the more right-wing thinkers in Fine Gael may find the current Government a bit more challenging should the Labour party start to flex its ideological muscles.

Political dynasties have long been a part of Irish politics and it is likely that they will continue for many years to come. The names contained in this book are some of the most instantly recognisable in the modern age. However, other dynasties have passed or died, and others will return in time. There is little doubt but that they have all had an enormous impact on politics and how we live our lives. It is a trait of many dynasties, whether they be local or national, that they try to use the same *modus operandi* and ape the characteristics or achievements of their predecessors. It has at times produced a certain amount of continuity. Dynasties often rely on being able to achieve high office, and this is not for prestige alone. There is little doubt that many fine 'would be' politicians lost a chance to run for various parties due to sharing a constituency with the son or daughter of a TD who filled the role. If that son or daughter goes on to achieve something then this is considered an acceptable price and proves the system works. However, where a dynasty fails to achieve office or promotion it can begin to rankle with local troops as to why they are there, and voters do, eventually, have a habit of asking themselves whether somebody else might not have done a better job. Generations of back bench TDs are unusual, and generally unacceptable to party organisations. It may allow a dynasty to survive in the short term, but without a high achiever in the family the risk of losing the seat is greatly increased.

Nonetheless, there can be little doubt that in an age when it is seen as commonplace and acceptable to deride politicians it is admirable for anyone to put their neck on the line. We may disagree with someone's policies, we may dislike someone's approach, most of all we may despise their politics, however we must never lose sight of the fact that no one has a monopoly on doing what is right. Little is black and white in politics, where most arguments involve numerous different shades of gray. Regardless of political views, the vast majority of politicians believe they are doing a good thing, and take decisions in good faith. There have been notable exceptions, but they remain just that, exceptions. Many dynasties have been involved in some very positive policies, and their members have done much good in our society, and where one member fails or is proven to be the opposite that is still not sufficient reason to ignore any positive effect.

Some argue that the 2011 Election may have seen the end of the political dynasty. I would not tend to agree. It may mean we will say goodbye to many of the established names we know, but there is every chance that new dynasties will rise and new families will establish their name at the end of the current generation. The reduction in Dáil size may end up benefiting those with a recognisable name as it will be more difficult for new candidates to become known. Certainly the old 144 seat Dáil was no better in terms of stopping a dynastic tradition. The truth is that, like any profession, a child learns from their parents. There is nothing unnatural about a child wishing to follow in their parents' footsteps. What is unusual is the propensity of the Irish electorate to so often seek out the security of 'the name they know'. The only thing that will change this is not a new electoral system or a change to numbers but instead a complete change in how the electorate assesses their politicians and evaluates them.

It remains open to debate as to whether Ireland would be any different without dynasties. We do not know who or what would have filled that void. We can say that we would perhaps miss some of the characters and personalities contained in this book. Ireland remains a local and personal society, be that for good or ill. A name carries weight in Irish politics, can be a burden once you get there, and brings with it responsibility and expectation that can either enhance or immobilise the bearer. There are certainly many chapters still to be written in this story.

Bibliography

Andrews, C.S., *Dublin Made Me*, Mercier Press 1979
  Man of no Property, Mercier Press, 1982
Andrews, David, *Kingstown Republican*, New Island Books,
  2008
Clifford, Michael & Coleman, Shane, *Bertie Ahern and the
  Drumcondra Mafia*, Hachette Books, 2009
Coleman, Marc, *Back from the Brink: Ireland's Road to Recovery*,
  Transworld, 2009
Collins, Stephen (ed), *Nealon's Guide to the 30th Dáil & 23rd
  Seanad*, Gill & Macmillan / *The Irish Times*, 2007
  The Power Game, O'Brien Press, 2000
  The Cosgrave Legacy, Blackwater Press, 1996
  The Sunday Tribune Guide to Politics, Tribune
  Publications, 1997
Downey, James, *Lenihan, His Life and Loyalties*, New Island
  Books, 1998
Duignan, Seán, *One Spin on the Merry-go-Round*, Blackwater
  Press, 1996
Farrell, Brian (ed), *The Creation of the Dáil*, Blackwater Press,
  1994
Ferriter, Diarmaid, *Judging Dev*, Royal Irish Academy, 2007
Finlay, Fergus, *Snakes & Ladders*, New Island Books, 1999

Fitzgerald, Garret, *All in a Life*, Gill & Macmillan, 1992

Gallagher, Jackie & Hannon, Philip (eds), *Taking the Long View*, Blackwater Press, 1996

Hannon, Katie, *The Naked Politician*, Gill & Macmillan, 2004

Kennedy,Geraldine (ed), *Nealon's Guide to the 29th Dáil & Seanad*, Gill & Macmillan / *The Irish Times*, 2002

Lenihan, Brian, *For the Record*, Blackwater Press, 1991

Maher, Jim, *Harry Boland: A Biography*, Mercier Press, 1998

Manning, Maurice, *The Blueshirts,* Gill & Macmillan, 1970

Minihan, Mary, *Dáil Spats*, Maverick House, 2005

Moody, T.W. & Martin, F.X (eds), *The Course of Irish History*, Mercier Press, 1994

O'Byrne, John, *O'Machiavelli*, Leopold Publishing, 1996

O'Mahony, T.P., *Jack Lynch: A Biography*, Blackwater Press, 1991

O'Riordan, Tomás A., *William T. Cosgrave*, UCC Multitext Project in Irish History

O'Sullivan, Michael, *Seán Lemass: A Biography*, Blackwater Press, 1994

O' Toole, Fintan, *Ship of Fools*, Faber & Faber, 2009.

Rafter, Kevin, *Fine Gael: Party at the Crossroads*, New Island Books, 2009

Reynolds, Albert, *Albert Reynolds: My Autobiography*, Transworld Ireland, 2009

Ryan, Tim, *Mara P.J.*, Blackwater Press, 1992

Walsh, Dick, *Inside Fianna Fáil*, Gill & Macmillan, 1986